Published by ECW Press
665 Gerrard Street East
Toronto, ON M4M 1Y2
416-694-3348 / info@ecwpress.com

Library and Archives Canada Cataloguing in Publication

Oliver, Greg, author
Father Bauer and the great experiment: the genesis of Canadian Olympic hockey / Greg Oliver.

Issued also in electronic formats.
ISBN 978-1-77041-249-1 (hardback); ISBN 978-1-77305-000-3 (pdf); ISBN 978-1-77090-999-1 (epub)

1. Bauer, David, Father, 1924–1988. 2. Hockey—Canada—History. 3. Hockey—Canada—Biography. 4. Winter Olympics—History. 5. Catholic Church—Canada—Clergy—Biography. I. Title.

GV848.5.B379O45 2017 796.962092 C2016-906354-2
C2016-906355-0

Editor for the press: Michael Holmes
Cover design: Michel Vrana
Cover images: © Weekend Magazine / e002505708 / Reproduced with the permission of Library and Archives Canada
Printing: Friesens 1 2 3 4 5

The publication of *Father Bauer and the Great Experiment* has been generously supported by the Government of Ontario through the Ontario Book Publishing Tax Credit and the Ontario Media Development Corporation.

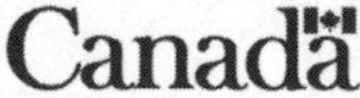

PRINTED AND BOUND IN CANADA

FATHER BAUER AND THE GREAT EXPERIMENT

THE GENESIS OF CANADIAN OLYMPIC HOCKEY

GREG OLIVER

This one is for my dad, who has called Kitchener-Waterloo home for most of his life. He taught me so much over the years, but the greatest lesson was how to stay strong by your spouse. Love you, Pop.

FOREWORD

By Jim Gregory, Hockey Hall of Fame Class of 2007

Without Father David Bauer, I would not be in the Hockey Hall of Fame. I would not have been the general manager of the Toronto Maple Leafs, or a vice-president of the National Hockey League. The Order of Hockey in Canada would have gone to someone else in 2015. Heck, Father Bauer even performed the wedding ceremony for my wife, Rosalie, and I, and baptized our first child.

So who was Father Bauer and why does he matter?

He was the most remarkable man that I ever met in all my years, and his story, told here in its entirety for the first time, is equally fascinating.

The Canadian Olympic hockey program, as it exists today, began under Father Bauer. The education programs in junior hockey have him at their core. He played a major role in the growth of international hockey and the resulting Europeans coming to play in North America.

He foresaw things. Back in the early '60s, he used to tell me, "You know, we're going to have problems. The Russians are getting too good. We're not going to be able to handle them. They don't have a professional league, so all their guys are on one team."

With an older brother, Bobby, who was a star on the Kraut Line with the Bruins in the NHL, David Bauer learned the game from some of the greats. He took that knowledge and mixed it with his personal experiences and beliefs to become the most unique of hockey men.

His ideas and perspective on hockey weren't pie-in-the-sky thinking; they were often proved right. I used to listen to him—on the ice, in the dressing room, in the office—as he shared tips. He would tell me things about hockey that you just wouldn't know if you were working in another job or just watching on TV. I never stopped seeking him out for advice.

My own attempts to play junior hockey at St. Michael's College in Toronto in the early 1950s may not have panned out—I was cut twice—but Father Bauer encouraged me to stick around and help out with the Midget team he ran. There isn't much I didn't get involved with, from running errands to organizing equipment to recruiting players. It all helped as I went on through hockey.

On Sunday, August 6, 1961, Father picked me up in the car he had borrowed from his sister, but didn't tell me where we were going. It was Maple Leaf Gardens, and we met with Stafford Smythe, who was running the team.

"Is this the guy you were telling me about?" Smythe asked Father, who nodded. Stafford looked at me and said, "What makes you think you can work in hockey?" That's how I got my job. He hired me right there, strictly on Father's recommendation. I left my job at Colgate-Palmolive and never looked back.

He had that sort of influence on countless people, changing lives for the better.

Father Bauer was the most knowledgeable, conscientious, caring person I ever met.

Now you get to meet him too.

INTRODUCTION

Wobbling behind his team's bench during a pivotal Olympic game with Sweden, blood dripping from a small gash above his right eye, Father David Bauer had a decision to make. He could allow his "Boys"—Canada's national hockey team—freedom to avenge the errant toss of a broken stick which hit their beloved leader.

Or he could practice what he preached.

He took the high road and changed the perception of Canadian hockey abroad.

"The whole team was quite incensed at the Swedish player throwing the stick at Father Bauer," recalled Paul Conlin, a left winger with the team that played at the 1964 Games in Innsbruck, Austria. "He got us under control right away and it never developed into an incident. In fact, I think the incident helped us quite a bit, helped our image quite a bit, or helped Father Bauer's image for sure."

An athlete all through his life, with a bashed-in nose to prove it, Bauer's strong grasp held back a couple of players who were heading over the boards, the Swedish player Carl-Goran Öberg directly in their sights.

Centreman Roger Bourbonnais's major recollection is Bauer's calmness through it all. "We really respected him, so you played his style, and that was discipline and perseverance and excellence in what you do."

Of course, history has a way of bending and adjusting to suit the current storyline, and martyrs aren't always what they seem.

Eight minutes into the third period, Canadian defenceman Barry MacKenzie crushed Öberg with a boneshaking and stickbreaking hit. The Nats on the bench roared in appreciation, giving Öberg the gears as he got up from the ice. The stick was tossed in frustration and anger at the yappy Canadian players. They ducked. Their coach did not.

Bauer, wearing black and his clerical collar, was immediately tended to by trainer Johnny Owen. Later it was worth a chuckle—most of the players had cut themselves worse shaving.

There was even a point later in the contest where Coach Bauer asked MacKenzie, "You going to get that Öberg back?" Jumping up from his seat on the bench to get on the ice, MacKenzie promised revenge. "Well, sit down then," said Bauer.

The thrown stick became part of lore, living on in a way that the game (a 3–1 win for Canada) itself didn't; perhaps if the "Nats" hadn't been so achingly close to a medal.

Sensing an opportunity to be in the spotlight he so craved, Canada's number one nemesis abroad, John F. "Bunny" Ahearne, the president of the International Ice Hockey Federation, decreed that Öberg would be suspended for a game, as would referee Gennaro Olivieri of Switzerland, who failed to penalize Öberg.

Speaking on behalf of the world of amateur hockey, Ahearne wanted to "thank Father Bauer for exercising control over his players on the bench after the incident."

After the game, Bauer did more than dismiss the accident—"I happened to be in the way"—and forgive Öberg; he invited the Swede to be his guest to watch the tilt between the Soviet Union and Czechoslovakia the next night. "He's a fine, clean-cut boy," said Bauer. The left winger and the priest were already acquainted, as Sweden had toured Canada for a series of exhibition games in December of 1963, and Öberg had even attended the Toronto Maple Leafs training camp in September in Saskatoon, Saskatchewan. "Little things like that happen in sport," said the 39-year-old Father Bauer. "I know Öberg very well, and I like him a lot. A little excitable maybe, but he is still a very fine boy in my book."

At the conclusion of the Innsbruck Games, International Olympic Committee president Avery Brundage presented Father Bauer with a special IOC gold medal for character and sportsmanship.

"I think Father really earned it for being the great person he is and the way he handled everything and everybody. It could have turned into a real donnybrook," said Canada's general manager, Dr. Bob Hindmarch, in his memoir, *Catch On and Run With It*.

During the medal presentation, Ahearne said Bauer "stood there cut and bleeding and under control. He also kept his players under control too. Not only that, but the next night he took Öberg to the Russia game as his personal guest and forgave him completely. If we only had more men in this game like him it would be a much better sport."

Amen.

Chapter 1

THE GREAT EXPERIMENT

It was *always* about something more than hockey. The public and the press may have focused on the end results—a couple of bronze medals in Olympic and World Championship play, a win in the hometown Centennial tournament, spirited and fair play, and a whole lot of heartache—but for Father Bauer, his dream, his Great Experiment, was about both education and his country. Hockey was merely a means to an end, a pathway to patriotism and to a better life.

At a sportsman's dinner in Medicine Hat, Alberta, in April 1966, Father David Bauer quoted American senator Robert F. Kennedy, who once said, "Part of a nation's prestige is won at the Olympic Games." He then shared his own thoughts on what that meant. "Our biggest problem is the task of making Canadians out of all of us," said Bauer. "We have to start someplace and we have to help our own Canadian athletes."

The Canadian Dream, if you will, was always a part of David Bauer, reinforced as it was by his brother Ray representing Canada (as a part of the Sudbury Wolves) at the 1949 World Championships, and then another brother, NHL great Bobby Bauer, coaching the Canadian hockey teams at the 1956 and 1960 Olympics.

It was a vision that he shared with the ultimate patriot, Monsignor Athol Murray of Notre Dame College in tiny Wilcox, Saskatchewan.

"God, Canada, and hockey. Not necessarily in that order," was his mantra. The chain-smoking, salty-mouthed Murray is often credited with inspiring Bauer with the idea of an Olympic team made up of students, but that is not the case. Murray and Bauer didn't become truly acquainted until after the team was formed in 1962, but that doesn't mean he didn't play a major role.

Barry MacKenzie, the national team defender, spent 22 years working at Notre Dame College after hockey, but first met Pere Murray in Father Bauer's dressing room. "We were playing against the Saskatchewan Senior All-Stars in Regina and Father Dave said, 'Guys, I want you to meet this guy. This guy is from Notre Dame, he's a passionate Canadian; he might sound a little bit off-colour when he comes in here.' Sure enough, Pere Murray delivered as promised—"somebody you couldn't help but remember." He also put his money where his heart lay. "He's a very inspirational speaker, and he said, 'I'm donating $1,000 to your program.' Well, he didn't have any money. He was always picking the pocket of everybody else that had ever been to Notre Dame."

Chuck Lefley was one of the later Nats, joining after the 1968 Olympics, but like them all, he came to know Pere Murray, who was not a fan of wearing his clerical collar. "I remember looking at him, and saying, 'My God, that's not how I think of priests or how they should look.' He had a pair of pants on, long underwear, unbuttoned down the front, and he had a cigarette in his mouth. He was just a wonderful character."

Like Murray, Bauer was first and foremost an educator. Their outside interests, such as hockey or politics, helped to make them more interesting priests. A quote once attributed to Murray became one that Bauer often repeated: "I am a little guy who could have very easily gone wrong but by the grace of God, I did a little work for Him."

A theme on the sports banquet circuit—Bauer and his Boys hit *a lot* of hockey dinners over the years—was the value of an education. It was a topic he spoke with passion about, particularly in rooms full of young, aspiring hockey players dreaming of playing the game as a profession. He knew he was in a tough spot, as the law allowed students to drop out of school at the age of 16, meaning that the hockey establishment of junior through the pros had no obligations to broaden any young minds with anything but slapshots and saves. "Of course every young hockey player here tonight should seek a career in the National Hockey League, but they should take an education with them," he told a crowded room in Lethbridge, Alberta, in May 1966. "It doesn't cost a cent [to] carry an education with you," he said. "Don't underestimate the value of an education. . . . It should be the most important thing in a boy's life."

That is not to say that Father Bauer didn't think that faith was important too, it's just that he wasn't the evangelizing type. The Basilian order believed so strongly in education and the whole person that he considered an individual's personal relationship with God only a part of their makeup. In fact, in his own words, the whole wonderful idea of an Olympic team made up of lily-pure amateurs who were enrolled at university wouldn't have happened without faith.

"Looking back, I'm tempted to say it was a giant act of faith," Father Bauer told Terry O'Malley, the loyal defenceman who played for all three of Bauer's Olympic teams—in 1964, 1968 and 1980—and then followed Father's lead to Japan and to a job at Notre Dame College. "It was crazy, and to my horror, in a way, it was accepted by the Canadian Amateur Hockey Association. We would begin in the fall of 1963. . . . We had no uniforms, no ice, no schedule, no base, no money. Nothing."

News broke of Father Bauer's plan in mid-August 1962, but it wasn't officially announced until the end of that month. Naturally, it was met with a wide variety of knee-jerk reactions, including the now infamous tirade by Dr. M. L. Van Vliet of the University of Alberta, who called it an "absolute farce." Respected sports columnist Scott Young of the *Globe and Mail* wanted to give it a chance, saying the "best news in hockey for years is that decision to start planning Canada's 1964 Olympic team now." Young thought the plan to "gather a team of reasonably amateur amateurs" hit many of the "2,163 suggestions on this subject I've heard since Canada lost the 1960 Olympics."

Bauer himself was pretty quiet in the press about what actually drove him to the national team concept, which was odd, given his penchant for gab and friendship with the Toronto scribes who had followed him to a Memorial Cup with St. Michael's College in 1961.

Grant Moore was not one of Bauer's Majors—in fact, he played on the rival Marlies—but did skate with the national team for a short while, and was one of many Father Bauer called upon as a taxi service when he was in Toronto. Those car rides were an examination into your soul, said Moore. "He could almost look into your mind, when you're one-on-one talking to him, and see what you were thinking."

Goalie Cesare Maniago said, "He'd always ask you the question, and he's waiting for that response, and he'd maybe help you along the way for the response that he wanted to hear." In short form, it was the BP—the Bauer Pause.

Years later, with the national team freshly dead and buried at the hands of Hockey Canada (and the National Hockey League—though you'll never find that on the record), Bauer worked with Douglas Fisher on a report to John Munro, Canada's Minister of Health and Welfare. Delivered in June 1971, it's a remarkable peek under the collar, and the contents, sprinkled as they are throughout this volume, give an impression of an introspective yet passionate man who did his part to do things right, on the ice and off.

After all, it was about more than just hockey:

> Within the context of the world struggles for power in which our freedom was and is at stake, Canada cannot play a decisive role but it can make real contributions of its own. It can do so, however, only if our leaders have seriously faced and thought out our aims and our capabilities. In the same context one can locate the role of our sports in the development of the human person who would one day be called upon to lead wisely in a turbulent world. Sport on the international level is certainly not just the carefree mixing of youths of all nations as it is sometimes pictured, nor is it just, as cynics might have it, a sort of irrelevant extension of the Cold War. Rather it is an opportunity to apply on a higher level. That same principle I spoke of before: Make use of technique, but let the spirit prevail. It is a chance to show to the world the true character of our people—on a secondary level, no doubt, but one which all the world watches and one

> which can "capture the fleeting idealism of our youth."
>
> And within Canada itself, strained and divided as we are, hockey, our national game, seemed and still seems to be one rallying point for most Canadians from coast to coast. No doubt, again, this is not of itself the deepest level, but it is one which can be made a focus for profoundly important national involvement and unity. The implications of this for our representation as a nation in international competition are considerable.

Having seen his brothers come up short in the colourful, unpredictable world of international play, Father Bauer knew all about heartache. He and his brother Ray travelled to Colorado Springs, Colorado, for the 1962 World Hockey Championships. They talked about what shape the 1964 Olympic team could take for Canada. "Little by little, as he talked and as we watched the tournament, it began to dawn on me that perhaps it would be possible to apply, with an Olympic team, the philosophy of sport that it had not been possible to apply adequately in Junior A hockey," wrote Father Bauer.

Also in attendance were important Canadian Amateur Hockey Association figures, including president Jack Roxburgh, and Gordon Juckes, the secretary who would remain a key cog in the Great Experiment until the end. The hockey bureaucrats liked the idea that the Bauers proposed, a national team based at a university, lily-pure without any trace of "shamateurism," a term that had come into common usage to refer to countries like Sweden or the USSR that paid its players to play hockey year-round while officially employing them in other jobs, like military service. They'd taken the idea back to the CAHA executive, and Father Bauer set about making it happen.

In his own house, St. Mark's College on the grounds of the University of British Columbia, he found support from principal Father Ed Garvey and Father Henry Carr. In particular, Bauer wrote that Father Carr's wholehearted belief made the Great Experiment seem possible:

> At that time he was 82 years of age, the oldest living Basilian. He had been Superior General of the Basilians and certainly

> the most important man in forming the Basilian approach to education. Back in the early years of the century he had been a coach himself and had led St. Michael's teams to national championships in both football and hockey. He saw at once what was at stake with regard to the proposed Olympic Team and encouraged me to go ahead with it. Father Ed Garvey, too, although not much involved in sport himself, had long been interested, as a philosopher, in the philosophy of sport and had written on this subject. He, therefore, also supported the idea.

"The impact that Fr. Carr had on him was very evident," said Father Ted McLean in 1988. "He believed that seminarians and the spirit they could generate could be combined, and successes were not only gained through the win-loss column."

Bauer made academic and athletic allies at UBC, too. Bob Hindmarch was a professor in the physical education department, and would serve as an unofficial assistant coach, general manager, and sounding board to Bauer. Bob Osborne of the department of education believed in it, as did Dean A.W. Matthews. A new arena had been in the works at the school in Vancouver for years, and the plan was just the kick-start that was needed to make it happen.

Aware of the politics involved in such a monumental change in direction, Father Bauer sought out the support he needed. Though he is not mentioned by name in the minutes from the CAHA annual meeting in May 1962, it's obvious he was a little bird speaking into the ear of President Jack Roxburgh. The members debated a couple of ideas: the old tried-and-true idea of a senior team for the 1964 Olympics, though none had applied; or the Canadian Army running a disciplined team using its soldiers. The minutes list another concept: "The president reported that there was one more idea for an Olympic team selection and that had to do with choosing a university team. He said that this idea had been passed on to him earlier that morning, and it was to take outstanding college players and transfer them all to one university and thus develop a team there."

From May to August, Father Bauer worked his magic, talking to all the notables, including Federal Health Minister J. Waldo Monteith, who ultimately provided some of CAHA's funding. He obviously did his job well; according to reports, Bauer's presentation at the August 26 meeting lasted just two minutes, and was followed by just 10 minutes of discussion, before it was approved.

The Great Experiment was on. By the time it ended six years later, Canada had had a truly national team, made up of players from across the country, from all walks of life, for the first time in its history.

Unfairly, perhaps, they were often referred to as "Bauer's Boys," even if he coached only a single season before turning over the reins to Jackie McLeod. "It was never my team," Bauer told reporter Jack Matheson in the spring of 1969, sitting in the Ottawa office of Derek Holmes (one of many whose lives were steered, in part, by Bauer). "It was Canada's team and I think it accomplished a lot. Not many medals, but I think we made Canada aware of quite a few things."

Though it was never about religion, in a way the Word was unavoidable. In Europe, the media loved Father Bauer, the priest behind the bench; and behind the Iron Curtain, well, he was an oddity in a culture where churches were off limits. His very presence and demeanor were enough, wrote Pierre Berton in *The Comfortable Pew*:

> When I use the phrase "walking sermon," I think of Father Bauer preaching to the largest congregation in Canada—the readers of the newspaper sports pages—about the Christian way of life. If the adjective "preachy" has taken on unpleasant connotations, it is because few clergymen have either the imagination, the drive, or the opportunity to do what Father Bauer did. They are the prisoners of their pulpits. If Father Bauer had had a parish, could he have left it to go to Innsbruck? Would he have had time, between the endless home visits, the Women's Auxiliary sales, the Men's Club evenings, the ringing telephone, and the demands of two weekly sermons, to select an Olympic hockey team, much less coach one?

Chapter 2

GROWING UP BAUER

Howie Meeker still remembers the games . . . The esteemed player, coach and broadcaster, with his unmistakable nasal voice and unbridled passion for the sport, used to skate on the pond at Victoria Park on the border between Kitchener and Waterloo in southwestern Ontario. The city kept the pond ideal for skating, both for pleasure and for epic games of shinny. At the time, Meeker lived within walking distance, on Eby Street.

The Bauers had a huge home in downtown Waterloo, also not too far from Victoria Park. Dave Bauer, the youngest of the six boys in the Bauer clan, loved to play hockey, just like his big brothers.

As if he were still using a telestrator, Meeker can describe the action from the 1930s like it just happened. "There'd be 25 hockey games going on," Meeker recalled. "They'd divide the teams. You always came with two different colour sweaters, a dark one and a white one, because you didn't know for sure what team you were going to be on. They kept it even, and they kept it clean, they kept it fun, because there were no boards."

With a couple of dozen games going on, there were many nets too. "Somebody's lunchbox or somebody's pair of boots" would serve as posts.

The ringleader, the top jock in their age group, was Bobby Schnurr, later related to the Bauer family through marriage. He lectured Meeker once, and once was enough. "Hey kid, what colour's that jersey that you got on?" Meeker replied that it was blue. "How come, when you get rid of the goddamned puck you always give it to a white? If you keep giving it to these guys all the time, your ass is out of here!"

Meeker said, "It's one of the first lessons I learned—if you pass the puck to someone, it's got to go to someone wearing the same colour jersey."

There was really only one true goalie, or one with equipment anyway, and he came from pretty good stock. George Hainsworth Jr. would be out there wearing his father's threadbare pads. George Sr., after all, had been a star with the Montreal Canadiens from 1926 to 1937, winning the first three Vezina Trophies for the league's best goaltender.

"It was a great time to grow up because it was wonderful hockey and the weather was cold enough to keep the natural ice," said Meeker. "Gosh, we must have had it from late November through to March."

Many of the boys on the ice were trying to emulate Kitchener-Waterloo's trio of NHL stars—on the same line, even, with the Boston Bruins—Milt Schmidt, Woody Dumart and Bobby Bauer. Through his uncle, Harry Wharnsby, Meeker had been fortunate enough to be a stick boy for a senior hockey team that had featured all three.

Hockey was a big deal in town. "I was interested in many sports and played practically everything going," Father David Bauer wrote in 1971. "Still hockey had a special pull. Not only was it Canada's national game and played with a special intensity in my home town of Kitchener-Waterloo; there was also the pull exerted by the image created by the NHL, made doubly strong for me by the fact that my brother was a part of it."

Upon winning the 1961 Ontario Hockey League playoff title as coach of the St. Michael's Majors, Father Bauer reverted into little Dave Bauer, a 12-year-old hacking around on the homemade rink on a tennis court beside the family home, trying out the skills brother Bob had shown him. Standing beside the John Ross Robertson trophy for the league champions, Bauer thanked his sibling. "He taught me the importance of hockey fundamentals when I was 12. I used to go to the Boston Bruin[s] training camp and we had a rink at the side of our house in Kitchener. All I've ever tried to do in coaching is pass on the fundamentals and strategy I learned from Bob."

It was more than just a makeshift rink at the Bauer residence at the corner of King and Allen Streets. There were boards, and the ice had lines painted on it; there were lights that shone at night, and a small changing room. At centre ice were the initials BHL, for Bauer Hockey League.

David William Bauer was born November 2, 1924, in Waterloo, to Edgar Joseph John Bauer and Alice Bertha Hayes, who married in 1912. There were 11 Bauer children in all: six boys—Frank, Bob, Eugene, Jerome, Raymond, and David—and five girls—Alice, Mary, Rita, Therese, and Margaret. Another sibling died at birth. David was the youngest boy, and three sisters followed him in the family tree.

While early education was at St. Louis Separate School in Waterloo, followed by three years at St. Jerome's College in Kitchener, there were many lessons learned on the sports fields, in church, and at the family business.

A. Bauer and Company on King Street in Waterloo was founded in 1888 by Aloyes Bauer. He was born in town to Karl and Sophia Bauer in 1861; his parents had emigrated from Bavaria first to Buffalo, New York, and then to Waterloo. Aloyes began work in his father's carpentry shop at 14 years of age. He was a hard-working man and managed to build and pay off the cost of his home before marrying Magdalena Kuntz in 1885. (Her family was involved in the Kuntz Brewery in town, and Aloyes managed it for a time.)

In 1917, the company's name was changed to Bauer Industries, just after it started making automobile seat cushion padding. The jump into the just-developing car industry proved to be a stroke of genius. By 1957, with Aloyes's son Edgar Bauer in charge and Waterloo celebrating its centennial, its plant occupied 200,000 square feet—compared to 16,500 in 1917—and had 170 people in its employ. A foam rubber padding manufacturing facility added to the available products as well. The original furniture part of the company spun off into Globe Furniture Company Limited.

Edgar Bauer spent 50 years in the family business, beginning with six months after his schooling at St. Jerome's College on the factory floor; he went on to become general manager, chairman of the board and president. He would use his wealth and influence to try to improve the community, an example he learned from his father, who spent 30 years on the Separate School Board, and a lesson not lost on his own children. First and foremost, in the political realm, he served as alderman in Waterloo from 1922 to 1925, and on the Waterloo Public Utilities Commission from 1947 to 1950. Son Frank also gave part of his life to public service, spending six years as a city alderman and one year, 1954–55, as mayor of Waterloo.

Businesswise, Edgar Bauer worked with the Waterloo Board of Trade and the Canadian Manufacturers' Association, and presided, at different times, over Waterloo Mutual Fire Insurance Company and Globe Furniture Company. Son Ray would be the next generation running the felt business, changing it to adapt to the times and offer different products. Edgar Bauer was also a charter member of Kitchener council of Knights of Columbus—he was made a Knight Commander of St. Sylvester by Pope Pius XII in 1957—and belonged to the Waterloo Young Men's Club, and was an honorary president of the Waterloo Baseball Association. In 1970, a separate school was named after him in Waterloo's Lakeshore neighbourhood, making him the first Roman Catholic layman so honoured.

As a young man, Edgar Bauer had played baseball and hockey, and records show that he registered for his Ontario Hockey Association card to play junior hockey in 1906. He'd pass down his love of both sports through his children.

Both Bob and Frank won a Memorial Cup with the St. Michael's Majors in 1934, and Dave would follow in 1945 with the Oshawa Generals, and again in '61 as coach of the Majors. With the Boston Bruins, Bobby would win the Stanley Cup twice as well. Eugene—known as Gene—was with the Ontario Hockey Association–winning Kitchener Juniors in 1935. Brothers Jerry and Ray were Waterloo Siskins, champs of the OHA Junior B division in 1940.

Alice Bauer was originally from Linwood, Ontario, a half-hour west of Kitchener-Waterloo, but lived in Waterloo most of her life. Despite raising 11 children, she found time to be active in the Catholic Women's League and was a member of the Carmel Guild. Her faith was very central to her life, first at St. John's Roman Catholic Church in Kitchener and then St. Louis Roman Catholic Church in Waterloo.

Though sports and religion were pillars of life in the Bauer household, education held a place above all—as a teenaged Dave found out. "In a sense the founding of the national team dates back to when I was 15 years of age. It was then that my father told me that I would be a professional hockey player before I got an education—over his dead body," Father Bauer wrote in his report to the Honourable John Munro. "During those years he also impressed upon me the fact that one day I would have to account to God for the talents he had given me, and that there was a priority in terms of the development of our talents that included not just my own self-fulfillment but also the playing of a role in the development of world peace. Even though, at the time, I rebelled against what my father said, I can see now that everything I have done since then has flowed quite naturally from his teaching, not because it was my father who taught it, but because what he taught was true."

Taken as a whole, the Bauer clan has been part of Kitchener-Waterloo for more than a century. "It's an iconic family, but very few people know about it," said Kitchener native Rod Seiling, who'd play for Father Bauer in the 1964 Olympics before a lengthy NHL career. Coming truly full circle, he now lives on Father David Bauer Drive in Waterloo, which divides Waterloo Park on the north from the Waterloo Memorial Recreation Complex and homes and business on the other side.

Bauer is a common enough name, from the Middle High German word *bur* or *bure*, which means peasant or farmer. But when most Canadians hear it, the skate company comes to mind. Since the Bauer Shoe Company and the Canadian Skate Manufacturing Company had ties to Kitchener, it was only natural to assume it was related to the hockey-playing Bauer. But it took marriage to make that happen, with Bobby marrying into the skate-making clan. The former member of the Kraut Line would even have his own brand of skate, but not while he was playing. That came while he was an executive.

While he was at St. Michael's College in Toronto, first as a student and then as teacher, it wasn't unusual for Father Bauer to bring friends, students, and his players back to the family homestead.

In March 1959, Edgar Bauer died, and a few of Father Bauer's players travelled with their leader to his father's funeral. Cesare Maniago, future NHL goalie, was one of them. "We went up there and met the rest of the family. It was the first time that I'd gone to a funeral—I'd been to Italian funerals when I was maybe 14, 15, 16 years old, and everybody's crying and wailing and the whole thing. Then I go there, and everybody's smiling, laughing. I just didn't understand this. So I'm asking Father Bauer, 'Why the big difference?' He goes on to explain, 'Hey, life is a cycle. You're born as a baby, you go through adolescence, you go through adulthood, and it just revolves back to like being a baby again. If someone has had a full, satisfying life, that's all you want them to have. You look at my dad, he was fairly old when he passed away, and we all knew that he had a good life. You're sorrowful in that he passed away, but at the same time you keep thinking, "Hey, he did have a good life."'"

A more positive event was held at the home following the 1961 Memorial Cup win by the Majors. Billy MacMillan, another St. Mike's Major, and later a member of the national team, recalled the Bauer home. "He would always take a few players out to meet his family. I was out there a few times," he said. "They would kid each other. . . . They seemed to be very close when I was there."

Like any large family, the relationships often seemed complicated to an outsider. "The Bauer family is a bit discombobulated," explains hockey-player-turned-lawyer Doug Buchanan. "One of Father Bauer's biggest challenges in life was negotiating between all his family members. Every time they would have a family feud of some kind, of course he was the arbitrator that everyone would come to, because he was fair, even-handed and logical."

Terry O'Malley, *the* disciple of Bauer's disciples, went to the Bauer house many times, and wrote about the experiences in an essay. David had a "feisty temperament" and "any family gathering that I experienced over the years was a lively and challenging affair with 'equal time' the operative word for holding court. Along with this feisty, argumentative bent, the family atmosphere seemed to endow him with an ability to engage people and to have a great sense of humour. However, his dad appeared to leave him with the lasting impression that 'he was responsible to God for the talents gifted to him.'"

The home itself, at King and Allen, was built by Aloyes Bauer across the street from the family business. "I never saw such a house with so many rooms in it," said Mickey McDowell of the Nats.

If the Bauer home in Waterloo was massive, the family cottage in Goderich, on the shores of Lake Huron, was a place to get away from it all. Edgar Bauer had bought it in 1938, and it was always packed with humanity—three cramped bedrooms upstairs in the two-storey building, and a pot-bellied stove keeping things cozy on cool nights.

Les Kozak was one of Bauer's early proteges, and offers an excellent example of both the highs and lows of a relationship with a young priest still trying to find the balance between advice and control. At age 15, Kozak had come west from Yorkton, Saskatchewan to St. Mike's, but fit in quickly through sports. He has vivid memories "of this priest in these flowing robes, full of energy, and he had very black hair, combed back. He was very trim and fit, and had almost a predatory look to his face—he was going after something and he was going to get it. He insisted that I come out and play for the football team." Kozak also worked hard at school, and would later study biochemistry; he recently retired from the Polish Academy of Sciences in Olsztyn, Poland.

There was something else missing, though. A Maple Leafs prospect, Kozak eschewed the hockey road, taking a left turn, entering a Trappist monastery near Worcester, Massachusetts. The left winger was restless and his competitive nature made for constant self-examination against others. At St. Mike's, Father Bauer encouraged students to seek out self-perfection. Taking the lesson to heart, Kozak got married against Father Bauer's advice, getting engaged just a couple of months after abandoning the monk's life. It caused a falling-out between priest and student. "I guess he said, 'Well, if he doesn't want to listen to my advice, so be it,'" said Kozak.

For Kozak, it was incredibly disheartening that someone so close to him could cut him loose, never even calling when Kozak's life was threatened during an AHL game between Providence Reds and his Rochester Americans, his unprotected head striking a metal post holding up the wire netting around the rink. A top neurosurgeon happened to be on call in Providence and was able to deal with the depressed fracture on the right side of his skull. Kozak played 12 games in the 1961–62 season for the Leafs, and 45 in Rochester, but gave up on hockey.

He also cut ties with Father Bauer, save a single phone call he placed while in the Vancouver airport years later to say hello. "He was a pretty controlling person. Maybe there are areas where that control was not properly placed," said Kozak.

But in the summer of 1961, having returned from his retreat to the monastery, Kozak was essentially Father Bauer's "chauffeur, chief bottle washer . . . whatever needed to be done" guy until Maple Leafs training camp opened.

Alice Bauer would spend much of the summer at the cottage, with various family coming and going based on their schedules. "Ray, for example, would come around almost on a daily basis, and his sisters came by. It was kind of a fairly rambling cottage on the top a bluff, way up overlooking Lake Huron," recalled Kozak. "We had some really competitive beach volleyball and other types of sports in the waves. It was an utterly relaxing spot for [Father Bauer]. He could go there and sit on a chair over the lake in the setting sun and read [in] his office, whatever he wanted to do, or just think. He spent a lot of time thinking."

What Kozak wasn't privy to was Father Bauer's thoughts about a different kind of hockey team that would represent Canada with pride, restoring the country's good name abroad.

Chapter 3

BOBBY AND THE KRAUTS

For the record, "the Kraut Line," the nickname for the high-scoring trio that powered the Boston Bruins in the 1930s, was not a reference to shared German heritage. No, it was a shortened version of the title tagged upon them—the Sauerkrauts—by an old defenceman, Albert "Battleship" Leduc, who was then coaching the minor-pro Providence Reds.

While history may have popularized their Germanic roots, what makes the threesome of Milt Schmidt, Woody "Porky" Dumart, and Bobby Bauer so unique is that they really did grow up together in Kitchener, Ontario. They managed to find fame together as well, in the NHL and in the Royal Canadian Air Force, never losing their closeness. When the 49-year-old Bauer died suddenly of a heart attack on September 16, 1964, reporters caught Schmidt by surprise as he was running Bruins training camp. "Bobby was my right arm in hockey, the brains of the Kraut Line," he said.

In March 1952, Bauer made a one-game return to the NHL to be a part of Schmidt-Dumart night. "They were as finely balanced a hockey line as I've ever seen," wrote *Boston Globe* columnist Victor Jones. "Bauer was the brains, both on and off the ice. If you were talking to the three and asked a question, Bobby always made the answer, with the other two just nodding their agreement."

That one-night stand, while the Bruins were still in the playoff hunt, is part of hockey lore. The Bs knocked off the visiting Black Hawks 4–0, and Bauer had an assist playing part-time with his old buddies. That assist, along with another from Dumart, came on Schmidt's 200th NHL goal. "The Krauts operated as a line for a period and a half. Bauer, lacking the condition of his other two mates, took only a half turn each time, with Ed Kryzanowski replacing him as he skated to the bench for a respite. But while they were on the ice the line showed flashes of its old brilliance. Bauer made the 'moves' as long as his legs held out," reads the *Globe* account. His legs might have been tired from the 30-minute pre-game ceremony alone; it was estimated that Schmidt and Dumart received cash and gifts totalling close to $20,000, including silver pieces, movie cameras, portable radios, and bikes for their kids. Bauer got a portable radio, sportswriters and broadcasters gave him a silver pitcher, and his wife received a clock. "We are happy to honor these men not only because they have been great players but also because they have been great citizens in peace and war," said NHL president Clarence Campbell.

Born February 16, 1915, in Waterloo, Ontario, Bobby was the second-oldest son. His early organized hockey experience came in the Kitchener-Waterloo area. Following in the footsteps of his older brother, Frank, Bobby moved to Toronto to attend St. Michael's College. He was a star for the Buzzers, the school's Junior B team, in 1930–31. For the 1932–33 season, Bobby played for the British Consols and the National Sea Fleas of the Toronto Mercantile League, winning the city title with the Fleas. The next year, he made the top team at St. Mike's, the Junior A Majors.

The 1933–34 Majors won the Memorial Cup as the top junior team in Canada. "That St. Mike's team is still regarded in many circles as the greatest junior team of all time," it was reported in the obituary of that team's coach, Dr. William J. (Jerry) Laflamme, a dentist who had been an Allan Cup winner himself and a referee in the NHL. "It graduated Reggie Hamilton, Pep Kelly, Art Jackson, Bobby Bauer and Nick Metz into the National League, Mickey Drouillard into the International League, and included outstanding amateurs like Don Wilson and Johnny Acheson." Though he never played professional hockey, it's worth noting that Frank Bauer, future mayor of Waterloo, was on that championship team too. Bobby Bauer contributed 10 goals and 5 assists in the 13 games of the Memorial Cup playdowns.

The Cup final started April 3 at the Amphitheatre in Winnipeg, against the Edmonton Athletic Club, known to all as the Athletics. The Majors had no trouble in the first game, winning easily, 5–0. The second game was much more dramatic. Edmonton tied it, 4–4, with two goals in the third period, including the equalizer with just 30 seconds left. The teams went scoreless in the first overtime period. In the second extra stanza, played to its 20-minute entirety, Jackson and Kelly scored for the Majors to claim the Memorial Cup.

Back in his hometown, Bauer skated with the Kitchener Greenshirts, and the team won the 1935 OHA title. Bobby also worked continuously on his golf game in the summer, competing in tournaments when he wasn't playing a round at his home club, Westmount.

By May 1935, he'd signed a deal to turn professional, originally with Conn Smythe and the Toronto Maple Leafs. From there it gets a little cloudy.

"Lefty Bauer, now claimed by Boston Bruins from Syracuse Stars to whom his alleged contract was sold or assigned by the Toronto Maple Leafs," *Toronto Star* sports editor Lou Marsh attempted to explain.

Years later, another *Star* sports editor, Milt Dunnell, shared his memories of Smythe's thoughts about missing out on Bauer to Art Ross, manager of the Bruins.

"The Leafs knew about Bauer, all right. They had him signed and sealed . . . and stashed away with their farm club at Syracuse. He was on the payroll of the Syracuse team when Ross drafted him. As Bauer and the Krauts grew in professional stature, Leafs were put in the position of having pulled a rock. Their pride was pricked and their pocket had been picked," wrote Dunnell. "'I was absent in England,' Smythe used to explain grimly. 'I had an understanding that no league meetings would be held while I was away. The old master (Ross) got them to hold a meeting. He drafted Bauer off the Syracuse list. If I had thought there was any possibility of a draft meeting while I was gone, Bauer would have been protected.'"

Dumart signed with the Bruins as well, though the plan was to move him from defence to left wing. As the story goes, the two then lobbied Ross to ink their buddy Schmidt, a centreman, to a deal too.

Harold Kaese, writing in his column, the Pulse, in the *Boston Evening Transcript* in March of 1941 recalled, "The Bruins got Bobby Bauer first, then Woody Dumart and finally Milt Schmidt. They drafted Bauer from Syracuse, Toronto's farm, in 1935, outwitting Connie Smythe."

The Maple Leafs' Smythe and Boston's Art Ross were bitter rivals. Stealing Bauer must have been sweet, but the prize got even better.

According to Schmidt, the Leafs had been after him too. Frank Selke wanted to sign him, but Smythe thought he was too small. He didn't know that Schmidt was only 16. Ross had turned over the Bruins coaching job to Frank Patrick in 1934–35, and Boston owner Charles Adams hoped that with Ross now concentrating fully on his general manager's job, he'd find more promising players for the Bruins farm system. When Ross was scouting Bauer and Dumart that season, they advised him to take a serious look at their young Kitchener Greenshirts teammate. "So it was," wrote Stephen Harris in the *Boston Herald*, looking back at the Boston teams of the 1930s and '40s in 1998, "that Ross and the Bruins acquired the trio that would comprise one of the greatest lines in NHL history."

In October 1935, the Bruins held camp in Saint John, New Brunswick, and all three—Bauer, Schmidt, and Dumart—were there, but still technically amateur, should they be deemed not up to snuff and sent back home. Schmidt, skinny and growing into his frame, returned to junior in Kitchener, while Bauer and Dumart laced 'em up with the Boston Cubs of the Can-Am league.

The three were reunited with the Cubs and then with the American Hockey League's Providence Reds. Bauer debuted for the Bruins in the team's finale on March 21, 1937, following Schmidt and Dumart into the NHL. "What must I do to stay with Bruins?" Bauer reportedly asked Art Ross. "Nothing but what you've been doing," he was told. "You'll play up here with the other kids next season."

From 1937–38 through 1946–47, minus three years in the military, the Kraut Line was one of the greatest trios in NHL history. The Bruins won two Stanley Cup titles, 1939 and 1941, and the Krauts were always in the mix of the leading scorers in the league—including finishing one (Schmidt), two (Dumart), three (Bauer) in 1939–40. As well, Bauer collected three Lady Byng trophies for his fair play.

"They were—and are—an attractive trio. When they first arrived here, they were all bachelors and inseparable. If you were looking for Schmidt, you could be sure of finding him if Dumart was around. If you wanted to find Dumart, all you had to do was find Bauer," wrote Jones in 1952. "They were as finely balanced a hockey line as I've ever seen."

Upon Bauer's death, Jones reflected on what made the five-foot-six, 160-pound Bauer different. "Bauer was an unusual hockey player in many ways. He was small, though not as small as [Aurèle] Joliat or [Cooney] Weiland or [Herbie] Lewis. He was fatter, and off the ice he looked like a Boy Scout leader behind his eye glasses. . . . He had an emotional effect, not only upon the fans, but upon his teammates. Because he was such a little guy and such an obviously nice guy, the women fans all had their maternal instincts working overtime in his support. And because his bigger teammates liked and admired him, they, too, spread their protective mantle over him."

That first year, all three stayed in a Brookline, Massachusetts, boarding house run by Mrs. Pearl Snow, with two other Bruins, Ray Getliffe and Art Jackson. They talked hockey all the time, discussing tactics that could improve their game. "Many a night, rooming together on the road, the three of us would kid and talk hockey until four o'clock in the morning," said Schmidt after Bauer's passing.

"We appreciated one another," Schmidt told Jeff Hicks of the hometown paper in Kitchener, the *Record*, in 2006. "We never had any dull time with one another. We never had any shouting matches. Jokingly, Bobby would say, 'Milt, I'm over here on the right side, remember me?' Or Woody would say, 'I'm on the left side and you're passing to the right side all the time!' And I would just say, 'Hey, I'm the centre ice man. Whatever presents itself, that's the way it's gonna go.'"

"I was blessed to play with two great guys," Milt Schmidt told Eric Zweig, author of *Art Ross: The Hockey Legend Who Built the Bruins*, in April 2013. "We always played together when we were healthy," Schmidt continued. "We never played with someone else when we were able to play. [And] we never had an argument. If we didn't think alike we sat down and discussed it. The majority won. There were only three of us."

Like the Three Musketeers of lore, it was all for one, one for all—even when their country called. With World War II raging, Dumart became the first NHL player called to active duty by the Canadian military on January 19, 1942. His mother, Lavina, got the notice in Kitchener, and had to find him on the road with the team in Chicago to deliver the message. It's not like it was unexpected. The Krauts had attended a two-week reserve Army camp in London, Ontario, the previous summer. They decided to go to war together.

Ross scrambled to fill the Bruins lineup, and the Krauts left the Boston Garden ice, carried off by teammates as the organist played "Auld Lang Syne." Years later, recalling the ovation, Bauer said, "It sort of grabbed me."

En masse, the three reported to the Royal Canadian Air Force together at the end of January; a brief controversy ensued when it became apparent that Bauer had lied about his age, listing himself as being 25, born in 1916, so he wouldn't be deferred. The "studious Bauer" was made a radio technician; Schmidt was named a physical instructor; Dumart, with poor eyesight, was assigned to an accounting post. "We've got a date with the Air Force at nine in the morning and we hope they'll take us. If we make the grade and we play any more hockey, it'll be with an Air Force team," said Schmidt at the time.

The RCAF knew what they had, and had the Krauts on skates almost immediately—the Bruins taking on the RCAF Flyers in an exhibition game in February, with funds going to the RCAF Benevolent Fund. During a practice in Montreal in early April, three thousand fans turned out just to see them work out at the Forum.

Having only missed a single game for injury during his NHL career, Bauer suddenly found himself snake-bit. During practice in March, he lost his legs and fell headfirst into the boards, fracturing his collarbone. With the RCAF squadron, which played in the Quebec Senior Hockey League, competing for the Allan Cup as senior champions of Canada, it was impossible to keep him off the ice, said coach Bill Touhey. The Port

Arthur Bearcats lost in five games to the Ottawa-based Flyers. *Globe and Mail* reporter Vern DeGeer estimated that during the finale the Krauts played 40 of the 60 minutes at Maple Leaf Gardens in Toronto.

"I never saw such competitive spirit among players as manifest by Schmidt, Dumart and Bauer," said Touhey. "Like three young colts taking their first pasture fling in the spring. I'd rather you didn't say anything about Bobby's bad shoulder until the series is over, but you have the facts. Simply can't keep him out of the lineup, that's all, and I can only hope he doesn't wind up in the hospital."

The hockey season over, the Krauts did wind up going in different directions. Bauer took an RCAF course in radio aeronautics at the University of Toronto. Dumart went to Trenton, Ontario, and Schmidt stayed in Ottawa. Such was their connection that when Dumart and Schmidt shipped off to England in December to act as physical training instructors, the Canadian Press story noted, "Off the ice or on, this is the furthest Schmidt and Dumart have ever strayed from Bobby Bauer, the right winger of the trio from Kitchener, Ont."

Bauer kept playing with the RCAF team in Dartmouth, Nova Scotia, when he could, though a fall in the dark while in Halifax severely injured his knee. In August 1943, Bauer sent a letter to his friend Wilfred Chagnon, a druggist in Newton, Massachusetts, who shared with the local paper that Bauer had just met up with Schmidt and Dumart in England. "We hope to be home soon," wrote Bauer.

All three got into action while in England, on the ice at least. For years, Bauer would carry around a photograph of a hockey rink on which they all played outside of London, England. Its construction had been scuttled as the war started, but the ice-making equipment worked, so 10 posts were erected to hold up a circus-tent-like fabric. "Dodging those posts," Bauer told DeGeer, "became an art in itself. It took two or three games to get used to them. You had to, or break your neck. And the lighting was so poor the puck must have looked like a coffee bean to the goalies."

Upon the war's conclusion, Bauer suited up in the Toronto league with People's Credit for a few games before returning to Boston for the 1945–46 season. The Bruins weren't the powerhouse they were before the war, and neither was Bauer. He'd already thought about a post-hockey career.

The families were not related, but Bobby's marriage to Marguerite Bauer—whose father, Roy C. Bauer, ran the skate company in Kitchener—meant that his next job was a certainty. For his current employer, however, Bauer continued to toil. He initially told Art Ross that he was done at the end of the 1945–46 season, but he came back one more year—and was named captain to boot.

That campaign also resulted in another milestone (and a final, third Lady Byng Trophy), in the birth of Robert T. Bauer—Bobby Bauer Jr.—in December. The Bruins were playing in Toronto when Marguerite delivered the baby in Boston. The *Globe and Mail* reported the news:

> Bobby didn't learn about his debut into parental ranks until a telegram came to the dressing-room from Boston just as he slipped perspiration-soaked equipment from his weary body after the tie. He let out a yell, accepted congratulations from teammates, then, in bare feet and clad only in trousers and [an] overcoat, slipped across the corridor into the [Leafs'] room and broke the news there.
>
> Enemies a few minutes before came forward to shake his hand and Bauer, in a rush to catch a train along with the rest of his team, shouted happily as [he] made for the door: "It's a son. My first—and he was born at 10:15 in Boston. Boy, am I happy."

There was much speculation about Bauer's future in hockey. He was linked to a Junior A franchise in Kitchener, backed financially—naturally—by Schmidt and Dumart, though that didn't come about. Instead, he wound up coaching briefly in Guelph, bailing on the Junior A Biltmores in November 1947, citing business commitments. Next, he suited up for the Kitchener-Waterloo Flying Dutchmen, a senior club, his amateur reinstatement coming in February 1948.

The Dutchmen, though they changed ownership and dropped the "Flying" name, would be his home, often reluctantly, until his sudden death in 1964. He served in all the roles, first as a player, then manager, president, coach. This was on top of his duties in the business world (production manager at the skate factory) and at home as a father (another son, Brad, came along in 1950).

Besides the influence he had on the men he coached with the Dutchmen, Bobby definitely swayed the hockey mind of his youngest brother. There were many occasions through the years that Dave Bauer was asked about Bobby and the knowledge he imparted. The Bauers believed in the "fundamentals" of the game. "I'm going to stress fundamentals and try to build a strong defence for a base to work with," Father Bauer said after taking over the University of British Columbia Thunderbirds in early 1962. The two all-important concepts that he learned from Bobby were "never give the puck away," and "never take your eyes off the eyes of your opponent."

His fame allowed for Bobby to promote skates with his stamp of approval. In 1949, you could get the Bobby Bauer Special for $21: "Designed and approved by Bobby Bauer himself, featuring boots of oil-tanned top grain leather . . . long counter supports . . . reinforced eye-rows . . . double leather at points of wear . . . felt padded tongue . . . fitted with Bauer 'Invictus' satin-finished blades. Sizes 6 to 12."

There were other business interests too, including an electrical company, and a hockey stick factory in Breslau, Ontario, in partnership with Dumart. Away from the ice, he continued to golf—his first heart attack came at the Westmount Club—and play squash, and he was active in the community with the Kitchener Rotary Club. He also ran the Waterloo Tigers, of Ontario's Intercounty Baseball League, for a time.

The ultimate honour came to Bobby Bauer in 1996 when he was, finally, elected to the Hockey Hall of Fame. The Kraut Line had been reunited once more, as Schmidt had been inducted in 1961 and Dumart in 1992.

Chapter 4

THE DUTCHMEN FAIL TO FLY

The first ice hockey competition at the Olympic Games actually took place at the *Summer* Olympics in Antwerp, Belgium, in 1920. Those Games, right after the First World War, saw Canada start with a gold medal. It was a familiar pattern until 1952, though at the Winter Olympics. Canada won six of the first seven competitions; that one loss, in 1936 to Great Britain in Garmisch-Partenkirchen, Germany, is another story, but suffice it to say that most of the Brits had Canadian roots or had played hockey in Canada.

The Winnipeg Falcons were the champs in 1920, with players mostly of Icelandic background. Having a team from a specific city or two in Canada would become a pattern, one that eventually wore out its welcome and resulted in Father Bauer's national team.

Generally, it was the best senior team in the country, the Allan Cup winner, that represented Canada abroad. There were occasions when it was maybe a second- or third-place team, often because the winners couldn't afford either the travel costs or the time off work. After all, back then, Olympians were expected to be amateurs, meaning that their primary source of income could not be hockey. To say this was an uneven way of doing things is a bit of an understatement. In his 1976 book, *War on Ice: Canada in International Hockey*, Scott Young lamented the very premise of Canada's representatives abroad: "Can you imagine another sport in which you win a gold medal and then tell the winner to get lost, you'll find somebody else to have a try next year?"

Not only that, but the Canadian Amateur Hockey Association generally only contributed $10,000 as a grant to the team going abroad, meaning that, for the right to represent their country, the players had to fundraise, hat in hand, to do the trip at all.

In 1952, the successful pattern of the Allan Cup winners heading off to triumph and returning to glory was fulfilled again, this time by the Edmonton Mercurys, who, you might have guessed, had a car dealership backing them financially.

In 1956, it was expected that the Kitchener-Waterloo Dutchmen, winners of the 1955 Allan Cup over the Fort William Beavers, would do the same, but it was not to be.

The Dutchies were coached by Bobby Bauer, and his brother Ray, running the family business, was one of the backers. Another was Pat Boehmer, who had gone to school with David Bauer and whose family had deep ties to the area, operating Boehmers Concrete since 1875.

The team was eager for the challenge and said it wanted to go to Cortina d'Ampezzo, Italy, two months before the official announcement came in August 1955 from the CAHA. It would leave on January 19 and return during the first week of February. Unlike previous years, the CAHA said that no exhibition games would be arranged ahead of time, citing "inadequate" monetary terms (though the Dutchies would end up playing two, one in Scotland and one in Czechoslovakia). The Games fell during the self-proclaimed National Hockey Week, so the CAHA could justify an extra 10-cent surcharge at all arenas, the extra dough to help the Dutchies. "It is the greatest hockey opportunity and privilege the Dutchmen will ever receive. We're sure they'll acquit themselves in a manner that will add to Canada's prestige in the hockey world," vowed Ray Bauer, past president of the team.

In the current era of easy international travel, it is quaint to see the *Globe and Mail* listing the "contingent of Kitchener hockey supporters" that were also going to cheer on the Dutchmen in the upcoming Olympic Games. "Heading, or it could be trailing (we're not sure which) the party will be R. F. (Spike) Kearns [outgoing president of the Ontario Golf Association]. . . . Other KW travellers are Mr. and Mrs. Frank Beibert, Mr. and Mrs. R.K. Ellis, Ray Bauer, brother of the Dutchies' coach, Ted Palowski and Dr. Jimmy Spohn, the team's physician." The team flew out of Malton Airport outside Toronto (now known as Pearson International) and the trip cost the CAHA about $17,000. A Trans-Canada Air Lines spokesman said, "It was the biggest sendoff ever seen at Malton," as the Dutchies flew first to Scotland, and then Prague, then Italy.

Gold was certainly expected, as the Dutchmen were a top team—not like the Senior B East York Lyndhursts, who had fallen to the debuting Soviet Union at the 1954 World Championships. After all, at the 1955 Worlds, the boys from Penticton, BC, known as the Vees dusted the USSR 5–0 and claimed the title. But the Dutchies, including names such as captain Jack McKenzie, Jim Logan and Howie Lee, with Denis Brodeur (father of NHL great Martin) in net, didn't have any international experience, though they had beaten the Vees for the 1953 Allan Cup.

Canadian Press reporter Ken Hetheral sent notice from Italy that all was kosher: "Canada's K-W Dutchmen are such prohibitive favorites for the Olympic hockey title that most of the pre-tournament speculation concerns the runner-up spot." And that's how it was for the early games, as Canada ran through Germany (4–0), Austria (23–0!), Italy (3–1), and Czechoslovakia (6–3). But the shocking upset to the United States, 4–1, threw everything into disarray in the round-robin tournament. The Russians were too much for everyone, beating the U.S. (4–0) and then Canada (2–0) to claim gold. The Dutchies finished third.

Jim Logan is one of the few still around from that 1956 team. He said Bobby was "a good coach" who preached an overall game. Though he was the leading scorer at the Games, Logan, who now lives in Sudbury, Ontario, downplays that aspect of the Olympic experience. "As you can imagine, it was fantastic. It was in Cortina, which was a ski resort at that time. They built the arena just for the hockey and the figure skating," he said. There was no Olympic village, so "we were spread out all over the place," Logan added.

In *War on Ice,* Young wrote that "the loss to the U.S. was psychologically the killing blow." CAHA President Jimmy Dunn limply said, "I am proud to say that although we were not successful in winning the Olympic title, the players and team executives were wonderful ambassadors for Canada at all times."

Like all the Dutchmen, Logan wasn't making a living from hockey. Following his education at St. Michael's College, he was in an accounting course at the time of the 1956 Games. There was certainly no advance planning or reports on the competition. "The Russians were very strong, but they all were in the Army, it was said," recalled Logan. No one knew the Russians would be as good as they were. "We didn't know anything. There wasn't any pre-scouting by anybody from the team like they have today. . . . We weren't familiar with any of the teams. We just dropped the puck, and away you go."

Canada and the United States boycotted the 1957 World Championships in Moscow in protest of the USSR's recent invasion of Hungary. In Oslo the following year, the Whitby Dunlops took top spot for Canada, and in 1959, the Belleville McFarlands did the same—it was Canada's 18th World Championship.

For the 1960 Winter Olympics in Squaw Valley, California, the K-W Dutchmen were actually the second choice for the CAHA, as the Allan Cup winners in 1959, the Whitby Dunlops, had declined to participate. Only three players remained from the 1956 lineup: Ken Laufman, Don Rope and Floyd Martin. Three others were eliminated because of their past as professionals: Bill Kennedy, George Gosselin and Dick Mattiussi. Reinforcements were called in from other senior teams, including Harry Sinden of the Dunlops, who'd go on to greater fame as a coach and manager in the NHL (though he got ill at the Games and was a non-factor).

And Bobby Bauer was behind the bench again, but that was not the plan at the beginning of the season. Post-1956, Bill Durnan had been the coach of the Dutchmen. He was a great athlete, a star fastball and softball player, earning wages in the game in the 1930s. But he was an even better goaltender, and would end up in the Hockey Hall of Fame in 1964—a result of just seven incredible years with the Montreal Canadiens—and with six Vezina Trophies as the best netminder in the NHL. Remarkably, he was ambidextrous, able to switch his stick and glove hands on a whim.

He coached in Rouyn-Noranda after quitting the Habs, and was with the Ottawa Senators of the Quebec Senior League, before ending up in Kitchener.

Durnan certainly had his successes in Kitchener, including the 1958 Allan Cup Eastern Semifinal, but he abruptly walked out at the end of December 1959, mid-season, in the midst of a losing skid, dropping 10 of 14 games. Goaltender Cesare Maniago, a Toronto Maple Leafs prospect after time at St. Michael's College, had been essentially loaned to the Ontario Senior Hockey League. "I basically was the floating goalie," he said. "I think I played with every team in the league that year through injuries to other guys. It was like, 'Have suitcase, will travel.'" Naturally, he was thrilled to learn the art of goaltending from Durnan, but was disappointed when he abandoned his post less than a month before the Olympics. "Bill had some problems. They let him go, and that's when Bobby took over," said Maniago. Durnan was cryptic, citing "not enough horses" with the Dutchmen.

The *Globe and Mail*'s Gord Walker called Bobby Bauer "Canada's Patriot of the Year" for stepping back in, setting aside his own business interests to lead the Dutchmen back to the Olympics. "What else could I do? . . . I couldn't see that I could do anything else. We have a club here—we can't let ourselves down," said Bauer. "I didn't seek the coach job," he pointed out. "You'll remember that meeting we had at Hamilton. The night before we tried for Joe Primeau, but he couldn't make it. Then at the meeting we called Hap Day and Ted Kennedy. Any of these men would have been ideal, but unfortunately, none was in a position to take it. That's when they put the pressure on me. I guess I thought about it, real hard, for three or four weeks, hoping something would take me off the hook. But something never did. So I did the only thing I could."

The whole setup for the Dutchmen was different than in 1956. For one thing, hockey minds had recognized that the sands were shifting in the international game, and a senior team wasn't necessarily a gimme for a gold. Given his experience with hockey abroad, Wren Blair of the Dunlops was brought in as coordinator of the Dutchmen. Blair, a notorious hothead, had a different style, admitted Bauer. "I'm not at all disturbed about Wren exhorting, or screaming at players from the bench. I don't care who does the exhorting. All I want to do is win. And if Wren's exhorting will do it, I'm all for it."

Olympic rules at the time meant a 17-man squad, including a spare goalie, but only 14 could dress each game, plus the spare keeper. "We won't name our team until the last minute," said Bauer. "If we did, and one of them got injured, we'd be in a bad spot. I'm taking some of our K-W team with us to keep them in shape. If I didn't, they wouldn't have any hockey until we returned home, and we've still got to finish our league."

So began the lobbying of the NHL for help, and the many "what ifs" that arose from the shuffling of players. The key figure in it all was George Dudley, the CAHA secretary-manager, who believed that an all-star team from the top senior clubs was the way to go, but he couldn't figure out how to get the funds to make it happen. A sponsored club from a particular city could pull off the trips cheaper, without flying in players from Vancouver or St. John's. "If we could get the Allan Cup team of the previous year as a nucleus that would be even better, but we'd have to pry the best players loose from other clubs," Dudley mused in 1958 to George Dulmage of the *Toronto Telegram*. He'd done some lobbying of the Progressive Conservative government in power in Ottawa, but hadn't been successful. As the boss of Canada's reps at the Olympic hockey tournament at Squaw Valley, California, Dudley knew his work was cut out for him and the team. "I'd like Canada to have its finest team there. We can't afford another Cortina."

While Squaw Valley was closer than Europe for the Ontario-based Dutchmen—who planned to travel by bus and train—it also eliminated the possibility of any extra income from exhibition games. Traditionally, fans packed the arenas in Sweden, Czechoslovakia, and even Russia to check out the Canadian teams. There was not the same expectation for the series of games planned on the way out to California. Instead, the exhibitions ended up being the kiss of death for a few who had thought they'd be Olympians.

Initially, new legs were expected from St. Michael's College in Toronto. Given that Father David Bauer was the manager of the Junior A Majors, his brother was coaching the Dutchmen, and another brother,

Ray, was again helping to finance the trip, it made sense. At various times, Dave Keon, Terry O'Malley and Les Kozak all were considered for the Olympics, as well as Maniago.

Father Bauer, without the support of his school, helped his brother by calling Frank Selke, managing director of Montreal Canadiens, about lending the Dutchmen a couple of players. One of the targeted players was Bobby Rousseau, a star with the junior Brockville Canadiens, a Habs farm club. Rousseau had had regular competition against senior teams, so it was believed he was better prepared for international play than an average junior. Cliff Pennington, the Winnipeg centreman, was also pried loose from the Canadiens for the tournament.

Keon got into a game with the Dutchmen during the regular season, and said he expected to play in Squaw Valley. "I was going to not play any of the exhibition games, but I was going to meet them about five or six days before Squaw Valley," Keon said. "Then about 10 days later, I was told I wasn't going to be going. I never really knew what had happened, but I didn't go. Bobby Rousseau went in my place."

If O'Malley had made the team, it could have meant four Olympic Games for him. He believes it was an academic issue, plus too much time away from school. "Dave [Keon] and I weren't the brightest on the academic side of things. We did okay, but didn't have that much interest in school," said O'Malley. "The principal wouldn't let us go down to play, which was one of those things. There might be more to it that I don't understand. Dave would have been a good addition in 1960 for sure."

With the approval of Canadiens president, Senator Hartland Molson, Selke okayed the loan of Rousseau and Pennington. However, when the two young players saw little action in Squaw Valley, it later created a rift between the Habs and the eventual national team program set up by Father Bauer.

The roster changes continued en route to California. Ted Maki had been a solid defender for the Dutchmen, and was rehabbing his knee. Still, he expected to be ready for the Games. "I was on the tour heading out west. At Moose Jaw, it was determined that I wasn't part of it because of my knee," said Maki, who would later coach the Canadian Interuniversity Athletic Union's Wilfrid Laurier Golden Hawks hockey team. "It was surprising." Being in Squaw Valley watching the Canadians claim silver wasn't much of a balm.

Maniago got further along the train-ride than Maki—both were included in the team-photo distributed to the press—but not to the Games themselves. "I was part of that team until we got working our way out west, playing exhibition games along the way," said the veteran of 15 NHL seasons. "We ended up in Vancouver, and that's when they decided that they were going to try to get Don Head to replace me. They wanted me to go back to Windsor; that's where Don was playing in the Ontario Senior League. I absolutely refused unless I was going to be guaranteed my trip back home and also a certain salary." The only plus in the ordeal is that Maniago helped lead the Chatham Maroons to the Allan Cup that spring.

In Squaw Valley, all teams ran into hot goaltender Jack McCartan of the United States, the surprising gold-medal winner. The schedule was wacky, bowing for the first time to demands of CBS and American television, with games from 8 a.m. to midnight, all crammed within a 10-day window. The expected battle for the gold medal, Canada against USSR, ended up being for silver when Canada won 8–5; the U.S. had already claimed all the glory earlier in the day with a 9–4 win over Czechoslovakia. Only eight of the original Dutchmen were on the squad in the final game, and many believed the constant turnover of players created turmoil.

By May, discussion about what to do for future international competitions began in earnest. The Ontario Hockey Association's annual meeting in Toronto proved to be a powder keg. Notable names in the room included chairman Wren Blair; Gordon Juckes of the CAHA; Ray Bauer representing the Dutchmen; Greg Currie, who coached the failed East York Lyndhursts in 1954; Harold Ballard of the Toronto Marlboros, also representing the Toronto Maple Leafs; George Dudley, Canada's Olympic convener; and W. A. Hewitt, who took teams to the 1920, 1924, and 1928 Olympics.

Ray Bauer preached practical patriotism. "In [the] future, the team should be called the Canadian Olympic team and not by any city," he said. "It's not fair to expect a single city to pay the bills. The Russians didn't have to raffle off cars to raise money to come." (The Dutchmen raised $40,000 over two years for the trip.) "We lost by one goal. I couldn't apologize for anything," Bauer said. "I'm very proud of the Dutchmen. There's more to competing than just winning."

Blair agreed with Bauer: "There is nothing to apologize for. We've lost before and we're going to lose again." For the World Championships, Currie proposed finding a coach, a manager and players that wanted to win, not old pros who were just out for a trip and a paycheque.

Ballard wanted the NHL to take over, obviously not understanding the complexity of amateur status, even though he had Olympic experience leading the University of Toronto Varsity Grads to gold in 1928, and to the 1936 West Toronto Nationals, which they lost to Great Britain's pseudo-Canadian team. "Let them take a week off and go over and give the rest of the world a darn good lacing. Take such fellows as Bobby Hull, Ralph Backstrom, Bill Hicke, Red Hay, Stan Mikita and Billy Harris—even if it costs money," he said. Ballard, for all his cantankerous nature as owner of the Leafs, saw the game's international evolution. After the 1972 Summit Series he offered up a million dollars for Soviet Valeri Kharlamov, and predicted that Russians would be in the NHL "within five years."

Juckes talked money. "If they want us, they have to pay some money. It's a disgrace that our team has to pay to build a club, go on tour and have $3,000 added for hotels and expenses and then have the Olympic committee take all the money. We get nothing and they take the gravy from our club."

Dudley knew something had to be done, as did everyone in the room. "Ours are the best 17 after 500 have gone to supply the needs to the pro leagues in Canada and the United States," he said. "And at the Olympics another 500 are eliminated because they are reinstated pros."

Juckes predicted the next decade of battles with international hockey and Canada's place in it. "It is essential to foster the international tournament," Juckes said, "but by a method not to sacrifice hockey in our own country. In the international years there's a way of solving the financial situation, but I'm disappointed in the way the Olympics are run. In Olympic years to come there will have to be some hard talking before we send a team over under the present rules."

How much of the discussion got down to David Bauer, teaching at St. Michael's, is unclear, but one fact stood out—the Bauer family had lost three championships in international play. The reason to return was not just to win, it was that it was a noble goal worth pursuing.

"We cannot hope always to win—no country can—but we can and do hope always to be well represented, to be seen at our best in every aspect of sport," wrote David Bauer seven years later. "If this is the case in all sports, it must be especially so in that sport which is most commonly regarded as our national sport. Canada, for a long time, dominated international hockey. That time is now well passed, and its passing must be seen as a good thing. The sting of international competition in hockey in recent years has played a large part in bringing many who are interested in hockey to take a long hard look at the structure of the game in Canada. The look may well lead to great improvements in the whole organization of hockey."

Chapter 5
CAPTAIN OF THE MAJORS

With a big brother playing in the league, Dave Bauer was on the radar of NHL scouts from an early age. He was only 16 when he was invited to Hershey, Pennsylvania, home of the famous chocolate brand and the American Hockey League's Bears. In October 1941, the Boston Bruins, fresh off a Stanley Cup win, held camp in town.

After apprenticing under Art Ross, Cooney Weiland had coached the Bruins to the championship. With Hershey's coach, Herb Mitchell, moving on to manage in Saint Paul, Minnesota, Weiland was sent down to the minors to run the Bears. With so much talent unable to make the seven-team NHL, the AHL abounded with potential. That included coaches, with the likes of Eddie Shore in Springfield, Ching Johnson in Washington, Tiny Thompson in Buffalo, Bun Cook in Providence, and Bill Cook in Cleveland—all future Hall of Famers. Weiland—Ralph to his parents—was assigned the task of putting about two dozen players through drills. Compared to some of the men, Bauer was a lightweight, only 135 pounds, and he had only played centre with a Waterloo junior team.

At the end of the camp, Bauer was invited to join the Boston Olympics, one of the Bruins' farm teams that played in town and from which call-ups to the big club were frequent. "Naturally I was tempted, and naturally my father was concerned," wrote Bauer. It was decision time. "This was where my problem with my father's teaching began. He viewed hockey as a means for the development of my personality, contributing to the growth of the physical and emotional side of my life within the framework of formal education. As for me, I could see something in that, of course, but I also saw hockey as a commercial enterprise, a way of making a good living. The strong pull exerted by the image-makers, even then, had so powerful an influence on me that I knowingly and willingly opted out of schoolwork in order to defeat the goals of my father so that I could be left to pursue my will in peace. My father was a strong-minded man, however, and not so easily defeated."

In *The Death of Hockey*, a 1972 book by Bruce Kidd and John Macfarlane, Bauer explains he turned down the Bruins offer "because when the world is in turmoil, the mind wants to know why. That's basically what happened to me." In October 1941, Canada had already entered the Second World War, as would the United States after the December attack on Pearl Harbor. "I wanted to get an education, not as an alternative means of getting the financial benefits I could get as a pro hockey player, but because it was important for me to see what one could learn about truth."

The compromise was to enroll at St. Michael's College in Toronto and follow in the skates of two of his brothers, Frank and Bobby. Important to Edgar Bauer was that "both formal education and sport were pursued with vigor and excellence."

The Catholic high school had been established by French Basilians in September 1852. The order opened St. Michael's College in Toronto in the basement of the Bishop's Palace on Church Street; the school thrived and moved in 1856. The new home was just outside the city limits at the time, on land known as Clover Hill, located near the current streets of Bay, St. Joseph and St. Mary. The estate was donated by the Honourable John Elmsley. The next step, in 1881, was an affiliation with St. Michael's College at the University of Toronto for post-secondary education. Two other satellite schools operated for a short while until, in 1950, the school moved to its current location at Bathurst and St. Clair.

Looking back 30 years later, Father Bauer could see that the training camp wasn't what he thought it would be. "But something had also started to happen within me. I knew now that I could play in the NHL, but I had been disillusioned by what I had seen at the training camp. I saw there an empty life, and seeing it somehow made me aware that I was looking for something more, for a life in which I could fulfill goals beyond myself, goals of world peace which had begun to occupy my mind more and more."

In fact, he called it a "traumatic experience" because "for years I had been thinking of my own future almost exclusively in terms of playing in the NHL and now suddenly I had seen that as insufficient." That realization would start him on the path towards a commitment to amateur hockey over professional sport, which is, at its core, a business first.

Starting Grade 11 in the fall of 1942, Dave Bauer found a new home at St. Mike's. He was back playing all the sports he'd loved in Kitchener—and given that such old pals as Bobby Schnurr had made their own way to the school, it felt a lot like home. Goaltender Pat "Smiley" Boehmer, also from Kitchener, would become a friend for life. New friends included Brian Higgins and Ted "Peanuts" McLean, both future priests as well.

"Schnurr to Bauer" was a common theme on the gridiron as the St. Mike's boys competed against other Toronto high schools in football, going undefeated the two years Bauer was at the school. The *Globe and Mail* previewed a clash between St. Michael's and Runnymede Collegiate with the promise that, beyond his hockey skills, "Bauer also is a football player of no mean ability, to dust off a phrase."

"I played Senior Football with him in 1943. However, he was a star and I a rookie, so I didn't really get to know him. We had an unbeaten season. Other 'stars' were Higgins, MacLellan, Wilson, Clark, Frezell, Odette, and his buddy, Bob Schnurr," McLean told George Gross in 1988. "The next year Dave led us to another undefeated football season, climaxed by two wins in Winnipeg where he, Bulger and Bandiera were standouts. By the way, the *Winnipeg Free Press* said, 'Teddy McLean was a standout in the games.' In fact, I had my jaw broken on the first play of the first game and didn't play again. . . . So much for press reports."

In the summers, Bauer would suit up for junior and senior baseball in Waterloo, where he was an effective pitcher. But it was hockey that was Dave Bauer's main love, and the school loved him back. "In all the long history of St. Michael's none have borne the title of captain more worthily than Dave," was a line in the recap of the school's student publication, the *Thurible*, in 1944. He was captain for two seasons, the first under coach Father Hugh Mallon.

No one could claim that Bauer played favourites, said teammate John McCormack, an Edmontonian by birth. "We used to fight. He used to say that Milt Schmidt was the best hockey player ever, and I'd say no, Neil Colville was," said McCormack, who'd play in the NHL against Bobby Bauer. "But now, I agree with him. I think Schmidt was better than Colville."

There was a challenge to balancing schoolwork and hockey, and not everyone could do it. But Bauer could. McCormack said he had his own issues, as did teammate Ted Lindsay. "All he wanted to do was play hockey. He didn't care about the classroom. He was just down there to play hockey—and he did a good job of it," said McCormack.

Lindsay confesses that McCormack's description is spot-on. "I think I was focused on where I was going. I wouldn't think of it then. I had a good brain, I had a good head, but hockey was my number one love—not books."

According to Lindsay, Dave Bauer saw a bigger picture, even then. "He was a priest then," Lindsay said, attempting to further explain. "He was a Father to every guy, every man in the school, he was a Father. He was going to save all of us. Super, super gentleman." On the ice, Bauer was equally cerebral, said Lindsay. "He was a mechanical hockey player. . . . He thought everything out, like he was in the class."

There was a little time for other activities too. Bauer dated, including one woman he was apparently serious about. Years later, when Bauer was teaching at St. Michael's, he took Terry O'Malley on a trip to Niagara Falls and introduced him to a woman who he had dated when he was a younger man. "I ended up the chaperon. She was absolutely beautiful," said O'Malley. "He wanted me present so that this very public meeting would not be misconstrued. He was a cautious man and very committed to his vocation." The girl's father had disapproved of a hockey-playing beau that would have no future, ending the relationship. The experience was perhaps another reason Bauer passionately pushed education, so that other fathers would look more positively on hockey players.

The Junior B Buzzers would frequently practice with the Junior A Majors at Maple Leaf Gardens, often before school started for the day. Phil Samis was one of those Buzzers, and he looked up to Bauer, captain of the main squad. "He was highly regarded," said Samis, who briefly played in the NHL before becoming a dentist. "He was a man's man, if you know what I mean."

Like Samis, future Hockey Hall of Famer Red Kelly used to watch the Majors and learn. He noted what Bauer was great at. "What stood out was along the boards, he would skate and get through. It would look like he'd be nailed or something, but he always seemed to be able to get through there."

Hockey was a way of life at St. Mike's, said Samis. "The Fathers played hockey. They had a rink there, and they all played hockey. It was quite interesting to see when the Fathers were out skating with their robes on, down to their ankles."

Bauer's numbers for his first season were decent; he notched 10 goals and 11 assists in 20 games during 1942–43, and another 10 in the playoffs. He was presented with the senior athletic cup for outstanding achievement throughout the year at the father-son banquet in May 1943. Like other high schools, St. Mike's athletes lettered in sports, and at the same dinner, the letter "M" went to Majors Bauer, Jerry Hickey, Cecil Schmalz, Jean Marois, Greg Carter and Bob Schnurr.

He was even better his second full year, with 12 goals and 37 points in 25 games. The *Thurible* commented how Bauer was the last to leave the ice after practice, desiring to continue working on his skills: "Friendly, considerate, unselfish, studious, he didn't know how to quit. A constant inspiration and a model, Dave is modest and unassuming. . . . On the ice he was a skilled winger, a hard skater, and a battler. 'Take it up the boards, Davey,' we yelled; and when he did, no opposition could stop him. He had a way of drawing out a goalie and a deadly accurate shot that made opponents squirm when he got in close."

Like his brothers Bobby and Frank, Dave Bauer would win a Memorial Cup. Unlike them, however, it wouldn't be for St. Michael's.

In the spring of 1944, the OHA Majors were neck and neck with the Oshawa Generals. They might have been the best two teams in the country, but only one could go through to the playdowns for the spot as the eastern representative in the Memorial Cup. As often happens in sport, a key injury changed everything.

John McCormack centred the team's top line, though in his own words, "We were pretty interchangeable. We had a good coach, Paul McNamara, and he just used his shifts, from A to B to C." McNamara, who'd had his own successes in the OHA, wasn't that much older than his players—just 22 when he took over as coach.

Bauer was a natural forechecker (once called a "human fly" in a newspaper), so his line, often between Bobby Schnurr and Joe Sadler, had different challenges. When McCormack went down to injury, away went the Majors' chance against the Gennies. "If he'd have been healthy, we'd have beat Oshawa," said Lindsay. "They had a great team, but we also had a great team. But we needed John to be our big centreman on our number-one line." Bauer got 12 points for the Majors in the playoffs. Oshawa then steamrolled over the University of Ottawa in a best-of-three series, waltzing to 10–3 and 11–1 wins. The eastern final pitted the Gens against the Montreal Royals. It was closer, with Oshawa taking the best-of-five series in four games.

With World War II raging, allowances were made for player losses, and the Memorial Cup challengers were each allowed call-ups. The Generals turned to their foes, the Majors, and scooped up Dave Bauer, Ted Lindsay, and future NHL mainstay "Old Hardrock" Gus Mortson on defence. Looking back, Ted Lindsay can see how adding three major stars could bolster a team, even if it was under the heading of "military replacements." It still goes on now, but through trades earlier in the season, as junior franchises divest older players for draft picks and prospects. "Hockey clubs, all hockey itself, always wrote all their laws, their rules, in pencil, so they could erase them if they wanted to change them. That was my philosophy on what they did with rules," said Lindsay, who was not yet "Terrible Ted."

"Old Hardrock" Mortson had played with Lindsay in Kirkland Lake, Ontario, and would later captain the Chicago Black Hawks for a time.

Ironically, Mortson had tried out for Oshawa two seasons earlier. "But I didn't click. Then I went home and spoke to the priest who was running our juvenile team and he made arrangements for me to enroll at St. Mike's," explained Mortson in the *Hockey News* in 1950. The Generals also had the Majors goalie Johnny Marois ready if needed to fill in for Harvey Bennett.

Lindsay said that switching squads, joining the foes, wasn't as strange as it might seem. "We played them enough through the year that we knew them pretty good. I kind of was a student of the game. Maybe a lot of people didn't think I was, but I was a student of the game. I knew [what] I was doing. I knew what you had to do to win."

Oshawa's opponent in the Cup was the Trail Smoke Eaters, commonly called the Smokies. The skaters from the small British Columbia company town, where Cominco and its smelting facilities were the major business, had battled their way to represent the West under coach Gerry Thompson. A very young team, even in junior hockey terms, the Smokies averaged 17.5 years of age, believed to be the youngest average ever for a Memorial Cup finalist. In goal was Bev Bentley, just 16, the nephew of NHLers Doug and Max Bentley. To get to the championships, the Smokies swept the Edmonton Canadians in a best-of-three series before moving on to a longer series against the Regina Commandos.

It was supposed to be a best-of-five battle, but instead the teams played eight games. Junior hockey historian Gregg Drinnan explained the issue on his website: "The first three games of the series ended up being tossed out when Paul Mahara, a Trail player, was found to be ineligible. In fact, the Canadian Amateur Hockey Association ended up suspending Mahara from organized hockey for three years for 'twice falsifying baptismal papers.' Only a signed confession by Mahara kept the CAHA from hitting him with the maximum five-year suspension." In the games that eventually counted, Regina won the first two, but the Smokies took the final three to move to the west final, where they eliminated the Port Arthur Flyers in three straight.

In the Memorial Cup final, the Generals drove home to victory over Trail with ease, 9–2, at Toronto's Maple Leaf Gardens, making it a home game for Oshawa, just a little less than an hour east of the city. Bunny

Morganson of the *Telegram* wondered if there were answers out there: "Coach Gerry Thompson of the Trail Smokies would welcome any sound and practical suggestion as to how the Oshawa Generals can be stopped, if possible, in their mad, terrific and super-duper dash to clinch the junior championship of the Canadian Amateur Hockey Association." Short answer? There wasn't one. The Gens took the next two—5–2, then 15–4 in a game that saw key Smokies, Frank Turik, Lorne Depaolis and Mark Marquess, go out with injuries. The Trail goalie, Bentley, skated to the bench at one point and asked to be pulled before his mates encouraged him to continue.

Game 4, on April 23, 1944—with tickets priced at 50 cents, $1.00, $1.50, and, for all service personnel, 25 cents—was notable perhaps only for the fact that there were three more Majors in the lineup—for Trail. Given the injuries, the westerners were allowed to call up three, and chose Bobby Schnurr, Johnny McCormack and Jimmy Thomson. McCormack said they didn't even met the Trail players until in the dressing room before the game. On the way to the ice, he overheard a fan say, "There go the sacrificial lambs." The final score was 11–4, and Bauer finished with four goals and three assists for the Generals.

Morganson of the *Telegram* was pleased for Gens coach Charlie Conacher. "It was his first Memorial Cup after two failures and he was very happy about it all. Chuck celebrated by getting into most all the pictures and should receive a contract any day now from Hollywood to replace Clark Gable."

The *Telegram*'s sports editor, J.P. Fitzgerald, put things in perspective a couple of days after the conclusion: "Oshawa Generals are Memorial Cup winners and worthy ones. It is bootless to argue whether they are as good as or better than past champions. Certain it is that as amended and bolstered for the playdowns by three St. Michael's boys they compare most favourably with anybody's team of any year. And without the St. Mike's addition they were quite a bit best in their OHA sections. The junior series was the one least of all touched by the war though now that the season is over its ranks will be riddled."

Many of the Majors, like McCormack and Mortson, looked back on St. Michael's Memorial Cup win, in 1945 over the Moose Jaw Canucks, as a career highlight, but for Dave Bauer, it was a non-issue. He played a single game that 1944–45 season before heading off to do his part for his country.

The *Double-Blue* newspaper at St. Michael's College School, noted his departure: "Dave Bauer, a young man who has endeared himself to the hearts of all St. Michael's fans and teammates, entered the service of his country on November 24." In the *Toronto Star*'s Look! Listen! column on December 6, 1944, it was reported that the centre had been called away: "Shun! Dave Bauer, St. Michael's junior puck star of last season, is now in the Canadian Army."

Bauer was assigned to #12 Basic Training in Chatham, Ontario. In 1996, Lt. Douglas J. St. Louis of Windsor, Ontario, recalled his time with Bauer in a letter to the editor in the *Catholic Register*:

> During the war years 1939–45, I was stationed to 12 B.T.C. Chatham, Ont., as an infantry instructor.
>
> Sometime in 1945, David Bauer, Canadian infantry, was sent to Chatham as a recruit to prepare to take part in the action then raging in Europe. I was fortunate to have this budding hero in one of the platoons under my charge.
>
> What an inspiration he was. Even though he had celebrity status, having taken part in a Memorial Cup championship, he was a man of much humility, quiet by nature and very unassuming.
>
> He and his good friend Ted Lindsay were both members of St. Mike's Majors, but because of wartime manpower shortages went on loan to Oshawa to become a part of the Oshawa Generals, the Memorial Cup champions.
>
> My remembrance of Bauer is witnessing him on his knees, fervently reciting his Rosary in the midst of the crowded quarters with many young men around. It was an act of much courage under the circumstances.
>
> We became very good friends and even doubled-dated a couple of young ladies from Mercy College in Detroit.
>
> I remember him with such affection, admiration and respect.

> He was a real hero of faith and conviction with such strength of character, not one to receive the accolades he so deserved.

All the Bauer brothers would serve in the Second World War: Bob and Ray were in the Royal Canadian Air Force, Jerry took to the Canadian Navy, Gene and Dave enlisted in the Canadian Army, and Frank was in the reserves. A cousin, Flight Sergeant Wilbert Francis Bauer, who had played hockey with the Waterloo Siskins, was killed in action in Europe—the news arrived back home in October 1942.

During his time in the service, Dave Bauer ended up playing a little hockey too, with the Ottawa Canadian Postal Corps, which played in the Ottawa National Defence Hockey League. There was also a short stay with the Windsor Spitfires of the Windsor City Hockey League. "I had a brief stint in the army just at the end of the war, which if anything increased my interest in education," Bauer wrote in his 1971 report. Upon his release from the military, Dave Bauer enrolled at the University of Toronto.

Chapter 6

GOD 1, HOCKEY 0

The University of Toronto Varsity Blues took to the ice for the 1946–47 season with two notable absences. "Varsity hopes suffered a hard blow when Dave Bauer and Ted McLean joined the priesthood," reported the *Globe and Mail*. "Bauer was a stalwart of last season's team while McLean captained St. Michael's College to the Memorial Cup finals in his last season of junior-age play." Hockey's loss was God's gain, but He had to learn to share.

John McCormack, who'd played alongside both McLean and Bauer at St. Michael's with the Majors, was not surprised, especially by fellow centreman Bauer. "He was orientated that way," said McCormack. "We had three of them on our team jump right into priesthood." (The third was Gerry Gregoire.)

Following Bauer's passing in 1988, columnist Ray Alviano of the *Kitchener-Waterloo Record* sought out people who knew Dave, not Father Bauer. One who shared his memory was Otto "Dinty" Stuebing, a minor baseball and hockey coach. "Ach David, why did you do it?" Stuebing asked Dave in his heavy German accent. "I guess you don't want to work for the rest of your life!" It was a story that Father Bauer told again and again "with great relish, a guffaw and belly laugh afterward," said Terry O'Malley. "He could laugh at himself."

In 1946, Father Bauer entered St. Basil's Novitiate in Richmond Hill to study for the priesthood. His first professional vows came on September 12, 1947. He was ordained at St. Basil's Roman Catholic Church in Toronto on June 29, 1953 by Cardinal James Charles McGuigan.

A man of the world before he had even travelled it, Bauer was concerned about lasting global peace. "At 19 years of age I could see that our system of education ought to produce more wise leaders than most other countries in the world because of the close cooperation between Church and State within the educational structures of most provinces in the Dominion," Father Bauer wrote. "All of this tied in closely with the lessons which I had learned from my parents and friends and especially with the teaching of the Basilian Fathers at St. Michael's where I then started into university."

Bauer returned to St. Michael's College at the University of Toronto to complete his undergraduate studies, graduating in 1949 with a Bachelor of Arts, philosophy major. He studied and took to heart the philosophy of Jacques Maritain and the writing of British Catholic historian Christopher Dawson, who explored the Christian past through modern popular culture and art.

Maritain, from France, was reared a Protestant, but converted to Catholicism as an adult. "To exist is to act" was at the core of Maritain's beliefs, and he emphasized the importance of the individual in the Christian community. (Efforts to share didn't always work. "He told me I had to read Jacques Maritain," said Dave Keon. "I think I read five pages. 'I don't understand what this guy's talking about . . .'") While on a trip with the hockey team to France, Father Bauer visited Maritain in a facility run by the Little Brothers of the Poor near Toulouse.

"Those of us who lived with Dave in the Basilian community believed he was a prince among his brothers, if not for his affability then for his inability to say a bad thing about anybody," wrote Father William O'Brien in 1996. "For instance, as an undergraduate, he had become enthusiastic about two great Catholic philosophers—Jacques Maritain and Etienne Gilson—who didn't incorporate hockey into their teachings. As a result, much of the conversation in Dave's presence ridiculed the athletic incompetency of Maritain and Gilson, leaving Dave no alternative but to defend his philosophy heroes!"

The desire to read and learn never left Bauer. Later, on trips abroad with the national hockey team, Bauer would be engrossed in any number of books. "He'd have two or three books on his bed, open, all the time," said Terry O'Malley. "He had a BA and his theological training, but he never really did post-secondary work at any high level. But he certainly got personally educated and he had wonderful mentors."

In the report to Munro, Father Bauer quoted Maritain, who he said was "writing of the significance of pluralism in society and the fear some Christians had of this sort of open competition in human society." Maritain said:

> As for myself, who believes that the idea of man propounded by the metaphysics of Aristotle and Thomas Aquinas is the rational foundation of democratic philosophy, and that the Gospel is its true living soul, I am confident that, in the free competition of which I just spoke, the Christian leaven would play an ever-growing part. In any case the responsibility for nurturing, strengthening and enriching a common democratic faith would belong no less to the priest, dedicated to the preaching of the Gospel, than to the teacher, dedicated to the scientific spirit, if both of them came to a clear awareness of the needs of our times. Moreover, since it is a question of a secular faith dealing with the temporal order, its maintenance and progress in the community depend primarily on lay apostles and genuine political leaders, who are indebted to the scientific teacher for knowledge of the factual conditioning of human life, but much more, certainly, to the priest for knowledge of its meaning, its ends and its ethical standards.

To the young Bauer, the teachings provided direction. "Ideas such as these rang clear bells in my mind when I was 20, just as they seem vitally important to me today. They, along with my own deepening religious convictions, led to my entry in the fall of 1946 into the novitiate of the Basilian Fathers. Since that time my life has been that of a Basilian: one year as a novice, several to complete my studies in arts and in theology with some teaching interspersed and since 1953 as a priest."

The Basilian Fathers believed in education, and Father Bauer got his teacher certification in 1951 from the Ontario College of Education. The Latin motto of the Congregation of St. Basil is "*Bonitatem et disciplinam et scientiam doce me*" from Psalm 119, "Teach me goodness, discipline, and knowledge." The foundation is explained further on the Basilian website: "Our motto is a biblical reminder of our role as a teaching community and the simple, foundational importance of goodness and discipline in our celebration of God."

In Father Bauer's world, there was *ludus* too. Sports were more than just for physical exercise. A higher-ranking Roman Catholic thought so too. "Sports are a school for loyalty, courage, endurance, determination, universal brotherhood and all the natural virtues. These in turn serve as a solid foundation for the supernatural virtues which prepare one for withstanding without weakness the weight of more serious obligations," said Pope Pius XII.

Ernie Goman of Waterloo was a lifelong friend of Bauer's, and was the manager of the Kitchener-Waterloo Dutchmen for years as well. "He [Bauer] was an individual of great ideas and had lofty aspirations for everyone, no matter what segment of society they happen to be from," Gorman told Ray Alviano of the *Record*. "He would challenge people to try to improve themselves and to seek greater heights. Right from the time he started playing sports, you knew he had the ability to lead and inspire people to accept him as an individual they would like to follow, whether it was in sports or other walks of life."

Rick Noonan was one of those followers of Father Bauer. A student at St. Michael's, he would help out the hockey teams, and then head west with Bauer to British Columbia, serving as the trainer for the 1964 Olympic team. After working in the UBC Athletic Department, Noonan was asked to manage the 1980 Canadian Olympic team. Through 30 years of friendship, Noonan said that Bauer was very much aware of how he could possibly be perceived, so he set out to be balanced. "The fact that Father was a Basilian priest, he used to worry about that a lot, that people would misinterpret that he was trying to turn everyone into a Catholic. But really, he was very ecumenical," said Noonan. "And you look at some of his teams, the year we won the Memorial Cup, there were more non-Catholics than Catholics. They all loved him equally."

Bill Holowaty was a UBC Thunderbird after the heyday of Father Bauer, but hockey was hockey, and Father would still come down to games and practices on campus. There was a magic about Father, said Holowaty, who would have his own life altered by Bauer when he followed his encouragement to go play in Japan. "It was almost intoxicating to learn about his philosophies. I think anybody within the clergy, certainly a Basilian priest, a Catholic priest, would be intimidating if you were not from the church or had religious views, but he was not that," said Holowaty. "Subsequently, I really found that was the beginning of making me more comfortable in so many scenarios, but just because—this wasn't a typical match, this hockey coach, this hockey mentor, who never put pressure on you to convert you to Catholicism, if that was what he might have thought. He really had such special hockey insight that it was easy to buy into."

Somewhere along the way, Father Bauer learned to listen. "One of the things that Father was famous for was just being quiet. You'd be talking to him and he would have what we called the 'FB Pause.' There would just be a break in the conversation," said Holowaty. "Early on, you would want to fill that void and ended up talking and maybe saying more than you absolutely needed to. But to this day, the idea that you learn more by listening than you do by talking is something that guides me, guides my kids. The comfort in that you don't have to blurt an answer out or comment right away, you're allowed to think about it and put together a well-thought-out statement or argument without having to rush into the conversation."

There were times when hockey was not a part of Father Bauer's life, but the same can't be said for his relationship with God and his work as a priest. Besides his time at St. Michael's College in Toronto as a teacher and administrator, he spent 27 years at St. Mark's College in Vancouver, BC, where he often led services. Those who knew him, like Terry O'Malley, say that he struggled and laboured on his sermons, his goal being to point things out to you, but still keeping the message relevant with a touch of humour. He excelled in small group situations, like Bible study discussions and seminars. Yet he was a very private person as well, rarely drawing attention to himself. There were other ways Father Bauer shared the Word, through remark and deed.

In 1952, the entire Bauer family was a major part of the establishment of the Carmel of St. Joseph Monastery in the Kitchener-Waterloo area. Bishop J. F. Ryan of Hamilton may have been the main conduit to invite the Carmel of St. Joseph nuns to the Southern Ontario area, but the drive and financing came from Edgar Bauer and his family. The monastery now sits outside the city proper, in St. Agatha.

St. Jerome's Roman Catholic Church in Waterloo was the scene where Father Bauer performed his first Mass as an ordained priest in the summer of 1953. Through the years, Father Bauer conducted Mass countless times, and it was not always in a traditional setting. At the Memorial Cup in Edmonton in 1961, Father Bauer held Mass in the motel, using a portable altar that had been borrowed from the Archbishop of Edmonton. O'Malley recalled a Mass at a small chapel in the French embassy in Moscow. Another occurred at a church in Prague, where "four rough-looking characters all of a sudden appeared behind us giving us scowls."

Such was the following of Father Bauer and his hockey team in Europe that, somehow, the locals would find out where he was saying Mass and pack the church. When he was coaching in Austria, he made a special request to celebrate Mass in the pilgrimage church of Mariatrost, and his Austrian players all attended.

But there were personal connections too, said Holowaty. "He did Mass one Christmas in our house, and some of his brother Ray's kids who were in Toronto were there. That was a special night."

Father Bauer was no saint, of course. The art of socializing in his era meant having a drink, and Bauer liked his scotch. A favourite brand? "As long as it was good," said Noonan, who spent many a night sipping with Father, especially over plans for the 1980 Olympic team. Brad Pirie was on that '80 team, and chuckled over the question of having a drink with Father. "Then he'd go from priest to truck driver."

Ross Morrison was one of the original Bauer Boys, and lived in the

Hockey House on UBC campus, where he had an upper bunk in the trailer that was attached to the back of the house. He said Father had another habit. "Sometimes in the middle of the night, the door would open and I would be lying there," he said. "It was pitch black, but I could feel this presence. He'd come in and reach under my pillow and take my cigarettes! I'd say to him, 'I know it's you, Father . . .'"

And he was great at taking things in stride. Should you speak the Lord's name in vain in the heat of the moment during a game, you would find yourself with a gentle hand on the shoulder: "Now, now, I do the praying around here."

Holowaty was a part of the 1980 Canadian Olympic program but didn't make the final team. He did, however, play in a number of exhibition games, including one against the Americans at the Corral in Calgary. Down by a goal, loose cannon Glenn Anderson spoke up in the dressing room: "We've got to start hitting the fucking net!"

"Just at that time, Father had walked in the door. As he's walking across the dressing room, he goes, 'Glennie, what type of net was that?' and he keeps walking right out of the room. Shock, but all of a sudden, everybody loosens up. I think they went on to win the game," said Holowaty. "He knew hockey players were hockey players, and the culture is such as it is. He would never make you feel that you couldn't be who you were. At the same [time], it challenged you to know that there's a place for that."

For a Roman Catholic, however, nothing is more special than an audience with the Pope, and that happened for the whole Canadian hockey team after Innsbruck. After a few exhibition games post-Olympics, the team arrived in Rome. On February 15, 1964, the Nats were received by Pope Paul VI in the Apostolic Palace in Vatican City. "The athletes wore their jackets with the Olympic emblem over the pockets. Father Bauer wore the same jacket over his cassock and Roman collar," reads the Canadian Press report.

The story that ran in the news only tells a small fraction of the tale, said Morrison, who didn't get to play at the Olympics because Bauer thought he was too unpredictable. For one, Father Bauer had crowed that he was in his element, and would be the focus. Yet there were Swiss guards at the Vatican who, upon being made aware that the Canadian team was there, started getting excited. "Seth Mar-tin? Seth Mar-tin?" The fame of Canada's greatest goaltending export had preceded him and overshadowed his coach.

Morrison stressed that meeting the pontiff was never a guarantee; the team was promised nothing more than a chance to be in the greater audience for a papal blessing. The team, including a photographer and a couple of others associated with the Nats, slowly progressed from checkpoint to checkpoint, stonewalled by bureaucratic priests with clipboards and stern instructions to turn admirers away. Stymied right near the end of the process, Providence intervened, said Morrison. "We were standing there, milling around, and this priest goes walking by with the long robes on, and the round hat with the big brim, with a briefcase." The priest overheard their frustrations, and introduced himself. He was from Chicago and was thrilled that an Olympic team was at the Vatican. "He goes over to this guy and gives him a raft of shit in Italian. It took about that long," Morrison said, snapping his fingers. "He spoke to this guy in Italian and that guy absolutely collapsed, so he had some stature, this guy. So in we go." The team was instructed to stand in a horseshoe and told that His Holiness would stop to bless the team, and then everyone should go to the main audience in the St. Peter's Square.

But that's not what happened. An ornate chair with a foot stool appeared at the opening of the horseshoe formation, and Father Bauer was addressed: "His Holiness saw who you were, and he wanted to meet the team." A short speech was read and Pope Paul VI came into the room.

Morrison was practically roaring in laughter at the next bit. The Nats had already seen many of the riches of the Vatican, but there goes Father Bauer, approaching the head of the Roman Catholic Church . . . with a postcard of the Canadian team and a Russian lapel pin as gifts.

In his mind's eye, Morrison could still see the trinket. "It was rectangular, and it was powder blue with a white snowflake in white, and in the top, in white, was 'CCCP.' They were like hen's teeth at the Olympics. There weren't many of them. To get one was really something. So Bauer gave this to the Pope, and of course, Bauer being as astute and knowledgeable as he was, the words he said to the Pope were, 'This is the Russian lapel pin from the Olympic Games, and we played the Russians, in furtherance to the benefit of the world, the interplay of cultures through sport.' He did a really nice job," said Morrison.

Each player got a brief personal audience with the Pope and was allowed to kiss the Piscatory Ring, and a photographer snapped a shot. Many of the players, especially the Roman Catholics, had brought rosaries and other treasures for the Pope to bless. (Morrison later gained the everlasting love of his mother-in-law by handing a blessed key-chain over to her.)

Outside the room, though, they returned to being a fun-loving hockey team, and razzed their leader. "Father, the guy's got rubies like this, and you gave him a little pin and a team postcard?"

Chapter 7

SCHOOL DAYS

In 1954, Father David Bauer received his first assignment, and it was a familiar one. Though the school had moved since he was a student—from Bay Street to a bigger campus at Bathurst and St. Clair—it was still St. Michael's College.

And in many ways Father Bauer, the teacher, was a lot like Dave Bauer, the student. Both loved their sports.

Bob Pallante was one of his students. "He was close to guys, he was like one of the kids. He'd be out there playing touch football with the guys," said Pallante, a defenceman who'd play four seasons for the Majors. "He was a good athlete. He was a good hockey player. He was a good football player. Whatever sport he migrated to, he did very well at. He was a very well-educated man, too. He was very cerebral."

Another player/student, Les Kozak, recalled being recruited to the football team by Bauer. He was hardly the only future NHL player who excelled in other sports at the school. A contemporary was Gerry Cheevers, the future Hockey Hall of Fame goaltender. "Cheevers kicked field goals, and he was cool as a cucumber, he'd never miss!" said Kozak. Father Bauer was good at all the sports, said Kozak. "He knew all the details and mechanics for every sport that was played in our culture. Tennis, baseball, football, and, of course, hockey—I think he played golf too."

During his lifelong friendship with Father Bauer, Terry O'Malley saw the priest excel in many sports. "Apparently he was a great football player," he said. "I remember seeing a picture of him and he was the quarterback for the team. He said to me one time, 'You know, if my fingers were just a quarter-inch longer, I'm sure I could have played in the CFL.'"

In later years, O'Malley and Father would golf together in Japan, often taking to the driving range for practice. The skills he had at St. Mike's were still evident. "I was out at the St. Mike's football field, just 'round the other side of where the rink is," said O'Malley, "and he'd take a ball and say, 'I'm going to put it right there at home plate.' He'd blast that thing in. It would be 150 feet, diagonally across the field, and he'd whack it out there."

In Grade 12, O'Malley came across many of the school's Italian students—Cesare Maniago, Lou Angotti, Gene Rebellato, Gene Ubriaco, and their buddies—playing baseball in a parking lot lower than the surrounding ground. "They were pitching, they were throwing and a fight broke out. Father was in a soutane, the black robes, and he runs over and tries to break it up—I can't remember who the fight was between. But it took all his strength to break it up. He said, 'What's the problem here?' The guy says, 'I'm pitching strikes and he's not calling them.' They had a guy behind the catcher, and they had steps, so that was your backstop. They were just playing catch and throwing strikes. These guys were good athletes. . . . He looks and he says, 'Strikes? You want to see strikes?' So he marches off 60 feet, tucks his soutane into his pants, and he's got street shoes on, and starts to pitch strikes. He could throw sliders, he could throw curves, he could throw heat—and he was doing this right-handed. Then, to our total astonishment, he started to pitch left-handed; he didn't have the heat, but he had curves and he had strikes. He turns to the guy and he says, 'Are those strikes?' And the guy says, 'Yeah, yeah, Father, they're strikes.' He says, 'Sportsmen call strikes. Now call strikes as it's supposed to be.' And he walked away. Everyone was agape because he was that good an athlete."

As in any boarding school, students face an immediate growing-up period, necessitated by living in a dormitory setting. "It was a melting pot," said hockey great Dave Keon, who'd come down from Noranda, on the Quebec side of the northerly Ontario-Quebec border. "We all boarded in residence. For the majority of us, it was the first time we'd been away from home. That was a really big thing to go through because most of us, for a little while anyway, we were homesick. It was always a process of trying to get better and trying to widen your horizons."

There was a priest living on every floor of the dorm, but that doesn't mean things were calm. Boys will be boys, said Gene Ubriaco, the small left winger from Sault Ste. Marie, Ontario. "We jumped out of the windows so many times that the second year we came back there, they put something on the windows that we could only open them up maybe six inches. Imagine hockey players with real students!"

Though the school was run by the Basilian Fathers, not everyone had time to talk about counsel. In the classroom at various times, Father Bauer taught ethics, religion, theology, and history and offered guidance. "He was the kind of teacher that inspired you," said John Gouette, who'd later become a teacher himself, and organize an oldtimers hockey league. "Everyone in the class, first of all, did well. He just gave everyone fair marks. . . . He recognized the individual student."

Future NHL player, coach and general manager Lou Angotti says that Father Bauer "was always upfront and a very honest kind of guy. He always was around to give you advice. He always took a personal interest in all the players that he was associated with."

Thomas O'Brien was not a hockey player at St. Mike's but was equally enthralled by the teachings of Dave Bauer in 1957. "I can still hear his gravel-truck voice coming from near his belt buckle: "'Don't play around with the bandwagon, or you might get mixed up with the music,' he said to me once," O'Brien wrote in his memoirs of his time at the school. "Look at those fire-darting eyes, from an angry Sphinx, maybe. Look at the chiseled nose, jaw, and forehead right from a granite quarry. And all the time he had a gentle way about him. He'd walk into a room and it would go quiet all of a sudden." The hockey stories found their way into Bauer's religion lessons, wrote O'Brien:

"Gentlemen," he'd say, and off he'd go about living one's life for Christ. "The mark of a truly understanding Catholic is living with Christ. Whether, when you're playing a bad game of hockey and getting booted all over the ice, you understand yourself better doing it in the name of Christ. You can be bagging groceries in a supermarket and be very much at ease with yourself, if you're living with Christ. You're doing your best in the name of God, and for the glory of God. That, my dear friends, is true prayer."

"Does that mean that smashing an opponent into the boards is being Christ-like," he asked one day towards the end of the school year. "Gentlemen, the game of hockey is a good legitimate sport and if a maneuver, such as a clean check, ends up with someone getting hurt, don't blame the game. Real hockey players play live, clean hockey, and that includes clean, solid body-checks, along the boards or at centre-ice."

He'd have half the room with their hands up all trying to cross-question him about what he meant and how they were to implement his thoughts. Only the stupid—and there was always one—would mutter something like "panty-waist" or "away off again, too fundamentalist—as usual."

At the same time as he was dishing out advice, he was taking it too. One of Father Bauer's mentors through the years was Father Henry Carr, a scholar, athlete, coach, builder, and leader of the great university tradition of the Basilian Fathers within Canada. Bauer was hardly the only one influenced by Carr. "Carr was also something of a giant in the domain of spiritual direction," explains a 1999 *Catholic Insight* story. "He wrote countless letters to priests, sisters, and brothers of religious congregations, sharing his insights into the works of the great spiritual writers, such as St. Teresa of Avila and St. John of the Cross, correcting false notions of holiness, encouraging anxious souls in their spiritual journey."

Carr arrived at St. Michael's College in 1897 as a lay teacher, and was ordained seven years later. He brought both hockey and football to the school and coached for years, including during his time as the superior of St. Michael's College, 1915–25. He also significantly altered the high school curriculum to set up students for university admission, and partnered the growing institution with the University of Toronto. His efforts helped open the door for all Catholics to seek higher education at what were initially mainly Protestant schools. The University of British Columbia conferred a degree of Doctor of Laws on Carr in 1955, and the accompanying citation credits his revolutionary contributions to education in Canada: "Very Rev. Henry Carr, C.S.B., a scholar of outstanding attainment, who throughout a lifetime devoted to the education of Canadian youth has been an inspiring and challenging teacher, a fearless champion of Christian principles, and a leader of great vision and discernment. His qualities of heart and his spirit of real Christian charity have brought him the affectionate esteem of generations of students and of all those who have been associated with him during his illustrious career."

In January 1957, Father Bauer was named assistant principal at St. Michael's College. Despite the additional duties, his interests on the field and ice remained important. "I began coaching football and hockey on a rather full-time basis," he wrote in his report to John Munro, Minister of Health and Welfare, in June 1971. "Prior to ordination I had coached football at St. Michael's College in the University of Toronto and as a part-time teacher at St. Michael's College School I had assisted Charlie Gerre with the St. Michael's Majors in the OHA Junior A division. Now as a reflection on the philosophy of sport gave way to action, I continued to work with the Junior A team but also coached a bantam team, and during the next seven years I coached in every division of minor hockey except one until I took over as coach of the Majors."

Chapter 8

MAJOR ACCOMPLISHMENTS

There are some who might argue that Father David Bauer's greatest contribution to hockey wasn't helping to create the Canadian national team or winning the Memorial Cup in 1944 (as a player) and 1961 (as a coach), but rather the shaping and molding of none other than David Michael Keon into a Hockey Hall of Fame–calibre player.

Yet, technically, Father Bauer was not Davey's boss. "He was never my coach. He coached the year after I left," recalled Keon from his home in Florida. "He was the manager of the team, but when [coach] Bob Goldham was unable to come to practice, Father ran the practices. He had a certain philosophy of how he wanted the game played."

That philosophy began and ended with checking—both giving and taking—and Keon is Exhibit A. "He and I went head-to-head," Keon said. "His big project was to get me, as far as I was concerned anyway, to change my philosophy of what I thought hockey was about . . . and [show] how his philosophy would improve my play. It took him two years to get through to me, get it into my head."

Just about every player around in those days has a story about seeing Father Bauer working with Keon. Terry O'Malley was playing midget while Keon was in Junior B and saw one of their sessions. Father wanted Keon to work on his backward skating, and Davey was having none of it. "They start to get into a bit of a shouting match and he kicked him off the ice," said O'Malley. Fast-forwarding to a reunion at St. Mike's decades later, he asked Keon if he remembered the incident, and eventually it came back to him. Back at the dormitory, Keon and Bauer had an impromptu wrestling match to solve the dispute. "He must have won that argument because Dave Keon ended up one of the best checkers to ever play the game."

There was one occasion where Father Bauer, the GM, sat Keon out of an important game just to get his point across. The dilemma then was: should the Majors lose, then Keon's belief in Father would have been even more tested. "I think Father Bauer's greatest player was Davey Keon; there's no question about it," said goaltending legend Gerry Cheevers. "How he played was really a Father Bauer–style player."

A two-way centreman, the five-foot-nine, 165-pound Keon would play a remarkable 22 seasons in the NHL and World Hockey Association, but even more incredible was that he amassed only 151 penalty minutes during his career.

Billy MacMillan has an example of how Bauer's checking lessons paid off for Keon. "Everybody playing against Bobby Orr would try to ride him off into the boards, keep him isolated where he couldn't go either way, or he could only go one way. Well, Keon could check Orr in the middle of the ice, and that's what Keon was taught by Father Bauer. Because he wasn't that big, and he had to be a great checker—and I don't mean hitting guys. He was just great defensively, they couldn't get around him." MacMillan and Keon were line-mates with the Toronto Maple Leafs from 1970–1972.

That isn't to say Keon wasn't naturally gifted or didn't work at his game. He did. More than most. Every Saturday morning while at St. Mike's, he would head out at 6 with twin brothers Dave and Bruce Draper, hop on the streetcar, and go to Maple Leaf Gardens, where a friendly attendant let them in to skate around in the dark, equipped with just their skates, sticks and gloves. "I came to understand that if I was going to get better, I was going to have to adapt to what he was talking about, which was to learn how to play without the puck, and to work when you didn't have the puck," said Keon, also quick to credit Goldham and Father Ted Flanagan. "That took a while to sink in. But when I came to the realization that that's what I had to do, then things improved."

In an interview in the *Hockey News* in 1959, Father Bauer talked about Keon. "Two years ago, he thought he could get by on goals alone," he said. "Then, he made up his mind he'd have to learn to check in junior hockey or spend two years in the American Hockey League learning it. He has applied himself and now he's a pretty good defensive player."

Keon and Father Bauer stayed in touch through the years, especially when Davey's NHL career took him through Vancouver. They talked on the phone often, including just before the priest's death in 1988. When Keon was inducted into the Hockey Hall of Fame in 1986, Bauer was one of the people he invited to attend. Rick Noonan, who'd been around Father Bauer throughout his time with the national team, saw their deep love for each other first-hand. In 1983 Keon was in Vancouver for an oldtimers game, and Noonan and his wife had the two in their car. When it was time to drop off Father at St. Mark's, they shared a moment. "Father got out one side of my car, went around, and was standing in front of the lights and Davey got out and went around, and there they were, in the lights of the car, and there was an embrace that just said, 'Thank you.'" Noonan said. "I'd like to think that if Father had played in the NHL, he would have been a carbon copy of Davey. They were the same size . . . same type of skaters. I think Father saw that in David."

Of course, Keon was just one of dozens of young men who improved their hockey at St. Mike's through the teachings of Father Bauer. And their vocal feuding was the exception, not the rule. "He had a really quiet discipline in school and on the ice. He never shouted or got upset," said future NHLer Arnie Brown. "He'd listen to you very closely and then he'd suggest some things."

But it came back to checking, always. And that included *being* hit safely. Rod Seiling, 1964 Olympian turned long-time NHLer, appreciated Bauer's efforts to keep them healthy. "The first thing he did, the first practice, he took and showed us how to protect ourselves," Seiling said, explaining the process. "When you go into the boards, get your hand up so your head hits the back of the glove, not the glass. That was the first. The second was, if someone was going to run you into the boards, how to take your stick and let them run into that stick rather than you. I found it quite interesting that a man of the cloth would teach that."

There was an art to being checked, stressed the coach. Get an angle on your man. Keep him to the outside and don't let him into the middle. The wingers came back to check. A strategically-placed stick between an opponent's legs could significantly slow him down.

Some other philosophies included having players switch positions to better appreciate what their colleagues were doing. That included the goalies, said Cheevers, who played 12 games as a forward. "I thought it was going to be fun until the first time, which was sort of a rowdy team, I went into the corner and all five of their players came in the corner with me. I took an exit left and watched myself from there on in. He said it would do nothing but improve your skating. I was a decent skater. He said, 'It'll really help your skating and your perspective on playing the game.'"

Immediately upon his return to St. Michael's College, Father Bauer was involved in the hockey program. That first summer, he was elected as St. Mike's representative on the OHA Junior A council, meaning he quickly got to know the movers and shakers in Ontario hockey, such men as Leighton "Hap" Emms in Barrie and Eddie Bush in Guelph—both of whom would play a part later in the national team scheme, for good or for bad.

Junior hockey, with energetic, hoping-to-be-noticed teenagers playing the game, was always rough and unpredictable. Players were expected to be tough, and wild melees weren't uncommon. Father Bauer's team was different, though, said Cheevers, especially when compared to a team like Bush's Hamilton Red Wings. "Eddie Bush was trying to run us out of the rink, and they just couldn't do it. Father Bauer, he didn't like the ploy, he didn't think it was right hockey. It was Eddie Bush, actually, and he threatened to pull the team out and everything. But all it was was a psych job and we beat them."

Bauer worked with all levels of teams at the school, both as a coach and a general manager. He knew all the players in the system and how they were doing in their classes. He had a key helper—Jim Gregory. The native of Dunnville, Ontario, had come to St. Mike's to play hockey but found he wasn't up to snuff; he could score, but just couldn't skate well enough. Mr. Bauer—not yet a Father—had just returned to the school himself and convinced Gregory to stay. It was the start of a great mentoring relationship. Gregory had a day job at Colgate-Palmolive and helped out with hockey at St. Mike's more and more as Father Bauer assumed greater responsibility around the school outside of sports. Since the Majors were sponsored by the Toronto Maple Leafs, Gregory was often charged with collecting money to keep the program running. Stafford Smythe, son of Leafs owner Conn Smythe, was his contact, and a friendship bloomed. "Old Man" Smythe used to call the visitor from St. Mike's "Pope" Gregory, and the nickname stuck for a long time.

In mid-1959, Father Bauer surprised Gregory with the question, "Do you love doing this? Would you like to work in hockey for a living?" Taken aback, Gregory replied, "Are you nuts? I'd crawl on my hands and knees." The priest took Gregory, newly married and making $73 a week, to Maple Leaf Gardens and Stafford Smythe. The fix was in, the decision made, but still Smythe put Gregory on the spot: "What makes you think you can be a hockey guy?" "Well, I do it for Father Bauer," replied the "Pope." Asked about a wage, he bluffed and said he made $90 at Colgate-Palmolive. Smythe hired him at $95 a week to be a pseudo-assistant manager both for the hockey system and also the family's gravel pit. Gregory would build the Leafs-sponsored "Protestant" junior team, the Marlboros, for a few seasons, including during the 1964 Memorial Cup, and, in the spring of 1969, was named general manager of the Leafs. He held that job through the contentious Harold Ballard days, and, once relieved of his duties in 1979, Gregory moved to a job with the NHL, eventually rising to vice-president. He was inducted into the Hockey Hall of Fame in 2007 as a Builder.

The Majors' relationship with the Leafs wasn't always smooth sailing. Often at issue was what came first: the interests of the player or the interests of the Leafs?

Goaltender Cesare Maniago of the Majors was in the middle of such a tussle in 1957 when he was summoned to the Gardens to face scout Bob Davidson, assistant general manager / coach Hap Day, and all-around jack-of-all-trades King Clancy. The hockey men wanted Cesare, who hailed from Trail, BC, to sign a C form binding him to the Leafs for $100. He wavered and they threatened: "If you don't sign it, we're going to end your scholarship and send you back home."

"Well, now they've got me in tears. I go back up to the school. I get a hold of Father Bauer and tell him the story," recalled Maniago. "Now he's absolutely fuming. He gets on the phone, and I'm in the office when he's on the phone, and he's talking to Hap Day." Day confirmed Maniago's story and Bauer turned into a protective papa bear. Maniago says, "I heard Father Bauer's response: 'Listen, if you ever try to do this again, to him, or any of our players up here, we will sever our relationship with the Toronto Maple Leafs.' Click, he hung up the phone. He pointed his finger at me and said, 'Cesare, you're not going anywhere. You're staying here.' I just beamed from ear to ear."

In junior hockey, the Memorial Cup remained the goal for teams across the country. The Majors had come close, but hadn't won the big prize in junior hockey since 1945. A young Dave Bauer was on that team briefly, before heading off to serve his country in the war.

Things came together in 1961. The same core of players—captain O'Malley, outstanding goalie Cheevers, future NHLers Larry Keenan, Arnie Brown, Billy MacMillan, Terry Clancy and Barry MacKenzie, as well as such future mainstays of Team Canada as Paul Conlin and Gary Dineen—stuck together through midget and Junior B, building bonds and learning each other's tendencies.

It wasn't hard to believe in Father Bauer as a coach, said Cheevers. "He was incredible. He was way before his time in running things. When we got together in our junior year . . . we knew we were going to win the Memorial Cup. I didn't know how good we were, but with his leadership, you just believed you were going to win."

The whole 1960–61 season was one of change in the OHA Junior A loop, with four of the seven teams installing new coaches. At St. Mike's, Bob Goldham resigned as coach of the Majors, citing business pressure. Goldham, a former Detroit Red Wings defence ace, had come on board in 1957 after coaching in Toronto's Junior B league. As the season neared, Father Bauer, having approached a few different candidates, installed himself as coach, while maintaining the GM portfolio.

With Father Bauer behind the bench, the Majors finished second in the OHA, lead by the league's second-best scorer, Bruce Draper, with 44 goals. The team had speed and endurance and knew the fundamentals of checking inside and out.

"We didn't have the best offence in the world, but we did have a great defensive system, and that was thanks to Father Bauer. That was what really carried us through, brought us onto victory," recalled Paul Conlin. "I don't think anybody would have picked us to win the Memorial Cup. Guelph was the big team that year. They had Rod Gilbert and [Jean] Ratelle and [Bob] Cunningham and [Dennis] Jordan in goal, Bob Plager on defence." The Guelph Royals, coached by Emile "the Cat" Francis, finished the regular season 11 points ahead of the Majors.

At the same time, things were changing behind the scenes that would make this the final time that the Majors would ever even challenge for the Memorial Cup. The balance between academics and hockey had swung too far towards the latter for the Basilians. For the most part, the players concentrated on the games, only learning about the unlikely future of the program through newspaper speculation—no one went on record until the season ended.

In the playoffs, everything came together for St. Michael's. The powerhouse team from Guelph, with ace Gilbert off for back surgery, was dumped in a grueling seven-game series (four wins for Toronto, two losses and a tie), and the Majors moved on to the eastern playdowns against the overmatched Moncton Beavers. Bauer worried about a letdown: "We may have left our mental edge in Guelph," he said after the game. "In our dressing room Monday, I noticed all of the talk was about the west and the final series for the Memorial Cup. Not too many of our players seemed to be worrying about Moncton, but they seemed to be looking ahead to the winner of the Winnipeg-Edmonton series. I know that Moncton will give it a tremendous try. I don't know anything about Moncton. The only player they have whom I've seen is Lloyd Gallant, a defenceman. He was with us early this year and played some games with our Junior B team. Then he got homesick and went back."

Father Bauer needn't have worried. The Majors, playing at home at Maple Leaf Gardens—tickets $1.00, $1.50, $2.00, or $3.00—won 11–2 in the first game, on April 19, and, with the series still in doubt, arrangements were made for a trip to Edmonton by trainer/manager Gregory. They were a confident bunch; the 6–2 win a couple of days later to earn the eastern nod is proof that it wasn't misplaced.

A rallying point for the team was paralyzed 13-year-old Tommy Smith, a super-dedicated Majors fan who had befriended many of the players when they came in for their own treatments at St. Joseph's Hospital. A photo ran in the *Telegram* of Smith with O'Malley and the Richardson Trophy at centre ice after the game. Initially, the players had lobbied to take Smith with them out west, but the teen's complicated schedule of appointments at the hospital made it impossible.

Before the Memorial Cup began, Coach Bauer preached caution. "We are winning but I don't like the *way* we are winning," he said. "We are acquiring bad habits and I don't know what to do."

After a sendoff at St. Michael's College, the team flew off on a Trans-Canada Air Lines Viscount to Edmonton, which was hosting the Memorial Cup for the first time. Edmonton teams had made five Cup finals, including a 1934 loss to St. Mike's, but had never won; a championship would have to wait until 1963.

At the traditional Memorial Cup banquet held at the Macdonald Hotel in Edmonton, Father Bauer rubbed shoulders with old buddies like Johnny McCormack and Ray Hannigan, and NHL hockey royalty such as Jack Adams of the Detroit Red Wings, Bill Gadsby of the New York Rangers, and Billy Hicke of the Canadiens, as well as famed scouts like Bob Davidson and Al Ritchie. But a couple of key men from the Canadian Amateur Hockey Association were there too—vice-president, series convener, and dinner chairman Art Potter, and secretary-manager Gordon Juckes; they'd prove to be far more influential on Bauer's next nine years than anyone not a part of the Majors, except maybe the young, five-foot-nine centre from the Oil Kings, Roger Bourbonnais. The Oil Kings played as a junior team in the Alberta Senior Hockey League, meaning the players were home most nights, which was especially conducive to getting an education. Bourbonnais was on his way to an economics degree from the University of Alberta, and dreamed of more—he'd study law after signing up for Bauer's Olympic program a year later.

On the ice at the Edmonton Gardens in Game 1, Gerry Cheevers had some excellent protection, and it ended 4–0 for the Majors, which the Edmonton newspaper called "dull." He was used to the defensive efforts. "Quite frankly, it was an easy team to play for. We never got bombarded," said Cheevers. "[Father Bauer] was a strict disciplinarian as far as checking goes. Our best guy in our whole Memorial Cup run was a guy named Larry Keenan, who was even a great checker in the NHL."

Game 2 was similar, a 4–1 win for Toronto. "That Cheevers is quite a goaltender," praised Edmonton coach Buster Brayshaw. "He held them in there. He's got terrific reflexes. He was down on one knee once in the last period and kicked out the puck with the other foot. I still don't know how he did it." Father Bauer wouldn't go quite as far in his plaudits: "He played quite a bit better than average," said Bauer. "He made some key saves. But don't forget that other guy [Paul Sexsmith] made some great stops, too. It's still a close series."

Looking back 50 years later, defenceman Arnie Brown can appreciate Father's line-matching skill. "He was a great strategist. The best line against the opposition's best. He outcoached the other team by the fact that he'd always somehow get the line that he wanted against that line. When we played in the Memorial Cup in Edmonton, that was very important. We had the two Drapers and Keenan playing, and they were the big line. Well, they tried to place their best checking out against them all the time, but he would somehow get them out there with the other lines."

With the addition of forward Stan "Sonny" Osborne, who'd been stuck at home with exams at the University of Toronto, the Majors took Game 3, 4–2. Osborne had been a mid-season pickup for GM Bauer, as the rival Marlies had cut him on New Year's Eve. The three goals and an assist in the third game made it look like a great decision. "He's got a big heart," said his Majors coach.

The Oil Kings battled back, though, taking Game 4 on May 1 by a 5–4 score ("We lapsed for 58 minutes. We were a step behind all night," said Bauer), and Game 5, doubling up the Majors 4–2. After that one, Bauer was confessional, wrote Mike Armstrong in the *Telegram*: "Father Bauer actually blamed himself more than any player for the loss. 'I didn't shift my players around soon enough,' said Father Bauer. 'Our forwards were playing better on defence, and our defencemen better up front. Bruce Draper was much more effective on the blue line than he was as a forward. Larry Keenan was playing hard but was off his game. But I can't be too unhappy when we shoot like that.'"

There was much going elsewhere in early May 1961. Just before the final game of the Memorial Cup, American Navy pilot Alan Shepard took his capsule 115 miles up into the atmosphere at 5,000 mph, making him the second man into space. Back on Earth, the Bay of Pigs Invasion of Cuba was still fresh on everyone's minds, and Father Bauer would seemingly rather talk to the press about it than hockey. Laurie Artiss, covering the series for the *Brandon Sun*, wrote Bauer "has to be the most refreshing coach to come along in some time . . . no hackneyed phrases for him . . . just absolutely gracious in winning, sympathetic with the opposition and such."

To take his young players' minds off things, the master strategist shook things up. The team moved from a hotel five miles from downtown to Edmonton's premier hotel, The Macdonald, for the night. During the day, he took them to a nearby lake, where they hung out as a team at a cottage owned by a St. Mike's alum and played baseball. "It was just a day in the country," said Coach Bauer.

The Majors' 4–2 win in front of 7,159 fans to claim the school's fourth Memorial Cup—a record at the time—was a last hurrah, predicted Armstrong in the *Tely*, months ahead of the actual announcement. "This was probably the last Memorial Cup the St. Michael's Majors will win because it will be the last one they will compete for," he wrote. "Majors' coach, Father Dave Bauer, added authority to the possibility of his team withdrawing from Junior A by admitting, 'there is substance to the rumors.'"

As for the game itself, Cheevers was a star, but the coach pinpointed another key moment. "The turning point came when Paul Conlin made the score 3–1," said Father Bauer. "The puck took a bad hop and Paul Sexsmith had no chance."

It was time to return home, preceded by headlines like the *Globe and Mail*'s: "ST. MIKE'S THUMP KINGS TO CAPTURE MEMORIAL

CUP." There was another celebration in town too, as the Buzzers from St. Mike's had won the Sutherland Cup as OHA Junior B champs. The last Buzzers win? Coincidentally, it was also in 1945, when the Majors had won their previous Memorial Cup.

Watching film of the team's return to Malton Airport is like going back in time. All the players wear ties. Father Bauer sports a fedora, carries a book, and is all smiles, a beatific grin if there ever was one. Lots of people are smoking. The players have to get their own equipment off the plane.

The 64-piece school band led the team in convertibles up Bay St. to Toronto City Hall, where Mayor Nathan Phillips welcomed the champion Majors and Buzzers. The papers estimated the crowd at 1,000, made up mostly of teenagers "armed with firecrackers, horns and confetti."

The players sported stetson hats, and Father Bauer presented the mayor with a 10-gallon hat and a hockey stick. The mayor gave the players what was called "freedom of the city," an invitation to the upcoming Civic Sports Banquet, and the promise of gold cufflinks emblazoned with the civic crest.

Alice Bauer also threw a reception for her son's team at her home in Waterloo.

On the road to the Memorial Cup, the Majors played 98 games. That was in addition to regular life, classwork and studying. It was too much, said the school, and Father Bauer believed the same thing.

At the end of the 1958–59 season, after the Majors had lost to the Scotty Bowman–coached Peterborough TPTs in a gruelling eight-game OHA final (three wins, two losses, three ties for the TPTs), he'd lobbied for a reduced schedule. "The situation is so serious with us that if we can't play a shortened schedule, we will have to serve notice that we will drop out after next season," Father Bauer told the OHA Junior A council in April 1959.

The Majors already played fewer games in 1960–61—48 to 54 by other teams. To make up the difference, six games counted as four-pointers for the Majors, but only two points for their opponents. "It's too taxing on our players if we have to go through a full schedule," Father Bauer also said. "Our standards of education have intensified. If we had beaten

Peterborough in the league final and gone on for another week, I'm sure we wouldn't have had one upper school student on the team pass."

Father Bauer had warned the team's financial backer, the Leafs, that a change was coming with a letter to Stafford Smythe. "My opinion is that sooner or later [the college] will see fit to discontinue the Junior A series because of its growing professionalism, its long schedule and rough play which so often results in unfavourable publicity difficult for the educational institution to handle gracefully," he wrote.

On June 6, 1961, Reverend Matthew Sheedy, the principal of St. Michael's College, made it official, and his press release alleged that the schedule "mitigates against effective schoolwork" and that the school's "efforts to bring about appreciable change seem to have been met with no success." Father Bauer was sought out for most of the comments. "This was not a hasty decision," he said. "That idea had been bandied about for years."

Decades later, in a 1987 interview with Father O'Brien, Father Bauer addressed the decision:

> Our General Council had talked about this for a long time and they talked to me about it. I suggested that some of our relationships may have been damaged a little bit if we left in a way that would sever our connection so abruptly. Hard feelings would arise from the league. At any rate, hockey as an institution had been poorer as a result of it but maybe that's because the entire world has become a marketplace. That spirit seems to be pervading everything.
>
> We were always trying to cut down on the violence, cut down on the length of schedules, cut down on the materialism of the whole thing. We regretted very much leaving because we knew that this [school] is a major recreational institution in this country. The 1961 season, I think we played 98 games. At that level and at that pressure, if you really look over the whole history of it, it's amazing the number of boys who did it and survived academically. It was amazing what could be done even with those difficult circumstances. You have to have mixed

> feelings about it. It would have been a good thing to remain to have that moderating influence on the sport, then to have the trickle-down effect and it permeates through. That seems to be absent but I don't know whether we could provide that if we were there today.

Defenceman Rod Seiling had only played a couple of games with the Majors that season, sticking mainly with the Buzzers. He recalled "rumours" of the impending decision to drop out of the OHA. "Sheedy didn't want his students at school being associated with hooligans," said Seiling. "I thought that was not reality, and he was someone who wasn't really in touch with what was going on. But we weren't privy to the politics behind the scenes and what was really going on."

The players that remained—10 were over-age and a number left for university—had little choice but to accept the drop from the OHA to a newly-formed five-team Toronto Metro Junior A Hockey League. Other competitors were based in the Greater Toronto Area—Brampton, Unionville, Whitby—as well as the Marlboros. In its single season in the TMJAHL, the Majors won the league championship under the guidance of coach Father Ted Flanagan and general manager Jim Gregory, but fell to the Hamilton Red Wings in the competition to represent the east in the Memorial Cup. Again, the school was not comfortable with the work/hockey balance, and withdrew completely from competitive hockey. (The St. Michael's Majors Ontario Hockey League team from 1996–2012 played at the school and then in nearby Mississauga but had no formal affiliation with the school.)

Almost all of the Toronto Maple Leafs prospects switched to Neil McNeil, another Catholic school in the city, with Gregory taking over as coach. "For that year, we looked at about five places to move the team," said Gregory, whose title was director of the Leafs amateur farm system. There were possibilities in Kitchener and Guelph. "We ended up staying and we went to Neil McNeil, a boys' school out in the east end, and we stayed there two years. In '64, we amalgamated the Marlboros and Neil McNeil and went back to the Ontario league."

As for Father Bauer, he learned of his assignment just days after St.

Michael's pulled out of the OHA, on June 10, 1961, when the superior-general of the Congregation of St. Basil published the annual list of appointments. With top-level hockey gone from the school, he was half-expecting reassignment, but the location was a definite surprise. Bauer was reassigned by the Basilian order to serve at St. Mark's College on the grounds of the University of British Columbia in Vancouver. "An official at St. Mike's said there was nothing significant to be read into Father Bauer's transfer to British Columbia," wrote the *Globe and Mail*, noting St. Mark's had no hockey team. "However, he has been the central figure in the year-long soul-searching consideration of hockey values in the school. St. Michael's withdrew from the OHA Junior A group last week."

There are many theories about what happened, and some still wonder if Father Bauer got too big for his britches. "Then they shipped him out to BC. I guess he was getting too much publicity," said Billy MacMillan, a right winger for the Cup champs. "We were sad to see him go. Hockey kind of went down for a while after that."

Terry Clancy had played for the champion Majors and would later join the 1964 Canadian Olympic team. He too wonders whether jealousy didn't factor into things. "I don't think a lot of the other priests liked that he was getting all the notoriety. They knew he was a good coach and I'm not saying everybody felt that way. But that was going through the school at one time."

Father Bauer, in his report to John Munro in June 1971, addressed the move:

> Needless to say, this was bound to affect my own position. I had been coaching for seven years and thought a change would be in order. I suggested therefore to my Basilian superiors that I be moved to something quite different. Still, I was surprised, pleasantly surprised, when my appointment was changed to St. Mark's College in the University of British Columbia. This was a real change. Vancouver was hardly a hockey hotbed; I was moving into a new level of education and I really did not expect to have much to do with hockey from [then] on. I could hardly have been more wrong.

Chapter 9

FATHER GOES WEST

St. Mark's College, the Basilian theological residence on the campus of the University of British Columbia, couldn't have been more different than St. Michael's. Located at the school's northeastern tip in the beautiful Point Grey area of Vancouver, the Pacific Ocean was a short jaunt away, and the Rocky Mountains loomed to the east.

Bauer settled into his role with the college, teaching ethics to the nurses and serving as chaplain at St. Paul's Hospital. His home was a modest room in St. Mark's, and the small student residence attached to the college would soon be a home to some of his players and lifelong friends. Officially, Father was Newman chaplain and dean of residence.

Terry O'Malley followed the priest from St. Michael's to UBC. "The order sent him out. You get these letters of assignment every spring. It's a tense time for all the priests. He got assigned to St. Mark's College . . . They were trying to establish at St. Mark's College what they had at St. Michael's College, which was an affiliation with the main university. Since the Basilian Fathers were the best men in education, some were sent out to UBC."

From the start of the school year, the *Ubyssey*, the student newspaper, predicted that Bauer would be involved with the UBC hockey coaching staff. The Thunderbirds were not a strong team, and didn't always see eye-to-eye with their coach. Al Stuart, a Vancouver schoolteacher by day, had taken over the team in 1960. His players called him "Brush," for his brush cut, a remnant of an era just passed.

In Bauer's June 1971 report to John Munro, Minister of Health and Welfare, the priest acknowledged that he had been approached prior to even heading west. "Before I left Toronto I received a letter from the athletic authorities of UBC, asking if I would coach the UBC hockey team in the following year. I wrote back that I would think about it and we could discuss it when I got out there. When I did get there I was reluctant to take it on but agreed to assist the coach."

The T-Birds didn't even have a place to call home. Any team tryout first consisted of showing up at a classroom or a gym to talk to the coach. Practices were usually at the two-decade-old Kerrisdale Arena, roughly 20 minutes from campus, mostly late at night; for games, players and a few fans would bus to the dumpy old Forum in Vancouver, opened in 1936 on the Pacific National Exhibition grounds. Other games or practices were at the North Shore Winter Club, in Chilliwack, which was known for its curling rink rather than its hockey surface.

Their foes in the Western Intercollegiate League included the Universities of Alberta, Saskatchewan, and Manitoba, all a long distance away. The team made do on occasion by playing exhibition games with nearer semi-pro teams and squads at American universities and colleges just over the border.

Mickey McDowell was from Vernon, BC. His father owned a car dealership in town which sponsored a team in the Okanagan Senior League. Young Mickey got to know the players and developed into a speedy, if small, forward. He played his junior hockey in Regina, Saskatchewan, and the Montreal Canadiens owned his rights. But McDowell never forgot the lessons imparted to him by the restless senior players who held day jobs and pursued hockey: "Don't be a hockey bum."

For a time, McDowell toiled in the senior league he grew up watching. "I could live at home and play very good hockey, make more money and have a job," McDowell recalled. The money in the pros was not enticing, and the idea of travelling across the continent to be stuck in Rochester, New York, was completely unappealing. At the time, the

Rochester Americans were co-sponsored by Toronto and Montreal of the NHL. "The players used to call it Rottenchester, because you could rot there," he said. Some of the AHL teams were loaded with talent and could probably handle the weaker NHL teams, like the Bruins, on a good day. But McDowell felt a higher education would serve him well, and chose UBC, enrolling in the fall of 1961. He didn't choose it for the hockey. "I looked at the university hockey team and said, 'Scratch that. They're dog meat. They're awful.' I wasn't going to play there after the [high level] hockey I'd been playing."

There were horror stories circulating among the players on campus about life under Al Stuart. "The coach they had at the time was a real piece of work," said McDowell. Some of his friends went to the school's athletic director: "We've got to get rid of this asshole. On top of that, we've got the best coach in Canada sitting here at St. Mark's."

The rebellious players had already approached Father Bauer, but he had declined to get involved or to pick sides. "It happened, however, that a number of the boys on the team lived at St. Mark's and they kept after me about it so that finally, after talking with [phys. ed. teacher] Bob Hindmarch and [UBC Athletic Director] Bus Phillips, I agreed to coach the team after Christmas," wrote Bauer. "Coaching in BC was to be a new experience for me, for this was one area of Canada in which hockey was not really a major sport."

In January 1962, players returned to campus and learned that Father Bauer had replaced Al Stuart, just as the official part of the season was about to begin. "Athletic department officials have released no official statement on the reason for the change," reported the *Ubyssey*. The *Hockey News* noted the coaching switch: "Father Bauer indicated he was reluctant to take on the job this year, but since the remainder of the season would involve only a couple of months' work, he accepted the appointment."

Bauer set out to recruit. "I got a call from Bauer. He says, 'I know you're on campus. I know you played. Just come to one practice,'" McDowell said. Local players such as Boone Strother, Ken Smith and Peter Kelly also came on board.

Others on campus, like Stu Gibbs, a defenceman who'd played junior with the New Westminster Royals, didn't commit. Gibbs recalls running into McDowell around Christmas, and Mickey enthused that Bauer had taken over coaching. "You should have stuck with us," scolded McDowell.

The schedule was already set, beginning with a pair of games January 12–13 against the University of Saskatchewan in Saskatoon. There would be eight Intercollegiate League games total, plus exhibition games with Gonzaga University, Summerland, and intermediate teams in New Westminster, Powell River, Nanaimo, and Victoria.

The *Ubyssey* introduced the student body to the new coach of the "usually hapless icemen" with a photo of Father Bauer. Oddly, he was standing in front of a calendar issued by Maple Leaf Gardens, featuring photos of the top amateur teams in Canada: the Trail Smoke Eaters and the Galt Terriers. Both teams would play into the future of the national team.

Bauer preached the basics: "I'm going to stress fundamentals and try to build a strong defence for a base to work with," he told the student paper. As well, he proved his knowledge of the pro game of the past, explaining that a combination of a Toronto defence under Hap Day and an offence under Toe Blake would be the best team hockey had ever seen. He also praised Joe Primeau, who had coached at St. Michael's College before graduating to run the Maple Leafs, as the greatest "psychological" coach in any sport.

Knowing that he didn't have the most skilled team, Father Bauer planned to close up the style the team would play. "We're going to stop stick-checking and throw a few more artistic body checks. We won't be vicious; we'll just impede our opponents' forward progress with the odd shoulder."

Bauer took an optimistic look at the future of UBC hockey. "With all the players coming up from the new junior teams in the province and with the good nucleus that we already have to build around, we could be giving the prairie boys a good run for their money in the very near future," he said.

The planned UBC winter sports arena was part of Bauer's rosy outlook, It was scheduled to open around Christmas 1962, but wouldn't actually begin operations until 10 months later.

"As it stands now, my players only practice three times a week in the middle of the night," he complained. "We just have to have more working time if we're to improve to the calibre necessary to bring home some honors."

Having played under such crusty retired players as George Agar and Bobby Kromm, McDowell found Bauer's approach a breath of fresh air. "He was *so* different than any coach I'd ever played for," he said. "I started going to his practices and realized right away, 'My God, this guy really knows what he is doing.'"

After just three practices with the new coach, and zero games, the T-Birds departed for a four-game series against the far more experienced clubs in Saskatoon (which had played seven exhibition games) and Edmonton, where the Golden Bears were the defending western champions. The roster had seven first-year players, and goalkeeper Bill Rayment was considered the strongest player on the team. Returning intact from the previous season was the line of Denny Selder, Bob Parker and Chern Singh. Bauer said that it was an "an experimental series" where he would try players in different positions.

The results were as expected; the Thunderbirds lost all four games, and were outshot 40–11 in one contest. "I shuffled the boys all the time and now they have found themselves, they know what they can do," said Bauer, changing the focus to the traditional rivalry over the Hamber Cup between Alberta Golden Bears and UBC, usually up for grabs in March. "I think we can give Alberta a good fight for the Hamber Cup," he said. UBC hadn't won the Cup since it debuted in 1950. "I was extremely proud of the fighting spirit the boys had. They just never gave up trying. I'm calling practices off for next week to give them a chance to get caught up academically."

A couple of weeks later, Coach Bauer said that his team was already better than the team he took to the prairies. "The boys are shooting better, skating better and playing better position hockey," he said. "We should win with a few breaks and if we play properly in our zone." He accepted the underdog title for the T-Birds, but stressed that it was about more than hockey. "It is important that they be happy with themselves. I think the spirit's there."

Ultimately, the Thunderbirds lost every league game and were 2–1 in exhibition contests. In the Hamber Cup, a two-game total point series against the University of Alberta, UBC lost 5–2 at the Chilliwack Arena, and 8–4 at the North Shore Winter Club; the overall 13–6 score was a drastic improvement over the previous year's 23–6 shellacking.

In his 1971 report to John Munro, Bauer summed up the season in one line: "In 1961–62 we were able to surprise a few people."

The 1962–63 season would be markedly different in the history of UBC hockey, and would force the *Ubyssey* to change its tune. "The teams of the past few years went seriously about proving the saying that there are more ways than one to lose a hockey game. UBC teams tried to find all of them," reads one report. "Spectators harbouring deep grudges or sadistic tendencies find certain outlets for their pent-up feelings. But the team combines this with hard checking and the occasional finely executed attack to become a team worth cheering about."

Paramount to the upcoming success of the new Thunderbirds were four recruits, players loyal to Father Bauer and to his nascent idea of a national team.

Chapter 10

THUNDERBIRDS ARE GO

When the 1962–63 school year began the talk wasn't about the prospects of the Thunderbirds on the ice, but the building in which they were supposed to play. The winter sports arena was originally scheduled to open for Christmas, but many things went awry. Initial plans, announced in December 1961, called for a $500,000 arena, with the university paying half, and the student union matching; the pact between the students and UBC dated to 1959. Not long after details were revealed, Senator Hartland M. Molson and his brother Thomas of the Molson brewing company donated $100,000 towards the construction.

The building site on the outskirts of campus was north of War Memorial Gymnasium and east of the football stadium, about a 15-minute walk from the gym. The facility was designed to be three storeys, with an arena that would hold a single hockey rink on a 195-by-85-foot surface and seat 1,500 fans, along with eight curling sheets (with seats for 200), a first aid room, a skate shop, a large dressing room, a press gallery, a lounge, and several offices.

Construction did not start as planned on July 1, and the site was designated for other use by new UBC president Dr. John Macdonald. The arena was in limbo. By November, things were back on track, though; the Canadian government had created a winter work program, which shared the financial burden, whereby 50 percent of labour costs would be paid by the federal government and 25 percent by the provincial government. There was a catch though—work had to be completed by April for the grant of $75,000 to be awarded at all.

The project was scaled back slightly, using a recently constructed rink in Esquimalt, BC, as a template, with the price tag of $500,000 split between the university and the students. The facility would have an Olympic-size hockey rink, six curling sheets, seating for 1,750, a coffee shop, and large dressing rooms. Bulldozers from Farmer Construction Co. got to work on Wolfson field, behind the "C" parking lot, at the end of November. The Alma Mater Society was granted a 25-year lease for the land. "I can't believe we're finally underway," said AMS treasurer Malcolm Scott. "After all the setbacks, getting started is an anticlimax."

The first event at the arena was a practice on September 12, 1963, a workout for Canada's Olympic hockey team, which was in itself a major surprise.

In March 1962, Father Bauer was in Calgary preaching at a retreat of students from St. Mary's High School. His brother, Ray, happened to be there on business as well. Still interested in international hockey, Ray convinced Dave and Father Jim Whelihan, a Basilian teaching at St. Mary's and coaching the school's hockey team, to accompany him to the World Championships in Colorado Springs, Colorado, the first such competition in North America.

The Allan Cup–winning Galt Terriers were Canada's representatives in the eight-team tournament, with the top teams, the USSR and Czechoslovakia opting to stay home, as well as the lesser-ranked East Germany. The Galt squad had been bolstered by many former Kitchener-Waterloo Dutchmen, the storied franchise having folded. Defenceman Ted Maki was one of those who made the switch from K-W to nearby Galt, and recalled the uncertainty going into the tournament. "It was all up in the air. That was pretty well a last-minute situation, the Russians especially. I don't remember the exact reasons for them not showing up." The Berlin Wall had been erected just seven months previously and tensions between the Iron Curtain countries and the West had risen. East Germany was not recognized as an entity by the host Americans, and the Russians and Czechs boycotted in protest.

In the end, it came down to Canada and Sweden for gold, and it is a game that lives on—in Sweden at least. Sweden had never beaten Canada in any hockey game that mattered, World Championship or Olympics. The Broadmoor World Arena was the scene for the matchup, which started at 4:15 a.m. in Sweden, meaning that most of the country woke up to hear the radio broadcast. Rookie goaltender Lennart Häggroth was the initial hero, and bolstered by two goals from Ulf Sterner, Sweden was up 4–0 in the second period. Canada battled back, and it was 4–3 as time ticked down. With Canadian goalie Harold "Boat" Hurley pulled in favour of an extra attacker, Nisse Nilsson shot the puck the length of the ice into the empty net. Legendary announcer Lennart Hyland's call of the moment is akin to Foster Hewitt's "Henderson has scored for Canada!" from the 1972 Summit Series. *"Den glider i màl,"* which translates to "it slides into the net," was the famous line. It was Sweden's third World Championship, but the wins in 1953 and 1957 were at tournaments without either the Canadians or the Americans.

Bob McKnight had been on the 1960 Dutchmen at the Olympics, and then Galt in 1962 and Trail for the following year's World Championships. "The teams were getting better all the time," he said. "When I came back from 1963, I can remember somebody from a newspaper calling me and saying, 'How good are these teams that you're playing against?' I said, 'Well, the better ones, the Russians, the Swedes, if they played the fifth- or sixth-place team in the NHL, the NHL would probably win six easy, two fairly easy and two would be barnburners.' And they laughed at me."

During the tournament, Father Bauer talked with the various coaches. He found himself surprised that the Americans, who finished third, were able to talk in detail about plans for the 1964 Olympic Games, while Canada did not even know what team would be representing the country in Innsbruck. Casually, Father Bauer mentioned that Canadian colleges had represented Canada in international competitions in the past, and perhaps it was time to consider that again. It was a stray thought that he also shared with the Canadian hockey power brokers in attendance.

"In Colorado Springs, Father Bauer had some exhaustive conversations with CAHA president Jack Roxburgh and executive director Gordon Juckes," wrote Jim Coleman in *Hockey Is Our Game*. "The consensus of opinion was that Canada must embark on a radical new course, even going to the extent of establishing a permanent team comprised largely of university students, supplemented by the best available senior amateur players. There was agreement in principle that such a team must have a permanent training base and that it should play a full schedule of games against minor league professional teams."

The importance of education cannot be dismissed. As a mentor to many students and players at St. Michael's, Father Bauer saw a desire for a select few to carve a path where hockey and school went hand in hand, which was not the professional hockey route. "Another thing that happened at this same time [fit] in amazingly well with these thoughts," wrote Bauer. "Several players I had known in Toronto, Billy MacMillan, Barry MacKenzie, Paul Conlin, Kenny Broderick and later Terry O'Malley, called me long distance to see if I could help them find a way to continue their education. They all had had the old C-form with the Toronto Maple Leafs and had been told that they would receive no further help with their education but must turn pro as soon as their junior days were over. After some discussion of this with Ray and with another friend, Pat French, we thought it might be possible to arrange interest-free loans for these boys and to bring them out to UBC."

Roxburgh encouraged the Bauers to present their idea for a national team at the annual meeting in May in Toronto at the Westbury Hotel. All the provincial branches of the CAHA initially endorsed the plan, and everything was given the go-ahead at an executive meeting on August 26 in Toronto.

"I think such a team will be a tremendous thing for hockey in Canada, and in the long run the professionals will benefit, too," Bauer told the meeting. "I think it is important that we begin to look on this team right away as a national club, and we might even drop the UBC name at once and begin to call them the Canadian team."

The Canadian Olympic Association gave its own approval for the team on October 14. Milt Dunnell of the *Toronto Star* congratulated Father Bauer on selling the idea to the CAHA and warned of the difficulties: "Maybe it wasn't such a hard sell as it sounded. Ordinarily, the CAHA is under the gun when Canada fails to win the hockey crowd. Canadians seem to think it's an endowment from heaven that their boys should bring the medals. They're slow to accept the truth that Europe's best now can beat Canada's mediocrity. Bauer has taken the CAHA off the hook, to a degree. If the college all-stars lose—as they likely will—Bauer will share the rap with the CAHA brass."

The harshest critic was Dr. Maury Van Vliet, who was director of physical education at the University of Alberta and the man behind the powerhouse Golden Bears hockey teams. Van Vliet complained to the parent body of university hockey, the Intercollegiate Athletic Association, about the expected powerhouse at UBC. "What has been done is to agree to a Father Bauer [an] all-star team representing Canada through a university that does not own a hockey rink, located in an area that has never produced a hockey player, with a team that has never beaten anyone," he wrote.

Roxburgh responded publicly. "Dr. Van Vliet does not know what he is talking about," he said. "The university and Father Bauer certainly have no intent to form a stacked UBC team to compete in the Western Conference. It will be a completely separate team representing Canadian college hockey. It is a coincidence that Father Bauer happens to be at UBC. Had he been at any other school, the plan would still have been carried out." It did foreshadow that first full season, 1963–64, when Father Bauer found himself constantly reminding journalists and fans that the UBC team was *not* the national team, even though there were players who would represent Canada on the squad.

At UBC, Father Bauer found an advocate in phys. ed. teacher Bob Hindmarch, who would become general manager and de facto assistant coach of the national team. Hindmarch worked with Bob Osborne, head of UBC's department of education, Dean A. W. Matthews, and the Students' Administrative Council to garner the necessary support for the program. Hindmarch was the key administrator that arranged for players to come west, transferring whatever university credits they had already obtained to UBC.

There was still a season of intercollegiate hockey to play before any

Thunderbirds would skate in their new arena. The 'Birds were a changed team. Key additions were four men who followed Bauer from St. Michael's to UBC, lured by the idea of playing for Canada. Three were defencemen—Dave Chambers, Terry O'Malley and Barry MacKenzie. Ken Broderick, 21, was the goalie. While Chambers left before the Olympics, the other three stayed loyal to Father Bauer right through the 1968 Games.

Broderick, raised in Toronto's west end, had played baseball with MacKenzie as 12-year-old boys, with the future Nats keeper as the pitcher that loved to throw curveballs and shake off the suggestions of his battery-mate behind the plate. In junior hockey, Broderick was a Toronto Marlboro, and had played against the Majors with MacKenzie, Chambers and O'Malley. Since he didn't know Bauer personally, the invitation to a powwow at the Bauer family cottage in Bayfield came out of the blue. "I don't know what impressed Father Bauer for him to invite me to be a part of the Olympic team. It came as a surprise," said Broderick. "I had just finished a program at Ryerson Institute, at that time, in graphic arts management, and I was working at Sunnyside Pool." After the 1968 Olympics, Broderick followed his brother, Len, into the NHL. Though Len only played a single game, Ken would suit up for a decade with the NHL's North Stars and Bruins, and the World Hockey Association's Oilers and Nordiques, along with many stops in the minors. Post-hockey, armed with a bachelor's and a master's degree after all the years representing his country, Broderick "tried a few entrepreneurial ideas that didn't pan out" until landing with the Tim Horton's restaurant chain, where he opened some of the initial stores in Buffalo and then moved into corporate as a district manager. He was instrumental in Tim Horton's commitment to helping minor hockey through its Timbits program.

Over the years, MacKenzie—"Bear" to his teammates—grew into one of the best bodycheckers in international hockey. "Barry just loves to hit," reads a 1966 *Winnipeg Free Press* story. "MacKenzie's reputation is known from Moscow to Winnipeg as a hard-hitting defenceman." His NHL career fizzled after just six games in Minnesota in 1968–69 after he had the temerity to ask North Stars dictator Wren Blair about when he could see his family again. Blair coldly replied, "I once went two years without seeing my family." Choosing not to suffer in the minor leagues, MacKenzie returned to the red and white, suiting up for the 1969–70 Nats, the rules against pros finally lessened. When the Great Experiment died, Bear turned to Father Bauer for advice, ending up coaching the OHA's Sudbury Wolves, playing and coaching in Japan, and then coaching, teaching, and presiding at Notre Dame in Wilcox. After Father Bauer died in 1988, MacKenzie's wife, Diane, turned to him and said, "What are we going to do now? You're going to have to make a decision for yourself."

The MacKenzies were hardly the only ones that had their lives shaped by Father Bauer. Exhibit A would be Terry O'Malley, his wife, Debby, and their family. It all started when O'Malley, a Toronto lad, decided he wanted to follow his buddies to St. Michael's College instead of rival De La Salle, where his brothers went. In line with his application, it was announced that they were full and were no longer taking entrants. O'Malley and a buddy snuck into the basement of St. Michael's College and made their way to the applications office—only to run into the same imposing priest that had just closed down the line. Their papers were accepted, though, altering O'Malley's life forever.

He was a part of the core that moved through bantam to Junior A, winning all along the way for the Majors. O'Malley thrived under Father Bauer and excelled under his guidance, whether it was with the Nats through three Olympics, playing and coaching in Japan, coaching and teaching at Notre Dame in small-town Saskatchewan, or coaching the UBC Thunderbirds in the mid-'80s. "O'Malley is not an ordinary hockey coach," cautioned Don Wells in the *Ubyssey*. "A mixture of traditional Irish Catholic, Canadian Olympic hockey hero and humanitarian philosopher, O'Malley is as much a fan of Mother Teresa as of Gordie Howe."

The likes of Broderick, Chambers, O'Malley and MacKenzie were a step above the usual recruits at UBC, but they couldn't play alone. Returnees to the 'Birds were Pete Kelly, Mickey McDowell and John McLeod, and newcomers included Gary Morris and Ralph Lortie.

The Thunderbirds got publicity abroad, probably for the first time ever. In a Canadian Press story spread country-wide, Father Bauer assessed his squad: "I can't help but believe we'll be stronger than last year." He was right. "As a result of Bauer's vision and recruiting efforts, the 1962–63 UBC Thunderbirds was undoubtedly one of the best teams in UBC hockey history," wrote Don Wells in *Flight of the Thunderbirds*, a book celebrating a century of UBC sports.

But first there was an adjustment process, as hockey found its foothold on campus. MacKenzie reminisced about a conversation with a taxi driver shortly after flying into Vancouver, who asked what he was doing in town. When Bear replied that he was there to play hockey at UBC, the cabbie responded, "So you play field hockey?"

Chambers only stayed a year with the program, working towards a Master's in physical education. With a ruptured spleen from his days on the University of Toronto football field, Chambers didn't think he could handle the rigors of international hockey. Instead, he went into teaching and then coaching. "Dave Chambers was a fine player who had been out of hockey because of illness and, as it turned out, never really recovered his strength enough to play in the Olympics," wrote Bauer. While Chambers was finishing his master's in 1967 at UBC, Bob Hindmarch encouraged him to seek the job leading the Huskies at the University of Saskatchewan. From there, Chambers coached at the University of Guelph, Ohio State University for two years, and then returned home to lead York University in Toronto. He also coached the junior Toronto Marlboros, Canada's gold-medal junior team, at the 1988 World Junior Ice Hockey Championships in Moscow and a couple of Spengler Cup teams. He served as an assistant coach with the Minnesota North Stars before getting a chance to run the show as boss of the Quebec Nordiques from 1990 to 1992.

Chambers considered some of the things he learned from Bauer, both at St. Michael's and UBC. "I think I always wanted to be a coach, so when I was being coached, I was thinking about what they're thinking about, how they run the practices, how they handle players. With some coaches, I might say, 'I wouldn't be like that guy.' But I liked Father Bauer, and he was probably the best one—I don't like to say who's best, because I had some good coaches."

The actual intercollegiate schedule for the 1962–63 'Birds was only

10 games, and didn't start until mid-January. Bauer set out to find more challenges, scheduled around classes and the weird practice schedule. "We practiced at Kerrisdale late at night, it was always late, sometimes it was 10 o'clock. It wasn't set hours. Then we played our games on the weekends," said Mike Smith, a Toronto boy at De La Salle College who'd played against Bauer's Majors. He was not one of the recruits that Bauer had planned for the national team. Coincidence had Smith heading to UBC to study, and he made his own pitch to be included on the team in the late summer of 1961.

Smith had read about Bauer's transfer in the newspaper. "I got a hold of him—at the airport actually—because I didn't have a place to stay. When I got out there, he finally got me into St. Mark's. That year, he took over the university team, which was a ragamuffin team, really." Smith played on the sad-sack 1961–62 Thunderbirds, and recognized the improvements that Bauer brought.

"I think my skills improved. Bauer imparted a lot of hockey skills to us. He demanded, well, maybe not demanded, but just because of his aura, the loyalty he had was amazing. We would go through the wall for him. He was quite a personality. It was a big deal for all of us playing with Bauer. Bauer was so well known, famous, that to me it was a big feather in my cap to play for him."

Stu Gibbs had played defence in junior, but lined up on left wing at UBC. He missed out on a chance to play for Bauer the first year, and eagerly tried out for the 1962–63 team. And he wasn't alone. "There was like 120 guys trying out. It was quite a riot. I've never seen anything like it. Father was pretty astute. He said, 'I can't sort out 120 guys,' so he had us all skating Kerrisdale Arena in groups of 20." The whittling down process was simple, recalled Gibbs. "He just took the guys who could skate. From there, he got it down to a reasonable number. Luckily I got down to the last 40 and then the last 20. It was an absolute thrill and a privilege to play for him."

Like Chambers, Gibbs would find a foothold in coaching hockey for a while. "I ended up going playing and coaching in Europe for a few years, probably [due in] a large degree to his influence. But I would say that year playing for him was far and away the pinnacle."

While the team played exhibition games against the likes of Powell River—a remote town on the northern Sunshine Coast of southwestern British Columbia that meant the team had to fly—Bauer always had the grander vision in mind.

An exhibition game was scheduled with the touring Russian national team on November 23 at Toronto's Maple Leaf Gardens. "This game will give our boys a chance to meet international competition," said Father Bauer. A number of players from the Metro Toronto Junior A Hockey League (which footed the bill) bolstered the six T-Birds that made the trip: Ken Broderick, who'd played plenty at Maple Leaf Gardens with the Marlboros; St. Mike's grads Terry O'Malley, Dave Chambers and Barry MacKenzie; and BC boys Pete Kelly and Mickey McDowell.

There was no lack of talent around Toronto, and Bauer had plenty of picking to do during the four days of tryouts/practice. Future NHL stars Ron Ellis, Pete Stemkowski, Mike Walton, Wayne Carleton and goalie Gary Smith were all in the mix, but also notable were soon-to-be Nats Paul Conlin, Billy MacMillan, Grant Moore, Gary Dineen, and Rod Seiling.

Bauer used the opportunity to scout the current crop of Russians, travelling an hour down the highway to his hometown to see the Kitchener-Waterloo Tigers lose to Russia 5–3. The All-Stars later gathered around a television set as their coach showed them how the Soviets backchecked and skated like the wind.

After the Russians beat the Hamilton Red Wings—a sort of reunited Memorial Cup championship squad—in Hamilton, 9–5, Bauer was quoted as being "amazed" by the Russian team. USSR coach Arkady Tchernyshev wasn't bragging, but merely pointing out facts, when he talked about his team. "Yes, our team is better than the one which came to Canada in 1957. . . . The players are younger and faster. I worked with both clubs. The oldest we have now is 24. On the other team we had players over 30. . . . I learned everything I know about hockey and so did the team from you Canadians."

"I was flabbergasted," said Father Bauer upon his return out west. "I don't know how long we can continue to pit amateurs against pros like the Russians who play hockey all year round. . . . I thought I was going about coaching scientifically but then I saw the Russians. They have two coaches, one who directs the team and another who shoots movies of every game." The touring Soviet team won eight games against one loss, to the senior Windsor Bulldogs (their fifth game in seven days).

The Soviets had changed from the squads he'd seen previously when his brother Bobby lead the Dutchmen into the Olympics. While they were still reluctant to shoot until they found what they felt was the perfect opportunity, the Russians had started to use their bodies much more and didn't look for a penalty when hit themselves.

Just watching the skilled Russians added a new level of stress to the priest, who was still planning for the hybrid UBC-Toronto juniors game against the Soviets: "I've spent a few sleepless nights and I'm going through a mental revolution."

The game was a debacle. The Soviets spanked Bauer's youngsters, 6–0. Valentin Kozin counted two goals, and diminutive goalie Viktor Konovalenko got the shutout. The press focused on the visitors. "Their checking, passing, skating and puck control made for domination of the game and, as in all previous cities where they played, they received a fine hand from the crowd," wrote Al Nickleson in the *Globe and Mail*. Dineen hit the post on a penalty shot, resulting in boos from the audience.

On the first weekend of 1963, the Thunderbirds went into Trail, a small British Columbia community where a mining company, Cominco, was the key employer. It also had sponsored one of the best hockey teams in Canada, the Smoke Eaters. The Smokies, a senior team, had competed abroad and won the World Championship in 1939 and 1961, both times in Switzerland; they'd also earned two Allan Cups as Canada's senior hockey champs.

On January 3, the Birds tied the Smoke Eaters 1–1, thanks mainly to the brilliant goaltending of Ken Broderick (41 shots) and the dogged checking that the coach preached. "This was a good indication that the collegiate level of hockey can be good enough for international games competition," Father Bauer told the *Vancouver Province*. "Just think, Trail is going to the World Championships next month and we were good enough to tie them."

Quiet and introspective much of the time, Father Bauer was not prone to gushing in the press about his team or individuals, but nor would he be disparaging. On occasion, however, his joy shone through. "To me it was a bigger thrill than winning the Memorial Cup with St. Michael's to see those boys play Trail," he said on his return to UBC. "I have never seen such hockey courage displayed." Bauer did not, however, say much about the 7–2 loss to the junior Smokies on the Friday night, or the 4–4 tie against the Nelson Maple Leafs on Saturday.

In inter-league play, the Thunderbirds stormed into Saskatoon and took two games from the defending western champion Huskies, 4–2 and 4–1. Any smiles, however, were wiped from faces when the Vancouver Canucks of the Western Hockey League pasted them 9–2 in an exhibition tilt.

Up next was the two-game series with the Alberta Golden Bears for the Hamber Cup, which UBC hadn't won since 1950. After a 13-year residency in Edmonton, the Cup returned to Vancouver, even though the teams split the games. The Thunderbirds lost 3–2 in overtime on a Friday night, but won 3–1 the next night to claim the Cup. Easterners like Mike Smith had little appreciation for the feat. "I just knew it was a big deal for us," he said. Gibbs, who grew up in North Vancouver, knew what it meant. "It was like a complete turnaround. Fans were coming out."

It marked a turning point on campus—winning has a way of doing that. The *Ubyssey* even wrote a love letter/editorial to the team on Valentine's Day 1963.

> Prior to last year when divine (or other) intervention brought Father Bauer to St. Mark's College to teach religion, UBC had taken up permanent residence at the bottom of the standings in the Western Canada Intercollegiate Athletic Association. The teams of the past few years went seriously about proving the saying that there are more ways than one to lose a hockey game. UBC teams tried to find all of them. This year's Birds, however, are a fast, tough team who make hockey worth watching. A weak offence is made up for by robust defence which takes delight in doing physical damage to adventurous forwards who try to get too close to UBC's goal. Spectators harbouring deep

> grudges or sadistic tendencies find certain outlets for their pent-up feelings. But the team combines this with hard checking and the occasional finely executed attack to become a team worth cheering about.

With 1,400 fans packing the North Shore Winter Club for games, the Thunderbirds kept things rolling and clinched their first western university title. The team finished the regular season with eight wins, a single loss, and one tie. Broderick really was the difference, with a 2.00 goals against average, as the team potted 42 goals, with 20 against. "Our team really overachieved," said Broderick. Mickey McDowell was the scoring champ, and defenceman Barry MacKenzie tied for the league lead in assists.

Up next was something completely new, and not just for the hockey neophytes of BC—the first national university championship. The four-team tournament was hosted by Queen's University and Royal Military College, awarded the initial championship as a tip of the hat to their collective history—the first intercollegiate hockey game was played in Kingston in 1885 when Queen's beat RMC 1–0 on a fenced-off area on frozen Lake Ontario. Games were at the Kingston Memorial Centre, with a 200-by-90-foot surface, bigger than any National Hockey League rink. The four squads were Sherbrooke University, representing the Ottawa-St. Lawrence Intercollegiate Athletic Association; the undefeated McMaster Marlins from Ontario; St. Francis Xavier, the champs from the Canadian Maritime provinces; and UBC from the West. Major Danny McLeod, the RMC coach and co-chair of the tournament, predicted right at the start: "McMaster is the club to beat."

The Thunderbirds went to Kingston without Father Bauer. He'd flown to Stockholm for the World Hockey Championships, but made it back for the games. "I came back from the world tournament," he said, "because of the way I feel about this team. These players have made more personal sacrifices than any other intercollegiate team."

The *Kingston Whig-Standard* newspaper made note of the Olympic tie-in for the T-Birds, and for many fans, the two teams were one and the same. "Father David Bauer, UBC coach, is expected to ice a strong club for the tournament. His Western Canada championship team will form the nucleus for Canada's 1964 Olympic team." Out west, Mike Hunter at the *Vancouver Sun* knew better: "Thunderbirds had been billed as Bauer's Bombers, Canada's entry in the 1964 Olympics, by eastern press and officials. In fact, they are an ordinary college hockey team made up of players many of whom may never make Father Bauer's UBC-based Olympic squad."

The Kingston newspaper, one of the oldest in the Dominion, featured the games prominently, including a front-page photo of Bauer shaking hands with Mayor W. T. Mills before it all started, but the fans did not turn out, even though the tickets were reasonably priced at 75 cents for general admission (25 cents for kids), up to $1.50 for reserved tickets. The third-place game, played hours before the final, offered free admittance.

In the semifinals, McMaster's Bob Pond scored 35 seconds into sudden-death OT to win 4–3 over St. FX. In the other, UBC beat Sherbrooke, 6–2, with four first-period goals. Size was a factor said Bauer after: "They're certainly no Alberta or Saskatchewan. Saskatchewan has two forward lines, all bigger than Sherbrooke's biggest man."

McMaster's team was in the stands watching the UBC-Sherbrooke game (with 700 or so others), and Bauer said that was in his mind after the early lead. "I wouldn't say we intentionally played easy," he said. "But we didn't take any chances. We didn't want to tell them (McMaster) anything we didn't have to."

As for the final to determine the first Canadian university champ, Bauer promised, "We'll play 'em tight and tough, like we have all year, with emphasis on the tough."

Roughly 1,200 fans turned out for the final. UBC struck first, with winger Ralph Lortie tipping in Dave Chambers' point shot early in the game. McMaster's star, Bill Mahoney, who would be named most valuable player of the two-day tourney, tied it in a scramble.

During the second period, the 'Birds got tangled up changing lines, and were whistled for too many men on the ice. Only seconds later, Jim McLellan scored for Mac. Mike Smith takes the blame. "You're talking to the guy that lost the game," he said. "[The linesman] nailed me when

I played the puck as I was coming off for a line change. The puck ended up around my feet, and, of course, I played it with my feet and got a penalty. They scored the winning goal there." Gen Hamada made it 3–1, and Pete Kelly got one back, but UBC never caught up. McMaster was the champion, 3–2.

"We were down. Nobody was breaking sticks or anything. We were down—we'd lost and that was it," said Smith years later. Bauer said something similar at the time: "I have nothing but the highest praise for McMaster—a good hockey team. I thought our boys played a fine game but we didn't shoot enough."

After the game, Terry O'Malley, the captain of the team, said: "We just weren't as sharp as we could have been, although we gave it everything we had. We haven't had a tough game like that since the Saskatchewan series a month ago. We'd beat them in a seven-game series."

The University Cup was presented to McMaster captain Butch Hyde by the Honourable J. Waldo Monteith, Minister of National Health and Welfare. For all the bravado of his MVP performance, Mahoney was ineligible for Bauer's Olympic dream, as he split a season between the Hull-Ottawa Canadiens of the Eastern Professional Hockey League, and the Clinton Comets of the United States Eastern Amateur Hockey League. He'd also been coach at Carleton University in Ottawa while he got his BA, before taking a one-year physical education course at McMaster.

One of the fans at the tournament was Ray Bauer. According to Father Bauer's report to John Munro, he wasn't pleased with the team he saw on the ice.

"All during that season of 1962–63 people kept referring to the UBC team as Canada's Olympic team. It wasn't, of course, but that didn't stop people from calling it that," wrote Bauer. "That didn't bother me so much in Vancouver since this was far and away the best team UBC had ever had in hockey, but I remember my brother Ray, after the final game in Kingston, being visibly shaken and indeed sick to his stomach at the thought of that team representing Canada. I had to reassure him that we had a very different team in mind and that I had been recruiting a lot of players."

Chapter 11

AN OLYMPIAN TASK

How much of a difference can 23 feet make? It doesn't sound like much, but put that extra area onto a hockey rink, spread out over a fast-paced 60-minute game, and it allows a lot more space for chasing pucks. The international game, as it grew and matured in the 1950s, favoured speed over spunk, conditioning over combativeness. The senior teams that Canada had been sending abroad couldn't adjust to the quicker tempo. They were usually part-time hockey players with day jobs, families, and distractions away from the rink. Trips abroad were time away from responsibility, hockey mixed in with a little hellraising and hoisting of the odd cold beverage.

When Father Bauer set out to create an Olympic team, he not only saw a need to create a national team, but he imagined a certain type of committed player who could excel on the larger ice surface. In general, North American rinks are 200 feet long by 85 feet wide, while European surfaces measure 210 feet long and 98 feet wide.

The sermon was the same in 1980 as it was in 1964. "No. 1, you have to be a skating team," Father Bauer told Wayne Parrish of the *Montreal Gazette* in late 1979. "We selected pretty well on the basis of speed and it's difficult to believe there are faster skaters around than Ken Berry or Glenn Anderson. We realize we've got some smaller fellows (18 of the

24 players are under six feet), but ultimately, you have to play on that big ice surface."

It wasn't easy, said Gerry Pinder. "You're playing teams that are very, very good with puck movement, very good skaters. So it was twice as hard once you got into the game because you're astounded at the size of the ice and then guys know how to use the ice surface in terms of a puck-possession game. It was a really big learning curve."

Another difference had to do with using the body to check; it was okay in your defensive zone, but verboten past the red line. For Canadian ruffians used to crashing and banging, that was as much an issue as the bigger rink.

"At the time I joined the team you still could not bodycheck on the offensive side of the red line," said Morris Mott. "So it was body position. It was all, keep your body between your man and your net. You are not going to run the guy but you are going to be in his way. And when I think back on it my checking really improved within about two years." Some called it "speed forechecking," the need to rush into the offensive zone and pressure the opposition, trying to poke the puck away.

Playing exhibition games only helped a little, said Jean Cusson. "[In Canada], it was definitely different hockey than we played in Europe. First of all, it was tougher hockey. The emphasis was on bodychecking. With Father Bauer, it was the start of the revolution of hockey—that's the way I look at it." The rules could change from game to game. One night might be traditional North American rules, and the next game was conducted under international guidelines, befuddling teams from the senior leagues.

Murray Williamson, a Winnipeg native who coached the United States national team, talked in 1967 about schooling college kids in a different game. "There is a big difference between college and international hockey. The gap is simply tremendous. We had to teach them completely new tactics. They learned more in the nine games we played in Europe than they ever did in some 60 games they played during a three-year span in college."

Yet for all the differences on the ice, hockey was still hockey. The puck moved along frozen water and was aimed at a net that was the same size as back home in Moosonee.

More of a repetitive issue was politics. There were the devious, oddly-named referees from lesser-hockey-playing nations whose every free second was apparently spent trying to figure out how to mess with the Canadian team. International rules had two referees and no linesmen, compared to one referee and two linesmen in North America.

"As far as the refereeing is concerned in international competition," Bauer said in 1966, "I would like to see more Canadian and American participation. I think this would help eliminate a great deal of the trouble that seems to arise each year."

It was such a constant lament from the Canadian coaches that it became a "boy cries wolf" scenario, and ended up being white noise to the press, which got tired of the whining—patriotism only goes so far.

In a *Toronto Star* column in October 1967, Jim Proudfoot had had enough of the bias of the international press, too, and of the Canadian Press news service for distributing reports from warped perspectives. "Canadians are only too willing to believe foreign reports, even though European sports writers are notoriously inaccurate and biased. This even applies when one of our teams goes behind the Iron Curtain. Everybody knows Communist newspapers are propaganda agencies, yet we swallow everything they reprint about what they term the brutality of our athletes. The fact, which anybody who's seen international hockey knows, is that Russian and Czech players employ tactics—spitting and kicking, for example—to which no Canadian player would stoop."

Referees can only call the game they see on the ice, and an odd call here, a questionable penalty or an ignored offside, is only one domino in a series of events that can alter a result. That offside may not factor into the game at all, or it results in a play that races down the ice in the other direction, a foe caught up-ice unable to get back in time.

To many, the true villain was the man at the top of the mountain—the Machiavellian maestro who acted as puppet master and czar. Perhaps you saw his mug shot in a "most wanted" photo at the local post office, or had seen his effigy burned in protest after a heroic act was overturned in the boardroom. Meet John Francis Ahearne, or "Bunny" Ahearne to the universe of international ice hockey.

Consider one of his pompous pronouncements, from May 1964, a slam at Canada, boldly delivered in person at a CAHA meeting in Montreal: "You criticize year after year," he told delegates from across Canada. "You criticize the refereeing, the playing rules and the method of determining placings in world and Olympic tournaments, but you never come up with proposals."

His rise to the top of international hockey was unlikely as making wine out of water. Back in 1933, the Irish-born Ahearne ran a travel agency in London, England. The British Ice Hockey Association didn't have much cash and needed office space, so he loaned it some of his excess. Elevated to secretary of the BIHA, he then ended up in charge of the English team sent to Milan for the precursor of the bigger World Hockey Championships. For the BIHA, he exchanged a couple of letters, and took charge of the European Hockey Federation and the International Ice Hockey Federation, where he stayed firmly entrenched until 1977. Though he didn't play the game, he served as manager for the British team in the 1936 Winter Olympics in Garmisch-Partenkirchen, Germany. That team, made up of a number of Canadians with ties to the United Kingdom, won a surprising gold medal over Canada.

If that were all, he wouldn't have garnered the suspicions of double-dealing through the years. He continued to operate his travel agency until 1970, just a stone's throw from the bustling Piccadilly Circus, and a customer was the IIHF and its members. *Want to go to Stockholm for the World Championships? Have I got a deal for you!*

In person, he was charming: never at a loss for words, Irish wit protruding from his bulging jaw and balancing his "elfin and impish" weight on the balls of his feet, he was "like a karate expert on the offence" and seldom sat still. Politically astute, the fiery Ahearne saw the emergence of the Soviet Union as a hockey power as an opportunity, not a threat; the Czechs were forced to comply with their Russian controllers for most of his reign. He muscled (weaseled?) his way into the good graces of the apparatchiki, condemning the greedy capitalism of the National Hockey League when it suited him, then bragging about the profits of the latest World Championship.

During a 1972 visit to Canada, Milt Dunnell of the *Toronto Star* caught up with Bunny. "I get 16,000 cheers when I visit the hockey stadium in Moscow," Ahearne estimated. "At Vancouver, I get 16,000 boos. They don't like me in Canada—simply because I apply the rules. Many of those rules were suggested by Canada in the first place, by the way."

At its essence, there was a "protect the game" nature to Canada's dislike of Ahearne, not all that different than the outcry over FOX Sports and its experimental blue, glowing puck. In 1969, Bunny proposed some wacky ideas: "I would like to see curved blue lines, curving away from the goalies so that the wings would have a chance to stay onside during an attack . . . [and a] small red light, mounted on a thick steel rod and extending up from the boards, to warn a player he is coming to the blue line so he isn't always looking down for the line." But in the same piece, he opined that the goal crease needed to be bigger, which happened; that there needed to be more space behind the blue lines, which happened; and that the red line should be abolished, allowing for two-line passes, which happened.

Ahearne could fight back. "Your people spend too much time worrying about what happens in two weeks of the year, during the world tournament. They don't spend enough time worrying over what happens in the other 50 weeks," he said at the end of 1968. "Poor old Britain went through the same thing in soccer. The pupils were beating the teacher. Your people will have to do what Britain did in soccer—correct the interior faults first. Canada has the youth. It has the climate. It has the ice rinks. It also has something it should get rid of—an attitude of 'this is our game; nobody can show us.' In my opinion, Canada's problems are at home."

Those were just some of the challenges that faced Father Bauer as he set off on his quest to restore honour to Canadian hockey on the world stage. Someone with a lesser disposition, prone to second-guessing and appeasement over achievement, would not have gotten past the idea stage, throwing up his arms in frustration and walking away.

Once Bauer got the go-ahead for the national team from the CAHA, having worked his magic, making believers out of the various board members and key hockey people across the land, it was full speed ahead.

An early call was made by Father Bauer to Bob Hindmarch at UBC.

"So, Mr. General Manager, what do you think of our prospects for the Winter Olympics?" the priest presumptively asked the teacher, who detailed those early days in the biography *Catch On and Run With It*.

From there, the laundry list grows. Who to pick? Where to play? Who to play against? Will fans show up? Where will the money come from for everything from sticks to plane fares? Where will everyone live while at UBC? What will the uniforms look like? Insurance? Doctors? Answers were found to all the questions, though by today's standards, with millions and millions of dollars tossed around to hockey players by billionaire owners, the results were downright comical.

The best example of adversity is the Hockey House. The first wave of players, Ken Broderick, Terry O'Malley, Barry MacKenzie, and Dave Chambers, had lived at St. Mark's College, just down the hall from their coach, Father Bauer. That setup wouldn't work with 22 players chosen from an overcrowded training camp in Edmonton in August. An old building on the UBC campus was available. It had been used as a transmitter station during the Second World War but hadn't seen much attention in the subsequent decade. It was closer to condemnation than salvation. But it would become, as they say, a home and not just a house through time.

"It was a derelict house," said Ross Morrison. "They said, 'You can have that house.' We said, 'Father, what the hell is that?' 'Well, we're going to have to fix it up, boys.' Jesus!"

Everyone helped out. "That was a real team-building experience, in that players with certain skills in the construction field were actually the guys that did the work to get his house in order," said Ken Broderick. New windows were installed, the house was painted, and even the married players who were staying elsewhere, Gary Begg and Bob Forhan, chipped in. "We were living under one roof—you can imagine that every moment that we weren't doing our own studies for the schoolwork, there were card games going on, conversations, activities, that the guys were always together," said Broderick.

Forward George "Snowy" Swarbrick of Moose Jaw, Saskatchewan, was the key. He was the only player not enrolled in school, and, as luck would have it, he had experience as a handyman, so was tasked with working on the house. A trailer was acquired to allow for more bunk space. "They pulled a side-by-side trailer in, and we joined it. I did some electrical work and just helped out on the thing until all the guys got back," said Snowy Swarbrick, who didn't stick around after the Olympics, instead turning pro, suiting up for the new NHL franchise in Oakland, and later with the Penguins and Flyers. "We were a little happy family."

Everyone shared a room, except Mike Smith, who was playing with the Thunderbirds. Rather than stay at St. Mark's, he fashioned himself a room in the basement, formerly the coal room. The living room was just another place for bunks.

Get Ross Morrison going on the stories, and he finds it hard to stop. "We had bunk beds that he had gotten from the school. [Father Bauer] said, 'We're going to get the mattresses as soon as we move into the house.' Everybody got two felt mattresses, they were about that thick," he said, his fingers a couple of centimetres apart, "so everybody got two. And he paid 50 cents per mattress."

Students needed more than just a place to sleep, of course. "We had to find our own furniture," said Terry O'Malley. "I still remember Marshall Johnston carrying a desk he found across this open UBC field." When the hulking defenceman saw his teammate's quizzical look, he just shrugged. "I had to find something to write on."

Charged with keeping the house running was "Ma" Byers, a German housekeeper, recruited from a Vancouver restaurant, where she had been a cook. In her 70s, she was a rich character, as described by Brian Conacher in *Hockey In Canada: The Way It Is!* "She was truly unique," he wrote. "The first time I even saw her she was carrying in a side of beef off the meat delivery truck. I offered to help, but she refused—maybe she thought I was too skinny. She was strong as an ox, and in spite of looking as if she was ready to collapse, she was always the first up, and kept our house in as good shape as she could with what she had to work with. She truly became a part of the team in the months she cooked for us, and some of our best moments were spent around the kitchen table."

Ma Byers did what she could with the food, but there was another necessity. "That house had one bathroom, so if you had an eight o'clock class, you had to get up at 5:30 to have any chance of getting in the bathroom," said Morrison. Some just took to showering later in the day, or found other arrangements. Eventually, a second bathroom would be installed between the trailer and the house.

As one of the few with a car, Broderick often took the housekeeper shopping. "I'd take her down to downtown Vancouver, to the grocery stores and the meat markets. She'd buy all the supplies and bring them back to the Hockey House," he said. "She was great. She had a very good sense of humour. Here she was living with 20-plus hockey players. She had her own room. But she was up at the break of dawn, cooking, doing everything for us."

There was not much of a budget to feed the boys. "Feeding us baloney sandwiches, feeding us exclusively baloney sandwiches. I'm not kidding you. For weeks at a time," recalled Morrison. "There was no menu board. It was, 'How do you want your baloney sandwich? With or without mustard?' Some of the meals we got, poor woman, she did a wonderful job—with no money."

Maybe they were short of food because of Terry Clancy. "She fed me. I used to go into the kitchen and I became one of her favourites. I'd just eat in there too, and go out where the boys were eating. I just kept her as a friend because I knew I was hungry all the time. We worked out a couple of times a day."

Bauer's Boys headed out to do their laundry, not all that different than any other college students. Broderick remembers a laundry run with Brian Conacher: "We loaded so much soap into the machine that we had an instant flood of soap suds all over the place in the laundromat. We weren't really domesticated . . ."

Though the Hockey House was convenient (and perhaps misnamed, as a couple of rowers would later move in), it was only one of the issues Father Bauer, Hindmarch, trainer Johnny Owen and the rest of the organizers faced.

Finances were always a problem. "There was no money on that team. Nobody got a nickel," said Morrison, recounting a regular conversation with Hindmarch, the keeper of the funds. "Bob, I haven't got a fucking cent!" Morrison would cry, and Hindmarch would hem and haw, asking what happened to the $20 he had provided two weeks ago. Eventually, a player might squeeze another $20 out of the stone. In his memoir, Hindmarch admitted that some of the money came out of his own pocket. Extra cash was out there if you were willing to do odd jobs: Broderick parked cars at the racetrack; O'Malley swept the streets; many worked at hockey camps in the summer.

Some money was supposed to come from gate receipts, but an unknown team without name players wasn't drawing. The CAHA coughed up an initial $15,000, which didn't take long to be spent on uniforms, equipment ($6,000) and, well, everything else a hockey team needed to run day to day.

Case in point was a two-game series with the visiting Saskatoon Quakers in October 1963, which resulted in a $600 loss for the Nats. Transportation for the Quakers was $1,600, plus another $300 for accommodation and meals. Getting the visitors to the games in Coquitlam and on the UBC campus meant paying $50 for a bus. The referees were $100, and the staff at the ticket windows and at the door were $50. Income was $762 for the Coquitlam game on a Saturday, $814 on the Monday. "We could bring in cheaper clubs," said the team's GM, Bob Hindmarch, "and charge less, but it would be lousy hockey. It would not give the Olympic team much of a test."

There were many backers around the country, some big, some small, many of whom remained anonymous throughout. The UBC *Ubyssey* reported that it had learned that a benevolent donor gave $5,000 to the cause. "You've got to give it to Bauer how he struggled to keep things afloat." said Roger Bourbonnais. "I remember hearing some story that he would meet with local Vancouver businessmen, and they would take their chequebook out and cut a cheque to keep food on the table."

Major contributors included Calgary newspaperman G. M. "Max" Bell, financier James A. Richardson and, perhaps most importantly, Ian D. Sinclair. As president of Canadian Pacific Railway, which was the world's largest transportation system at the time, he was able to arrange for free or discounted flights, trips, and hotels; Bauer in particular made use of the complimentary flights, travelling extensively through the years. Bell, Richardson, and Sinclair would all be involved in the nascent Hockey Canada in 1969 as well, along with Charlie Hay, an oil executive whose son, Bill "Red" Hay, would play in the NHL and follow his father into both oil and Hockey Canada. There was also family—Alice Bauer supported her son with a donation right from the start, and Ray Bauer was both a donor through Bauer Industries and a sounding board for his little brother.

In 1967, Richardson talked about why he supported the Nats: "The team is every bit as important to Canada as the national flag. . . . This team is the symbol of our great nation."

Rick Noonan, who was a Bauer loyalist from beginning to end, said his mentor and friend knew which button to push to encourage chequebooks to emerge. "He was a pretty good nationalist, so I think he touched their Canadian heart," said Noonan. "Though we like to think that the Americans have all the nationalism to themselves, Canada, I don't think we're a great nationalistic country, but we certainly can come to front when hockey's concerned."

Through the National Fitness Council, the federal government managed to dig up $25,000 for the team in November 1963. In a story in the *Ubyssey* after the announcement, Hindmarch admitted that the plight was worse than he had let on. "We soft pedalled it because we were sure we were going to get money through the Canadian Amateur Hockey Association, but we didn't know when and we didn't want our creditors pressing us." Companies provided equipment on the basis of an IOU, and some would forgive the debt, patriotism winning out over capitalism. "But we don't want to appear to be in the position of being beggars so I'm glad the money came through," Hindmarch said.

Judy LaMarsh was in charge of the Health Portfolio at the time, which included amateur sport, and would become a major supporter of the Nats in person if not with funds. She made an effort to meet the team, arriving at the Hockey House for a dinner served by the players. "It was a very official occasion," wrote Conacher. "We all got dressed up in our 'Sunday go t'meetin' clothes, washed behind our ears, shined our shoes, and generally tried to look like the epitome of bushy-tailed Canadian youth—nothing to suggest it was a pitch for money. No one was even allowed to smoke in front of the reformed minister, who had kicked the habit." Years later, LaMarsh would ask Father Bauer to be a part of the National Coaching Certification Program.

Mickey McDowell, a UBC Thunderbird who'd play with the Nats, believes he was there at the genesis of the coaching program. The team was in Rosetown, Saskatchewan, and he walked by a restaurant where Father Bauer was having lunch with the mayor and other local dignitaries. Later, after an afternoon nap as a part of his pre-game ritual, McDowell noticed his coach alone in a coffee shop, looking sullen. Asking what was wrong, McDowell learned that the politicians were not happy. "We come in here and draw four to five thousand, and off we go, and we don't leave anything," Bauer said. McDowell suggested the team host a minor hockey clinic.

Father Bauer approached McDowell in the dressing room later at his stall. "You are not going to believe how well received that idea was," said the priest. So began a concerted effort for the Nats to be a part of the bigger picture of Canadian hockey and its development, even if the players weren't always fans of getting up early to help out. "I didn't think anything of it until I'm sitting on the bus at 7:30 the next morning, and Hank [Akervall] and [Bob] Forhan walk by and I hear them saying, 'Who the fuck's idea was this?' I thought, 'I'd better keep my mouth shut!'"

Another challenge was time. Both Bauer and Hindmarch were still working day jobs, which meant a delicate balancing act, taking turns on recruiting trips or presenting speeches.

It's important not to downplay Hindmarch's role in the whole affair, said Terry O'Malley. It was the future Dr. Bob—he earned a doctorate in education at Oregon in 1962, just a couple of years after completing his master of science degree at the same school—that dealt with the UBC administrators, arranging courses for the players, switching things around if necessary, getting credit for work at other universities approved for transfers. "He knew everyone within the university establishment and he was a good salesman at it as well," said O'Malley.

Few would argue that Hindmarch's association with the national team would propel his career. A native of Nanaimo, BC, he was a star athlete at UBC, excelling in football, basketball and baseball, and earning the Bobby Gaul Award in 1953 as the top athlete on the Point Grey campus. Hired as a teacher at UBC, he would later coach all three sports, as well as hockey—he's still the school's top coach, with 214 wins. He also taught at UBC and became a full professor in 1974.

The Olympic experience would help Hindmarch see a larger world. The UBC teams he was involved with, including his time as director of athletic and sport services, were international travellers, heading abroad for competitions—particularly to China, Japan, and Korea. He instituted exchanges of coaches and teachers as well, and hosted many a visiting team. He was also vice-president of the Canadian Olympic Association for 16 years, and was the Chef de Mission at the 1984 Winter Olympics in Sarajevo for the Canadian team. In 2009, he was inducted into the Canadian Olympic Hall of Fame.

"Bob was very political. I think he was in the right place at the right time," said Noonan. "He certainly owes anything he did . . . to Father Dave, because Father Dave was the one who put him into hockey."

But for all Hindmarch did—and he did a lot, along with the trainer, Johnny Owen (already a legendary figure at UBC), and Noonan, who was a jack of all trades when it came to the team and was trainer when Owen was working on other Thunderbird commitments—it was Father Bauer's team, and they were his "Boys."

And the players weren't all that different than their new leader, said Brian Conacher, hockey royalty through his father Lionel. Conacher played for the Nats in Innsbruck and the next year at the World Championships in Tampere, Finland, after a junior career as a Marlie and a year at the University of Western Ontario in London. When the rules were loosened about professionals playing international hockey, he returned after a couple of rocky years with the Maple Leafs, though he did earn a Stanley Cup ring in 1967.

"Father Bauer was renegade. He was taking players that were on the fringe, players like myself that had decided to go to university instead of just jumping in to turn pro and ending up in the Central Hockey League, or, back in those days, the Eastern Professional Hockey League, and ending up 25 or 26, no education, no opportunity, no nothing," said Conacher, who was considered a renegade himself. In 1970, his memoir/treatise on hockey's future, *Hockey in Canada: The Way It Is!* ruffled feathers, as it called a spade a spade and condemned the NHL for its vise-like grip on players.

Giving players an option to pursue an education and play hockey was very revolutionary at the time, and Father Bauer was up to the challenge. He also knew that molding those other renegades into a strong national hockey team was quite a different challenge.

Chapter 12

THE INNSBRUCK INCIDENT

When does a group of individuals become a team? When the roster is named? When it builds a house together on a university campus? After its first game?

Or how about when it first dons its uniform? For Canada's national hockey team, that day was November 12, 1963, when it beat the Melville Millionaires 6–1 in Melville, Saskatchewan, in front of 1,700 fans. "All of a sudden you had a maple leaf on your chest and you knew that you represented your country and it certainly made you feel very differently than any other hockey jersey that you had worn before," said Ray Cadieux, a speedy right winger from Ottawa. Prior to joining the Nats, Cadieux had a bachelor of commerce degree from the University of Ottawa and a master's from Laval.

A photo made the newspapers of Henry "Hank" Akervall wearing the new duds. Primarily red with white and blue lines, "CANADA" was across the chest in white letters with blue outline, with a white maple leaf also outlined in blue; a second maple leaf, with "CANADA" written on it, is on the left sleeve. Akervall himself was an excellent example of the type of intelligent athlete the program was attracting. A native of Port Arthur, Ontario (now Thunder Bay), he first caught the attention of Father Bauer in the OHA with the Hamilton Tiger Cubs. Three years at Michigan Tech later, including an NCAA championship and a partial season in Finland, where Bauer saw him again, the defenceman was invited to be a part of the Great Experiment. Akervall would just play a year with Canada, through the 1964 Games, before moving back home. In Thunder Bay, Akervall was a key figure at Lakehead University. He coached the Norwesters men's hockey team and rose to become the school's athletics director.

The Nats had already played a few games in a makeshift uniform—the word "Canada" wasn't on the original. Its first official game was in Chilliwack, BC, on October 1, against the Western League's Vancouver Canucks. For the record, Ray Cadieux scored the first-ever goal for the national team in a 3–2 loss to the professional team. Cadieux would prove to be a goal-scoring accountant that the *Winnipeg Free Press* described as a player who "loafs until he gets the puck and then he strikes like a cobra." Games followed against the Seattle Totems, a 3–1 win for the national team on the University of British Columbia campus, and the Portland Buckaroos, a 4–0 loss in Victoria, a ferry ride away.

The UBC student newspaper, the *Ubyssey*, did its best to introduce the newcomers living at the Hockey House in the fall of '63. "Except for a few hockey names, the remainder of the team will be unknown to most UBC fans," offered up Roger McAfee. "These notable exceptions are Brian Conacher, son of one of Canada's all-time great athletes, Lionel 'Big Train' Conacher; Terry Clancy, son of 'King' Clancy, a former defensive giant and now an executive in the Toronto Maple Leaf organization, and Gary Dineen, cousin of Bill Dineen, who had several successful years with Detroit of the National Hockey League." It also did its best to cover the "regular" Thunderbird hockey team, now coached by Dennis Selder, with a stronger recruiting class than ever before because of the publicity the school had garnered from its appearance in the national finals.

As for the coach, Father Bauer was realistic about his Nats, always careful not to hype: "We may lack some scoring punch, but we'll sure be tough," he said.

The exhibition games kept coming: a seven-game western-Canadian tour in November, a post-Christmas trip to southern Ontario, including a game in Maple Leaf Gardens against Sweden, its six-game tour marking the first time the country had played in Canada; in fact, it was the first time any international hockey had been played on Canadian soil. Czechoslovakia was in town at the same time and played both the Nats and the Swedes in what the CAHA called the Golden Jubilee Tournament. After first week of January, the Nats had only lost eight of their thirty games. Not bad for a team put together so quickly.

Getting to Canada's media centre of Toronto meant Father Bauer was in the spotlight. "I know a lot of people have scoffed at us, particularly in Toronto," he said. "But these boys are dedicated and patriotic. They're working hard because they feel it's an honour to represent their country."

The timeline had been the biggest challenge, he added, not knowing a player-led uprising was just days away. "We must compress into a few months what the good European clubs have done in five years."

An incident in Sudbury on January 3 helped team unity tremendously.

To hype a game between Canada and Czechoslovakia, Bobby Forhan was interviewed in the *Sudbury Star*. Forhan had played in town before, for the senior Wolves, under coach Peanuts O'Flaherty. The native of Newmarket, Ontario, had played his junior hockey in Guelph. "O'Flaherty was a great guy. I liked [playing] for him," said Forhan. "He stressed defence, just as Father Bauer does, and they have a different personality, but they're both nice to play for." With the senior hockey Kitchener-Waterloo Dutchmen, Forhan had been to the 1960 Olympics and the 1963 World Championships as a pickup for the Trail Smoke Eaters. At 27, he was senior man with the 1964 Nats, his wife working while he pursued a BA in phys. ed. at UBC.

The newspaper ads billed the contest as "The Game of the Year! International Hockey At Its Best!" Father Bauer talked to columnist Ted Saunders to promote it. "These boys have given up a year to make this team possible and I don't think it is fair to break it up now," Bauer said. "The club is showing great improvement and is better than what I thought possible when it was first suggested."

It was not international hockey at its best, a 4–0 win for Canada, though it was a success at the gate. With 6,731 in attendance—the biggest crowd in Sudbury history—gate receipts were $11,000, with the CAHA getting 70 percent.

"The game was chippy right from the start and sticks were carried at shoulder level most of the night," wrote Saunders. "A total of 33 penalties were handed out and most of them were for infractions caused by illegal use of the stick. Slashing, crosschecking, tripping, highsticking and kneeing were most of the penalties imposed." During the final 12 minutes, there were 13 penalties.

"You'd have to be a sadist to enjoy the show the visitors put on. The only thing they lacked was a boxing ring," wrote Paul Patton. Only two of the Czech players stayed for the traditional handshake.

Referees Hughie McLean and Lou Maschio never had control. At least not like Father Bauer did after the game.

"That was the dirtiest hockey game I have ever been in, in my life. And I played when the benches cleared and there were brawls," said Ross Morrison, a junior Marlie brave enough to befriend some St. Mike's Majors and hang out in their dorm. He'd been recruited from the University of Michigan, and spent what would have been his senior year with the Nats, before heading back to graduate. Later, in Innsbruck, Father Bauer recognized that Morrison's combustible nature wouldn't do, so he didn't play in the Olympics. Dave Merrifield, a centre who'd played at North Dakota, was another who had a run-in with Bauer and, unable to stick to curfew while abroad, was sent home—by boat, so as to avoid scrutiny by the press.

Through all the nastiness in Sudbury, Father Bauer had instructed his charges to not retaliate—and the Czechs recognized it so they turned dirty. Between the second and third period, Morrison and others made a plea to their coach: "Father, why don't you go for a walk for the third period? Because this is getting out of hand and these guys have got to know they can't take liberties."

"If I hear any more of that, you two guys will be taking those uniforms off and you won't be going to Europe," Father Bauer said.

Days later, when the team was in Toronto, there was a heart-to-heart talk in a Westbury Hotel room, the players laying out their concerns of balancing the hockey they knew how to play with being prim and proper representatives of their country abroad. One incident could forever mar Bauer's image, they argued, so maybe it would be best to stay home, or at least not play in the exhibition games before the Olympics.

"Father Bauer went from that meeting to a conference with CAHA executives and officials of the touring Czech team. The Czechs apologized for Sudbury, and promised that there would be no recurrence," wrote Scott Young in *War on Ice*. "Father Bauer took that promise back to his players. They agreed to leave for Europe as scheduled. All this was secret at the time, although it leaked out later in Innsbruck."

Before the Nats left for Europe on Christmas Day to play 10 games prior to the Olympics, there was much talk about further additions to the team. The nationalistic card was a natural way to entice the Maple Leafs and Canadiens into handing over prospects, but it didn't work out. One of the players apparently dangled by the Habs was Yvan Cournoyer. "I don't want to disturb this team any more than necessary," said Bauer. "Least of all I don't want to push any panic buttons."

The ace in the hole was goaltender Seth Martin. The man from Trail, British Columbia, had already carved out a reputation as the greatest netminder of his era, leading the Smoke Eaters to the 1961 World Championship, and returning twice more in losing causes. He'd made an impression.

"I had . . . a hero in hockey, a Canadian goaltender named Seth Martin," wrote Vladislav Tretiak in his autobiography. Czech goalie Jiri Crha, who made the NHL briefly in the 1980s, was also a fan. "I can say that he influenced me very, very much," said Crha. "Because back then—fortunately, we had great goalies too, like Vladimir Nadrchal, he was older than Jiri Holecek, all these guys—but before these guys, I tried to get as much information from Canadian hockey, but it was almost impossible to get any." Martin also popularized the face mask in Europe.

While he might have been nicknamed "the Magician," Martin was not a braggart. He'd met the team at UBC, travelling down on occasion from Trail, but never suited up for the Nats until overseas. He fit in quickly.

They didn't know Martin's legacy, admitted Marshall Johnston, who hailed from Birch Hills, Saskatchewan (thus the nickname

"Hayseed"), and joined the Nats after four years with the University of Denver Pioneers. "We played a lot of exhibition games . . . but before the Olympics . . . Seth was with us," Johnston recalled of the trips to Czechoslovakia. "These are old rinks and everybody's smoking and the haze was thick. And Seth comes onto the ice, and I couldn't figure out what the crowd was chanting, but the chant was, 'Mart-een, Mart-een.' The Czech crowd was chanting for him. Of course, he'd been over there before with Trail. They were well aware of him."

His fame carried special privilege too. While Hindmarch was known to occasionally sit in the lobby looking for troublemakers coming in after curfew, allowances were made for Martin, who was both older and better connected. When confronted one late night after being out with friends, Martin gave the team a choice: "I'll tell you what, why don't you just give me the return portion of my ticket and I'll go back to Canada tomorrow . . ."

Martin considered the differences between European and North American hockey in a 2012 interview. The larger ice surface meant more room around the net, and with so much passing, there were so many angles to consider. "I always said I had to play backwards because instead of going out on the angle to cover it," he said. "I backed up because I knew darn well that most of the time they weren't going to shoot from there, they would pass the puck around until they got a surer chance to score. It changed my concept of playing goal." Martin became a student of the way the Europeans played hockey, studying them in action when he was not in the net himself. "As a Canadian I would think, 'Well, he's going to shoot now.' He wouldn't shoot, he'd pass it off." Generalizing, the Russians and Czechs played a puck-control game, and the Swedes and Finns didn't pass as often or as crisply.

Goalie Ken Broderick had carried the Nats until this point, but didn't feel slighted by Martin's arrival. "He had the type of personality . . . you just had to like the guy," said Broderick. Pushed further down the list was Richard Broadbelt, known as "Beaver" or "Beav" to teammates, who'd been a product of the Montreal junior system. Broderick and Martin would share goaltending duties at the Olympics, often with one playing two periods and then switching for the last—Father Bauer feeling that it was good to keep both fresh.

The other last-minute addition was Rod Seiling from Elmira, Ontario, whom Bauer insisted he'd had in mind all along. Seiling was a defenceman playing junior hockey with the Marlies, under Jim Gregory. He knew only a few of the players he was joining. "Fitting in wasn't a problem," said Seiling, who would play 18 years in the NHL with the New York Rangers, Toronto, Washington, and Atlanta. "You always feel uncomfortable because you're supplanting someone who has been with the team the whole year. But I never noticed any ill will; I wasn't shunned by the team. My take on things was that the team members thought that I gave them a better chance to win."

Getting there was half the battle, recalled Seiling. "I was supposed to play two exhibition games, but only got to play one because the weather didn't cooperate. When I flew over, I was supposed to fly Toronto-London, London to the Continent, and join the team there. I ended up in Scotland, then on a bus to London, sitting around waiting in London, waiting for the fog to lift, both in London and in the Continent. I got to fly to Prague and I got put on a train to Bratislava. I got there just in time for the game. Played the game. Next morning we were on a bus to Innsbruck for the start of the tournament."

Seiling did miss some of the eye-opening moments for the Nats, memories treasured as much as medals.

The Canadians weren't quite travelling rock stars, but they were close, said Paul Conlin, who'd won a Memorial Cup with Bauer's Majors, and used the educational opportunities with the Nats to become a lawyer. "They seemed to love Canadians, but they didn't love the way we played hockey." There were countless postcards to hand out and other trinkets, though security in Russia would shoo away youngsters who crowded around the Nats. "We had a difficult reputation to overcome. The teams in the few years before 1964 that represented Canada in the world tournaments and that had been heavily penalized and loudly criticized throughout Europe. The media was very anti-Canadian because Canadians were the hooligans . . . the roughnecks. That was a reputation that we had to overcome and we tried hard to do that. I think we managed to do it, but it took a few years."

There were other brushes with fame, said winger / carpenter George Swarbrick, recalling a chance encounter with Ingemar Johansson, boxing's Swedish heavyweight champ, on a German ski slope. The Nats caught his eye with their matching winter coats, striped and sharp-looking. "We met him on one of the slopes and had a nice talk with him. Then from there, we walked back to our hotel in Füssen, and it was 32 degrees or so, big snowflakes. Real nice. The next day, we got on a plane and went into Russia, and it was 40 below. It was something else."

The team was hassled repeatedly behind the Iron Curtain. An interminable customs delay at the airport prevented them from arriving at the hotel until two in the morning. There was odd food and worry about constant surveillance. In fact, Canada's ambassador to the USSR, Robert Ford, who hosted the team for a soiree at the Canadian embassy, told Bauer and Hindmarch their rooms would be bugged, with the Soviets looking for an edge in the hockey games, while the players' rooms would not.

"Having seen the movie *The Manchurian Candidate* shortly before leaving Canada, Roger Bourbonnais and I were ready to believe the worst," wrote Brian Conacher in *Hockey in Canada: The Way It Is!* "In the best James Bond tradition we searched the room for booby traps and hidden recording devices. We didn't find any."

On the ice in the USSR, an exhausted Canadian team lost 8–1 to the main Russian squad before 15,000 fans in Moscow's Sports Palace, and then 2–1 to a secondary team. Father Bauer made no excuses for the crushing defeat. "The Russians were better. We were weak in all departments, except maybe goal. I'm not going to say anything that will take any of the glory off the Soviet win. Our men are young and this is good experience for Innsbruck."

Off the ice, there were other . . . complications. A couple dozen of the Nats hockey sticks never made it to the rink, and a bunch of lapel pins to be given out also disappeared. Yuri Gagarin, the first man in space, came into their dressing room one night, drunk and dishevelled, shaking everyone's hand and mumbling "Ya, ya."

Morrison shared a story of breaking away from Bauer's watchful gaze. "We got loose in Moscow, a couple of us. Well, not really loose.

We were in this big, old Russian hotel, the Metropol, with the lobby and the marble columns, classic, cavernous place. When you got up to your floor, there was an old lady sitting at a desk in front of the elevator. She was checking you in, making sure everything was right." Later, they snuck down to the grand ballroom, with a massive chandelier hanging overhead, hid behind a pillar, and ordered Russian champagne. Morrison remembers a well-to-do Russian family looking at them oddly, sneaking their drinks, and despite the language barrier, "it ended with us all shaking hands, people being people."

Following a 6–0 loss to the Czechs in the town Brno, near Prague, a handful of Nats were determined to find a beer hall. Through much sign language, they were able to explain to a taxi driver that they needed a drink. They were dropped off at what appeared to be a deserted venue, but upon closer inspection, the thirsty Nats smelled beer and made their way through the darkness of a lobby, through a long curtain to a bustling room.

"We walk up to the bar, and the bartender comes over—it's a big, long bar—and whole place goes dead quiet. Here's six guys with these bright red jackets and black ski pants on, and the ski boots we had. The guy looks at us, and we said, 'Beer?'" said Morrison. "We weren't there 10 minutes before you couldn't put your hand on the tables because it was all steins of beer."

A final exhibition game took place on January 21: a 3–2 win by the Canadians over Czechoslovakia's B team. There was one more pre-Olympic game, but it was a laugher, a 14–1 rout of Yugoslavia. Goalie Anton Gale saw 87 shots, to just 11 for Martin and Broderick. It was technically a play-in game to the actual tournament, the top eight teams in the championship bracket. Competing for gold were Russia, Canada, Sweden, Czechoslovakia, Finland, the United States, Germany, and Switzerland. Most notable about the rout was a telegram from the students at St. Michael's College in Toronto to its alumni: "Congratulations on your victory over Yugoslavia. Be assured we are all with you. Wish you continuing successes and the ultimate championship. Good luck Father Bauer, Clancy, Conlin, Dineen, MacKenzie, O'Malley, Seiling and the entire team."

"I've never felt sorrier for any person in my sports career than I did for Ken Broderick when he was called off the bench to replace Seth Martin with about seven minutes remaining in the biggest game that any of us had played in our lives," wrote Conacher. Notable for international hockey, only one penalty was called, a five-minute major for drawing blood on Vlastimil Bubnik with a hook to Hank Akervall.

Still, it wasn't over yet. Bunny Ahearne publicly stated that Canada would take gold over Russia if both teams ended up with 6–1 records, though Russia only needed a tie. All it would take was a win by the Nats in the final game of the Olympics. The other game of meaning that day was Sweden versus Czechoslovakia, which would be played after the Canada-USSR tilt.

Coach Bauer had done his part to fire up his team, wrote Conacher, beginning in the dressing room after the loss to the Czechs. "As we sat there in a state of exhausted shock, Bauer started to put the pieces of defeat together so that we could turn them into victory tomorrow. We lost a battle and that wouldn't change, *but* we could still win the war."

With Martin still achy, Broderick was in net, and the Canadians started well. George Swarbrick scored at 5:57 of the first period, and they held on till 10:41 of the second, when Boris Mayorov snagged a rebound off a shot by his brother Yevgeni, and put it past Broderick. Three minutes later, Bob Forhan put Canada up again with a hard shot from the right wing. Towards the end of the second period, Conacher was called for elbowing Alexander "Rags" Ragulin. The Canadians survived the vaunted Russian power play, but Vyacheslav Starshinov tied it up just after the penalty expired.

To start the third, Coach Bauer played his ace, putting Martin in net, hoping his magician had one final act. But the Canadians, running on gasping hopes and dreams, just didn't have the gas. Veniamin Alexandrov counted one on Martin, and that's how it ended, 3–2.

"Every player played his guts out in the last period and no one will ever be able to say that the 1964 Canadian Olympic Hockey Team quit under pressure," wrote Conacher. "When we staggered back to the dressing room at the end of the game, many of us in tears, we knew that we had faced our moment of truth and were beaten by a better hockey team that day."

There were tears, and an attempt to sing "For He's a Jolly Good Fellow" to Father Bauer in the dressing room. "It sounded as if it was coming from the bottom of a well," wrote Milt Dunnell in the *Toronto Star*. "They had to cry but they were trying to sing."

The game itself has mostly been forgotten in the controversial aftermath. The Russians claimed gold with an unbeaten record, but what of the other two medals? Sweden defeated Czechoslovakia in the finale, 8–3, meaning that three countries were tied with 5-2 records. It came down to the tie-breaking method, goal differential. But should it have been the difference in games between the three or four top teams? Or all eight teams? The Canadians, assured by representatives from the CAHA—especially Art Potter—believed that they had a medal, and headed to the award ceremony expecting to hold bronze. Based on the goals for and against the top four teams, Sweden was +1, Canada -1, and the Czechs -5.

There were separate IIHF meetings on the issue. The first occurred with three days left in the tournament, as it appeared that a tie between two or three teams was likely. At that meeting, it was decided that a tie would be broken by taking into account goal differential for all seven games. The Canadian Press reported that goal differential would settle any ties, but didn't specify whether it would be based on all the teams or just the finalists. In a second meeting, held during the Czech-Swede game, Potter, a member of the IIHF council, made his case that it should be based on only the top four teams. He was outvoted 6–3, with Russia and Czechoslovakia both supporting the Canadian position.

There was no time, however, to tell Canada's hockey players; the meeting ended with only 10 minutes left in the Sweden-Czechoslovakia game, and the Nats had already left their hotel on a bus for the medal ceremony. Gordon Juckes of the CAHA met them and told Father Bauer, "The rules have been changed and you're not getting any medal."

It was left to the priest to explain to his followers what had happened. "In the system that was in place prior to the Olympics, we should have ended up third, calculating goals for and against only for the top four teams. That was because you didn't really want to blow out Switzerland or some of the lesser teams in the Group A bracket," said Broderick. "Father Bauer's philosophy was just, 'Let's just win the game against the lesser teams and don't worry about running up the scores, and don't get hurt.' Based on that theory, we didn't try to beat up on the weaker teams."

Under the *new* criteria, Sweden was +31, Czechoslovakia +19, and Canada fourth at +15. "The shepherd and his flock have been fleeced!" quipped Marshall Johnston.

Father Bauer had a tendency to always look on the bright side, and said fate, or Providence, had played its part. Defenceman Barry MacKenzie was a little more to the point with his post-game anger. "If you tell me this is Providence, I'm going to punch you in the nose." Fifty years later, Broderick said, "That was a bitter pill to swallow because we felt that we had earned at least a medal position, and to have Bunny Ahearne, who was no friend of Canadian hockey, change the rules right at the last second . . . he was really close to the Eastern Bloc teams, so somebody over there knew how to screw Canadians, I guess you might say. They succeeded."

One Canadian actually got a medal. On February 9, there was a reception for the hockey teams where the extra hardware was handed out. It wasn't a packed house—the silver Swedes had already left for home and the Canadian players boycotted. Bauer, trainer Johnny Owen, and Art Potter were the only Canadians at the event. Coach Bauer went onstage to get a ceremonial cup for Seth Martin, deemed the best goalie in the Olympics, giving up just five goals on 150 shots during the 12 periods he played.

Shortly thereafter, Ahearne announced a special gold medal for Father Bauer, honouring his actions in controlling his team after being hit in the head by the broken stick of Carl-Goran Öberg during the game against Sweden. "For me, he set the finest standard of behaviour. He was generous in his thoughts, he was magnanimous in his actions. The standard he set will be rarely exceeded," said Ahearne.

"The hundreds of players and officials attending immediately broke into thunderous applause," reads the Canadian Press story. "Father Bauer, sitting in a back row, gazed at the floor. Owen, sitting next to him, stood up and applauded, but Father Bauer pulled him back on the seat."

Never one to back down from a challenge, Ahearne appeared at a CAHA meeting in Ottawa in May 1964 and addressed the decision to include all eight teams in the tie-breaking method. "Read the rules. They've been in the book since 1908 with only minor changes in 1960 and 1963," he challenged. "I'm not saying that this method is perfect. . . . If you have any ideas for improvement, put them forward."

The Soviet Union topped the medal standings at Innsbruck with 25, followed by Austria, Norway, and Finland. Canada only managed a single gold, in the four-man bobsled, and two bronze. Post-Olympics, the Nats actually played on, and toured Europe a bit. There were games in Italy and Germany, all for fun. The highlight, by far, was an audience with Pope Paul VI at the Vatican. They were therefore somewhat sheltered from the noise generated over the screwjob until arriving home on February 22 where they were greeted by family and friends—and the press—in a lounge at Toronto's airport. Dineen, a local boy, was interviewed. He said he'd lost 10 pounds during the overseas tour, and that the trip "was the greatest experience any of us could ever have had."

Father Bauer was careful with his words, saying that more experienced referees were a must. There had actually been a crack-of-dawn all-referee emergency meeting in Innsbruck on February 4, the IIHF trying to establish standards after the wild USA-Canada game. As for the fourth-place finish on goal differential, the priest rued not knowing that rule from the outset: "I think this is something that should have been decided before the tournament."

Jack Kinsella of the *Ottawa Citizen* said it was "one of the rankest shuffles since Hitler took over Austria." Andy O'Brien of the *Montreal Star* said it was a "typically screwy international hockey tournament finish. . . . We keep being reminded of Baron de [Coubertin]'s words that it doesn't matter who wins, but defeat still hurts in the winter field we should at least occupy as a strong competitor."

Dick Beddoes of the *Globe and Mail* took CAHA president Art Potter to task for vowing to never let a Canadian team play in Europe again. "It was the pouting reaction of a man-child who picks up his puck and goes home if he can't win," Beddoes wrote. "The Canadians guided by Father

David Bauer were good by Olympic standards, but they weren't good enough to win." (Fast-forward to May 2005, and the IIHF decided to award Canada a bronze medal for 1964, since they would have medalled in the World Championships, had they been held that year.)

The student-scholarship aspect of the national team was explored post-Olympics. During the school year, nearly every player had to drop a course or two—the workload and travel were just too much to keep up. "We are keenly aware of the scholastic penalty the boys paid, and are all the more proud of them for paying it without complaint," said Potter. "We know they'll make [up] the grades next year that representing Canada cost them this year."

Roger Bourbonnais shared his thoughts with the *Edmonton Journal*. "Put it this way. We all were proud to represent Canada and the experience is one we could not duplicate. The cost was a university year for most of us, but it was worth it—even if the scholarships were a reward which in the end meant little—and we are not complaining."

Education doesn't just occur in the classroom. In a chat with the *Globe and Mail*'s Jim Vipond during the Games, Bauer raved about the opportunity to go behind the Iron Curtain. "I know 21 young men who are better Canadians for their visit to Russia and Czechoslovakia," he said. "This was worth one year's formal education to the boys. . . . Their entire reason for the venture was fulfilled. Many of these boys arranged to take two summer courses each last year just to play on this team. Others postponed plans to turn professional. All agreed it has been worth it."

The Olympics in 1964 was not the media giant it would become years later as television invaded virtually every home (Canada versus Russia was on CBC Radio), but it was still news and it captivated Canadians. Each of Miss Olga Bies's Grade 4 and 5 students at Percy Merry School in Milton, Ontario, wrote a letter and made a poster supporting the Canadians in Innsbruck. Three were chosen and sent off. In May, Father Bauer replied. "Last week Miss Bies received a package from Father Bauer containing coloured photos of the team and himself," reported the *Canadian Champion*. "There was one for each pupil, also a letter thanking the children for their good wishes. The children were thrilled and quite happy to receive this souvenir picture and letter."

Father Bauer no doubt was trying to sow the seeds for future Nats. He committed after the Olympics to sticking with his program, and the CAHA approved in May.

"We've shown we can be good losers in Europe—now we have to go back and prove we can be good winners," he told Bob Scott of the *Montreal Gazette.* "I think Canadians will support this type of project. We were well received everywhere we went overseas. I have no complaints—even about going behind the Iron Curtain. We played hard throughout and turned in a greater effort than anybody expected us to."

The next decisions were out of his hands—who'd turn professional, and who would stick with the program . . . which was about to pick up and move halfway across the country.

Chapter 13

RED, WHITE, AND MAROON

There was a variety of reasons for moving the national hockey program from the University of British Columbia to the University of Manitoba in Winnipeg. They ranged from the altruistic—the idea of the Nats making their home in the centre of the country to boost patriotic fervour—to base economic considerations. And in 1964 the returning Olympians were faced with a number of challenges, not the least of which was whether to stay in the program and loyal to Father Bauer.

Terry Clancy was one who said no. "You coming to Winnipeg with me?" asked Bauer on the flight home from Innsbruck. Clancy was direct: "Nope, Father. As soon as I get off this plane, I'm turning pro. I've had enough of the Olympics." King Clancy's son would go on to a decade-long pro career, but took his coach's evangelistic education to heart and finished a degree in business with a mishmash of credits from UBC, both universities in Ottawa—Carleton and U of O—and Wilfrid Laurier University in Waterloo, Ontario. Now retired from work as a stockbroker and selling insurance, Clancy says he always felt a little chill from Bauer after he left. "I used to go to some of the events he was at, and I think he was a little miffed that I didn't join him in Winnipeg."

Others who *did* join Bauer weren't always there physically—school, work or family issues keeping them away. Broderick, the goalie put in the unwinnable situation in Austria, kept studying in Vancouver and made the three-hour flight when called upon. "I would go to Winnipeg for weekend games, exhibition games, special meetings," said Broderick, who eventually got a degree in physical education with a major in recreation. "Over the Christmas period, we used to get an international tournament, and I'd play there and then go to the world tournament. I just wanted to stay at UBC and finish."

Broderick doesn't remember exactly when he learned the team was being relocated, but he had no say in the matter. "We were never part of the discussion. All of a sudden, he just said, 'Guys we're going to move the team to Winnipeg.'"

The turnover and turmoil left the national team in limbo to a degree, with the next Olympic Games three years away. A unique solution was agreed upon, and the Nats merged for a season with the Winnipeg Maroons. Recognized as one of the best senior teams in Canada, the Maroons, formed for the 1950–51 season, were well-travelled and familiar with all the quirks of the international game. The Maroons were a decided step up from the Western Hockey League teams that had comprised the majority of the challengers for the team in British Columbia.

In his book, *Forgotten Heroes: Winnipeg's Hockey Heritage*, Richard Brignall addressed the strength of the Maroons: "The team would always have a group of former NHL players to pick from in the city when the Allan Cup play-downs started." In early 1964, with the Nats abroad, Maroons were on the road to the Allan Cup. After coming up short in the finals in 1961 and 1963, the third time was the charm and the Winnipeg squad finally took home the prize.

For Maroons goalie Don Collins, the Nats moving to town made sense. "We had brought a lot of the European teams into Winnipeg, like the Russians and the Czechs. We'd been bringing them for a long time. We started with the Russians before they had Tretiak in goal; they had a little guy by the name of [Viktor] Konovalenko then, and [Alexander] Ragulin and [Viktor] Kuzkin and [Boris] Mayorov. The Czechs had [Václav] Nedomansky before he escaped. I think he figured it would be a good place for them because we had a pretty good following with Maroons."

The Maroons coach was Gord Simpson, who had just retired as a defenceman, taking over the reins from Bill Juzda. He was a quintessential senior player of the time. After junior hockey in Winnipeg, he spent a season in Toronto with the Marlboros, and then three years in a senior league in the Maritimes. He returned home in 1952 and was a key figure with the Maroons for a dozen years.

It was Simpson who was charged with making it all work, as Bauer kept his day job at St. Mark's College on the UBC campus—and Simpson kept his at Supercrete Ltd., which made and sold cement. Simpson points the finger at CAHA secretary-manager Gordon Juckes for the decision. "[Juckes] amalgamated the two teams together, you might say. He came to us."

Years later, Juckes gave credit where credit was due, as "the national team in the beginning was fortunate in obtaining the volunteer services of the men who so ably looked after the affairs of the Winnipeg Maroons Hockey Club. Bud Holohan continued as general manager and Gord Simpson coached the club. There was a generous response from the Maroons noted not only in Canada, but also in Europe as a result of two highly-successful visits overseas in recent years. They would be most happy to help Canada build a 'national team'— also try to win back the world title at Finland in March 1965."

When Father Bauer announced the merger with the Maroons, there was intial misunderstanding. Many saw it as a return to the selection of the top senior team in the country as Canada's representative abroad. In truth, it was a stop-gap measure, a way to keep much of the core of the national team together for a year as new, younger blood was recruited. Bauer, aware of the flawed perception, called the merged squads "the beginnings of a truly national team."

Education, as always, was as important to him as hockey. "It is necessary to use the reinstated pros because the students won't know until March if their marks are good enough to allow them to compete in Europe," Bauer said. "It is not fair to ask the players to give up a year of university."

The world championships were still months away for Simpson and his merged team in the fall of 1964. With roughly 30 players available, it seemed he was part travel agent, part coach, trying to figure out which players were available at what time. "It was a pretty difficult for all of us, because the boys were still going to college or going to university, and of course, the members of the Winnipeg Maroons hockey club, they all had jobs, anywhere from salespeople to, one was a detective, a general manager of a company—they all had jobs," said Simpson. "It was pretty tough to amalgamate them, really."

Adding to the challenge was Simpson's loyalty to players he had played alongside for years versus the soldiers dedicated to Father Bauer who were eschewing professional careers to keep The Great Experiment going. Some Maroons admitted they were in over their heads. In *Hockey Towns: Stories of Small Town Hockey in Canada*, Derek Arbez told Bill Boyd, "I had a job and a family and there were some real good players. I suppose if I'd been a better player I'd have been on it, the national team, and gone overseas with them, but I didn't."

Simpson said that Bauer kept his distance. "He really was a good guy in management. He wasn't pushing anything on me at all or anything like that. He just stayed in the background. Sometimes I'd have to talk to him about what he thought." But first he would have to find him.

Collins explains that Father Bauer would be in town for significant exhibition games, often against Central League teams or touring European clubs. "He wasn't here all the time. He was all over the place—down east, and out in BC, trying to keep track of everything, I think—trying to look for other players for the program for the next year. He had a vision, there was no doubt about it. It was good because he was trying to put together a team that would be together all year, which was very hard. He was getting his players from all over Canada, which was good, because then he was getting some real good amateurs. That was the only way to fly. I know with our guys, we had a pretty good senior hockey club, and there was a lot of experience there."

Even lining up practice time with a full squad was almost impossible. Collins remains in awe of the commitment of the student athletes. "We practiced about four nights a week, so those kids would go right from school to the rink, then get back into the books. It's a hard life when you're trying to get an education when you're trying to play hockey." It's important to remember that at the time four Nats were enrolled at University of British Columbia, five at the University of Manitoba, one at the University of Western Ontario in London, and another at the University of Toronto.

Behind the scenes, the management of the Maroons stepped up to help—and Bauer must have known that going in. "For the next few years we are going to need help from an organization already in operation," Bauer said in August 1964. Bud Holohan was general manager of the Maroons, and would stay involved with Father Bauer in the role of educational advisor, encouraging the players to develop their mental and moral skills as well as their physical attributes; Holohan also served as president of the Canadian Amateur Hockey Association. Terry Hind, well connected with the sports community in Winnipeg, was team president and another key figure. Charles "Chas" Maddin, the father of filmmaker Guy Maddin, was manager on the bench. His son profiled the Maroons in his film *My Winnipeg*, a partial-documentary that also resulted in a book of the same title.

Guy Maddin addressed the importance of hockey in his household: "I was even born right here in this dressing room. Look at it. Born during a game between the Winnipeg Maroons and the Trail Smoke Eaters. I was bundled up and taken straight home after the game and brought back a few days later to watch my first complete contest. My dad worked behind the bench for the Winnipeg Maroons, the 1964 Allan Cup winners, senior hockey champs in the days of the Original Six."

The Nats/Maroons had an ambitious 40 exhibitions arranged prior to heading overseas to the World Championships in Finland. Most were against teams in the Central Professional League and the Saskatchewan Senior Association. In 13 games against CPL teams like the Minneapolis Bruins and Tulsa Oilers, the Nats finished 8–4–1. Overall, their record on the "road to Tampere" was 24–11–2.

It was a game, however, against the touring Russians that generated the most attention. The game took place on December 13, 1964, in Toronto's Maple Leaf Gardens. The Soviets shut out the Canadians 4–0. For the foreigners, it was just one stop on an eight-game tour. For the home team, it was Exhibit A in scheduling complications. Exams at the University of British Columbia kept goalie Ken Broderick away, as well as defencemen Paul Conlin and Barry MacKenzie. Even Grant Moore, the former Toronto Marlboros captain, couldn't get away from his exams at the University of Toronto for the game in the rink where he shined so brightly a year before.

Canadian coach Gord Simpson knew there was a lot of work ahead, logistically and practically: "We're going to have to drill quite a bit yet if we're to beat the Russians. I think we have the material. But all national team players should be stationed in one locale, and not scattered about the country."

Though the Gardens' rink wasn't of international dimension, the game was played under international rules. At the time, Simpson dismissed that factor as an excuse: "It was the Russian pattern that upset us, not the rules. We've played our last 18 games under these rules, but never with a set lineup. These Russians can fly, they can bump, they're agile, they set up their plays well and they're well-built. And I was disappointed in our inability to put the puck in the net. We had chances early in the game and missed, and they didn't give us many after that. We hope to get films of the game and study them."

A totally different kind of exhibition game took place at the Gardens on February 28, 1965, when the Nats, pretty well set for Tampere, Finland, took on a team of National Hockey League oldtimers put together by Hank Goldup. The veterans were mostly Toronto-based, and included Long John Henderson in net; Bob Goldham, Wally Stanowski, Gus Mortson, and Ivan Irwin on defence; and forwards Barry Cullen, Jack McIntyre, Danny Lewicki, Gus Bodnar, Brian Cullen, Sid Smith, Ron Hurst, John McCormack, Earl Balfour, Cal Gardner, and Harry Watson.

During the 2–2 contest, which saw the Nats fight back for the tie, the crowd of 7,943 "applauded both sides at the end of each period" reported the *Globe and Mail*. Post-game, Bauer was pleased. "We were very happy. The game more than served its purpose. No game (in the world tournament) will be as rugged as this, except the Russian game," he said, praising the opposition. "These fellows were good National Leaguers . . . most of them were great National Leaguers. You never lose that touch. And in their own end, that defence was pretty rugged."

For some of the Nats, it was a chance to get back in action; Barry

MacKenzie and Gary Dineen hadn't played in nearly six weeks. Never one to hold in his thoughts, Dineen was outspoken before the team left for Finland. "I think a great many Canadians are hoping we'll lose so they can say 'I told you so,'" Dineen told the *Globe and Mail*'s Rex MacLeod. The 21-year-old had starred with the Toronto Marlboros and was the property of the Toronto Maple Leafs. He'd frustrated GM Punch Imlach with his refusal to report to the minor-league team in Tulsa. "When I first joined the Canadian team I was told I'd be doing something good for my country," Dineen said. "I didn't believe it, of course. I said to myself, 'This is for Gary Dineen, a chance to travel and enjoy myself.' I changed my mind when I got over there. Now I believe it. Canadians don't realize the importance of these tournaments to people in Europe. It's not just a hockey game or games. It means a lot of Canadian prestige."

Dineen also expressed dismay with the scheduling. "This year, for instance, I hadn't played a game from Jan. 17 until we met the Old-Timers in Toronto on Feb. 28. So, we have one game together and then leave for Finland to play against the best in the world, teams that have been playing and practicing for months. And they wonder why you lose. I'm not trying to make excuses, I'm just being realistic."

While the Nats were playing in Toronto, Simpson already had a "B team" of sorts overseas, made up primarily of Maroons. When Bauer, in Toronto, was asked about a loss by the Nats in Moscow, the newspaper reported that he "seemed pleased" with the 5–1 score. "I thought they would lose worse than that."

The trip to Europe can be submitted as Exhibit B of the complications the team faced. Its plane left Winnipeg and stopped in Port Arthur, Ontario, to pick up Henry Akervall. Next, Grant Moore, Ricky Hay, and others got on board in Toronto. "It was kind of a mishmash team that went for the pre-tour for three weeks prior to going to Tampere," said Don Collins. "Even some of the older fellas, they couldn't make it for the whole six weeks . . . so they ended up coming over and replacing a lot of the guys that were on the pre-tour, which were mostly such Maroons as Lou Joyal, Elliot Chorley, Ron Farnfield." Besides games in the USSR, the "first shift" played in Finland and Sweden.

Fifty years later, Simpson still rues some of the choices he was forced to make when putting the World Championship team together. "There's a decision that I had to make. . . . Marshall Johnston was going to school in Winnipeg, and Fred Dunsmore, who was my best friend . . . I had to decide which one of them was going to be playing in the World Championship. It was a tough decision all around, really, because they're both excellent hockey players." Simpson chose Dunsmore over Johnston.

Collins, who served as Broderick's backup, sympathized. "It was very tough for [Simpson] because, well, some of the old guys looked better than some of the young guys. He had to try and walk a fine line, which was very difficult for him. He was trying to do the right thing by the young guys and he knew that they were going to be there, and we were going to be gone the next year, most of us. He had to get rid of a lot of the older guys."

The final world championship team for Canada was comprised of nine players from the 1964 Olympics (Gary Begg, Roger Bourbonnais, Ken Broderick, Brian Conacher, Paul Conlin, Gary Dineen, Bob Forhan, Barry MacKenzie, Terry O'Malley); Grant Moore, captain of the '64 Memorial Cup champion Marlboros; and seven Maroons (Reg Abbott, Gary Aldcorn, Don Collins, Fred Dunsmore, Al Johnson, Bill Johnson, Jim MacKenzie).

IIHF president Bunny Ahearne was not impressed, interviewed just before the tournament began. "Look at the team you have here in Tampere today. There are five reinstated pros and another five who played in the English National Hockey League five years ago. If that's progress you've got to prove it to me."

The Nats finished fourth. For the first time in a tournament, Canada lost to the three major powers: Russia (gold), Czechoslovakia (silver), and Sweden (bronze). The wins came over East Germany, the Americans, Finland, and Norway.

"I played against the Swedes and the Russians after they got bombed by the Czechs. I told Simpson, 'I'm here for a holiday! I did my work before this thing started. I'm just supposed to sit on the bench!'" said Collins.

One of the reasons the Nats partnered with the Maroons was their international experience, yet that, too, became an excuse.

Post-championships, Bauer said such former pros as Al Johnson and Gary Aldcorn were thrown off a bit by the larger European ice surfaces. "Skating is most important when you are playing the Europeans, and that extra ice makes a difference with some of our people who otherwise are excellent players," said Bauer.

Winnipeg Free Press sports editor Maurice Smith was along for the trip. He wrote that the only impressive game the Nats played was against the East Germans, an 8–1 trampling, dismissing shutouts against Finland (4–0) and Norway (6–0) posted by Broderick. "Canadian Amateur Hockey Association officials had vainly hoped that Canada might attain a second-place finish. Their aspirations were dashed by a team that seemed to lack fire and at no time played like a well-knit unit," explained Smith to readers back home. "Their inability to live up to their reputation as one of the world's hockey powers had European spectators shaking their heads in disbelief. Their general ineptness in their attack brought down the fable that Canada is a serious consideration in world tournament play."

The on-ice performance wasn't the only flame-out by Canada. The IIHF declined the country's request to host the 1967 World Championships, to coincide with the nation's centennial.

After the World Championships there was talk of dropping out of the 1966 tournament, which was set for Ljubljana, Yugoslavia, simply to better prepare for the 1968 Winter Olympics. Canada could miss both the 1966 and 1967 series and remain in the A Pool for the Grenoble Games.

Bauer predicted that it would "be very difficult for Canada to win the World Championship any time within the next few years." The priest said that others shared his feeling that it might be best to step back, but it was never an official CAHA position.

Naturally, he found a bright side. "I'm quite happy with our showing considering we only put this team together three weeks ago," Father Bauer said. "Our coming here served its purpose in that it gave our younger boys a chance to play together in international competition. We didn't expect to win the championship. Of course, we always hope but, after seeing the Russians play in Canada, if you were a realist at all, you couldn't help but expect them to win."

Looking back, Simpson summed it up like this: "Playing in the World Championships, trying to put a team together, competing against teams like Sweden, Russia, and Czechoslovakia, they started in summertime and prepared for the World Championships or the Olympics. . . . Now we're really trying to put a team together . . . and run all year round, the same way. We just couldn't do that with the way we were doing it."

Dineen was the leading scorer for Canada in the tourney, with 11 points (Czech centre Jozef Golonka had 15 to lead all skaters), but he was disheartened. "Canadian people have a nonchalant approach to these international tournaments," said Dineen. "There's no unity of purpose. You get the idea you're falsely representing your country."

Chapter 14

JACKIE'S BOYS

Following the failed experiment with the Maroons, it became clear that Canada's national team needed new direction.

Pere Murray, the colourful priest who founded Notre Dame College in windswept Wilcox, Saskatchewan, in the 1930s, was in his office, shooting the bull with Father Bauer and Al Ritchie, a Regina-based scout for the New York Rangers. They ran through the pluses and minuses of the current set-up, and considered players who could be added to the team. They also talked about a coach. Father Murray had an idea and called Swift Current, home of an old Notre Dame Hounds star.

Robert John McLeod answered the phone, though no one but his parents called him that. To most, he was "Shakey" or Jack or Jackie. The tremendously-memorable nickname was achieved honestly. When he was seven years old, in second grade in Hazlet, Saskatchewan, McLeod was stricken with polio. After six months in bed, he slowly made progress, overcoming the paralysis of his chest muscles. Soon he was out on the outdoor rinks in ramshackle gear, magazines for shin and elbow pads. He got further schooling in hockey and life at Wilcox's Notre Dame College, where he was a top athlete. "The polio condition bothered me when I made junior. I'd bend over to tie my skates and the upper part of my body would shake like I had a bad chill," McLeod recalled in 1966. It was Baldy Smith, a teammate on the junior Moose Jaw Canucks, that tagged him "Shakey."

The five-foot-nine, slender right winger had a knack for scoring, but only lasted parts of three seasons with the NHL's New York Rangers. He spent summers back home in Saskatchewan, where he was a top-notch baseball player. Much of his hockey path took him to such smaller outposts as Cincinnati, Saskatoon, and Vancouver. After a decade, he gave up the pro game and operated two stores in Swift Current. He also was a salesman of light aircraft, a nice complement to his own hobby as a pilot.

Most importantly, he regained his amateur status as a hockey player. Shakey served his country well internationally, performing in three consecutive World Championships. In 1961 in Geneva, he was with the Trail Smoke Eaters, and was leading scorer as the Smokies won the title; it would be Canada's last until 1994.

Though the Canadian representative—Galt Terriers in 1962 in Colorado Springs, and Trail again in '63 in Stockholm—didn't win, McLeod gained an appreciation and understanding of the nuances of the international game that would serve him well as coach of the Nats from 1965 to 1970.

Ted Maki, a teammate on the 1962 Terriers and 1963 Trail teams, said McLeod was "a good stick-handler. He knew the game, he understood the game."

Murray didn't say a lot to McLeod on the phone, but asked him to come down for a visit. That August day, McLeod flew down in one of the planes he had access to, landed in nearby Corinne, got a ride to Wilcox, and altered his destiny. The sales pitch to the aircraft salesman was straightforward: "We need a coach for the Nats."

"I had a meeting with them, and another meeting that night with my family, my wife and children, to discuss it. My wife and kids agreed it would be quite a challenge," said McLeod, who spent two days in Wilcox getting to know Bauer. "Not so much being interviewed as, I think, he was getting my philosophy on life."

As columnist Dick Beddoes put it, "Last spring Father David Bauer romanced him to run the national team, an idea that appealed to McLeod's sense of challenge."

Officially, McLeod took over in September 1965 in Winnipeg. Being new to coaching at a major level, McLeod was initially a little . . . shaky. "But he was a good coach. He was very fair. And he listened like we did to Father Bauer," said goaltender Ken Broderick.

Bauer was listed as "special advisor" for the national teams from 1965 to 1968, while his day job was at St. Mark's College at the University of British Columbia, 2,000 miles from Winnipeg. The national team really was McLeod's job. He ran the team and sought out the players. Help came in the form of the Canadian Amateur Hockey Association, with which he shared office space. The CAHA took care of the nuts and bolts, like booking travel and paying bills. Phil Reimer, a veteran Winnipeg newsman, was added to deal with publicity.

Being coach also meant that he had to sit through the annual CAHA meetings. McLeod's dry, prairie sense of humour seemingly helped him cope. "We were under their umbrella," he said. The bluster was evident, with every province sending a representative to the assembly that wanted to be heard. "There always is in those organizations, isn't there? A lot of hot-air guys. I think they treated us pretty fairly, but we didn't have any money."

Those CAHA minutes provide an interesting peek into just how cash-poor the Canadian national team was. This is from the team's preliminary balance sheet prepared by chartered accountants Parker, Quine & Company, for April 30, 1967:

ASSETS	
Cash on hand	$100.00
Accounts receivable	$2,470.70
Office equipment	$378.30
TOTAL ASSETS	$2,949.70

LIABILITIES AND DEFICIT	
Bank overdraft	$2,634.52
Accounts payable	$1,999.16
Provisions for accounts not yet submitted	$2,423.24
Advances — overseas account	$8,734.36
TOTAL LIABILITIES	$15,791.28
DEFICIT ACCOUNT	$12,842.28

Equally fascinating are the revenue and expenditure lines from the same report. Some samples of the revenue include the grant from the Department of National Health and Welfare ($48,200), travel money from the tournaments in Colorado Springs ($5,000) and Europe ($9,926.74), advertising in the team's yearbook ($2,495), and revenue from the broadcasting, TV and radio, of the World Championships ($4,877.92). Operating expenses included salaries for management ($10,336.80) and trainers ($5,379.20), and promotion and press conferences ($8,536.04), as well as ice rental ($2,376), equipment and uniforms ($6,783.25), and maintenance of the equipment and uniforms ($1,293.76).

"We used to play exhibition games around the country, just so some of the people could see our team, and make some money too," said McLeod. For the year that ended April 30, 1967, the Nats brought in $144,928.82 in gate receipts for games in Canada, but $42,914 went towards the teams they played, transportation ate up $32,159.26, and meals and lodging $7,757.45. As for the referees about whom McLeod always seemed to complain, the expense line was $485.50. International travel, lumped together with lodging and baggage fees, added up to $29,368.84, along with $497.85 for the trinkets that the Canadian team became well known for handing out to fans young and old.

Setting up the games was a hassle, McLeod said at the CAHA annual meeting in May 1967. "Last year in Montreal it was decided, in order to get better competition for Canada's national hockey team, that the branches were going to go back and during the summer consult their different leagues and form all-star clubs, and we would go to different parts of the country and play these teams and they in turn also would come to Winnipeg. We have a very hard time in Winnipeg with the

Winnipeg Arena in respect to hockey games. It is tough to ask for practice time at all times and play eight or nine games in the Arena throughout the whole winter and we did a lot of touring last winter across Canada, which is very hard on our boys. They go every weekend and when we contact the different teams or branches with regards to getting the All-Star team back to Winnipeg there was very little cooperation; in fact, we were only able last year to get Kingston to come to Winnipeg to play hockey and I am sure Kingston went out of their way to do it because it was late in the season and we were getting hard up for games before we went overseas. We did bring Drumheller into Winnipeg and they came to Winnipeg with twelve hockey players, which wasn't too good with our crowd. It didn't set too well with the sportswriters and news media in Winnipeg either. This hurt us bad when they didn't show up with a full team."

While Father Bauer didn't attend to the day-to-day dealings of the team, he would show up when he could, sometimes on the road, sometimes in Winnipeg.

"We got along right off the bat," said McLeod. The amiable priest wasn't a micromanager. "He did help me out scouting players. He asked me to run the club. Don't get me wrong, he gave me a lot of good advice, and I was more than willing to take it, let me tell you. He was very good. I ran the hockey club and he was there to help."

On the road, Bauer and McLeod would occasionally share a room—and hockey talk. "He was a pretty sound sleeper. We both were," said McLeod. "We spent a lot of time together, Father Dave and I. On the buses, on the aircraft, and everything else, you get to spend a lot of time together and pass on ideas."

They were able to form a bond with other hockey men, too. "We both became pretty good friends of [Anatoli] Tarasov, the Russian coach," said McLeod. "It's funny how that works, I often look back on that, too. Hockey is hockey. . . . Things just seemed to work out. He was not very fluent in English, but he spoke a bit." Instead, they might talk through a chalkboard, diagramming plays. "He had his ideas, I had my ideas, and Father Dave had his ideas, so there you go."

One of Shakey's ideas was that he could still play—and he could.

When the Nats found themselves shorthanded, like at the 1965 Walter Brown Tournament in Colorado Springs, Colorado, Father Bauer said McLeod provided the team with a new spark by coming out of retirement and lacing on a pair of skates. "We'd be short or something, and I practiced with the boys every day; I'd put on the uniform and the equipment," said McLeod. "I was in pretty good shape."

Herb Pinder recalled the fun in practices. "You could only score by shooting it off the post. Shakey played with us. He was older and slow, but he could shoot it off the post."

Shakey was ahead of his time, said Gerry Pinder. "He did things that they weren't doing until several years later in the National Hockey League, in terms of our practices. Not only were they good practices that mixed in power play and penalty kill, and the ability to play a puck-possession game, because our opponents were all puck-possession teams. The NHL was for the most part 'dump it in.' The Russians were puck-possession, so were the Swedes, Czechs, and Finns. He had us, in practice, reversing, regrouping, backing deep, and reversing, pass the puck back to our d-men in our own end, all kinds of things that were revolutionary because of our opponents, what they did. They weren't doing that in the National Hockey League. If you remember, the National Hockey League really started to change after they had several series against the Russians."

Future filmmaker Guy Maddin was nine years old when McLeod took over the Nats; fortunately Guy's father, Charles, still had a lot of pull around the Arena. "I was in the dressing room a lot for the coaching. That was kind of before hockey coaching was invented, right? There wasn't a trap, or anything like that. They worked on the power play," he said. "But chalk talk usually consisted of Shakey McLeod throwing the chalk at somebody, and, 'They'd better f'n work hard!' He was good with the players."

The fact is that McLeod didn't have a green-as-grass locker room; he had lawyers, teachers and accountants, along with some new blood. "I guess the leaders on the team were the coach and then Marshall Johnston and Fran Huck and Mo Mott, maybe Terry O'Malley and Ray Cadieux," continued Maddin. "But it was a lot of silent leadership. There was some rah-rah in the dressing room, but it was kind of just intelligent people realizing what they had to do."

Chuck Lefley was brought into the system in 1969, and he didn't get to see much of Father Bauer. "Shakey was a very passionate guy. He really wanted to win and he would do anything. He was almost a polar opposite to Father Bauer. Father Bauer was very calm and Jackie was the one that would excite you, get you going when you weren't going," said Lefley. "He was a wonderful man. He really understood, because he had older players—and when I say older, I'm talking late 20s—and he had some 18-year-olds that he had to deal with, and he did it all great."

Winnipeg Free Press columnist Jack Bennett was initially a skeptic. "I recall now how sorry I felt for him," he wrote of the initial hiring. "I had good reason to think the Nats simply wouldn't play for anyone else but Father David Bauer. I wasn't, however, alone in my thinking. Many of the team's friends and critics thought the same."

But the Nats bought into what Shakey was selling. "This is as closely knit a hockey team as you'll want to find," wrote Bennett. "The veterans are young in years and the rookies are talented and willing pupils. Most important, they like the coach. Like him! That's an understatement, if there ever was one. They'd skate through the walls of Winnipeg Arena for Jackie McLeod."

There was a divide in the team that wasn't necessarily evident to outsiders. "Some of the western guys felt that there was a bit of a division between the team, the western Protestants recruited by Jackie McLeod, and the eastern Catholics recruited by Father. That's oversimplifying it, but there was some truth to it," said Herb Pinder, who would be in the western camp, given his upbringing in Saskatoon and the fact that McLeod brought him and his brother Gerry into the Nats fold. "Fran Huck was a Catholic so he didn't fit the mold, but by and large, there were those that were recruited by Jackie and those who were recruited by Father, and older and younger, Catholic and Protestant. There was a bit of that on the team. I didn't care, I was so friggin' happy to be there."

Chapter 15

CZECHS AND REFEREES

The free-spirited, guitar-playing, fun-loving George Faulkner was Newfoundland and Labrador's gift to hockey—and to the Nats. Undoubtedly, he is the greatest character to ever suit up during the Bauer years.

Coming out of the Maroon experiment, fresh blood was necessary. New coach Jackie McLeod and manager Father Bauer had a pretty good idea where talented players were in the country, and the challenge was signing them for the national team and convincing them to stick around for the 1968 Winter Olympics in Grenoble, France. The program, although lacking in medals, never hurt for publicity. It was an easier sell than in the past, but not everyone knew about Father Bauer and the Nats.

In the spring of 1965, Bauer was at a coaching clinic in St. Andrews, New Brunswick. Midweek, there was a spirited game between the coaches, and George Faulkner, who was there as a coach and had impressed on the ice, was summoned. When Faulkner was told that Father Bauer wanted to see him, he said, "Who's Father Bauer?"

There's a good reason he didn't know Father Bauer, said Faulkner. Newfoundland had entered Confederation in 1949. As the last province to join, and the furthest east geographically, it has always stood apart physically—Newfoundland is an island, while Labrador is on the mainland, east of Quebec—and culturally. "Back here in Newfoundland, we weren't members of the Canadian Amateur Hockey Association, so we weren't really up on things that were happening in the rest of Canada at that time," he said.

Father Bauer surprised Faulkner when he asked: "How would you like to play with Canada's national team?"

Born in Bishop's Falls in 1933, Faulkner is still considered the greatest hockey talent to come out of the province. At 15, he was playing in the Grand Falls Senior Hockey League. With only six NHL teams, there wasn't a lot of opportunity for Faulkner. His rights were held by the Montreal Canadiens, a perennial powerhouse. (It's tough to crack a lineup with the likes of Doug Harvey, Rocket Richard, Tom Johnson, Jean Beliveau, Boom Boom Geoffrion and Dickie Moore.) George's brother, Alex, did play for a short while in the NHL with the Detroit Red Wings. Instead, George Faulkner had starred for junior and senior teams in Quebec and Newfoundland. He's most remembered for his decade as player-coach of the Conception Bay (NL) CeeBees—four-time Herder Memorial Trophy winner as provincial senior hockey champion. That's where he was when the Nats came calling.

"Totally unexpected" were the words Faulkner used to recall the invite. "I was 33 years old then. I said, 'Yeah, I'd like to, but I'm arena manager and playing coach of the CeeBees back in Harbour Grace." He got on the phone to Frank Moores, who would later become premier of Newfoundland, but at the time, operated a company responsible for putting the ice in Harbour Grace arena. "Oh, you've got to go. If Father Bauer asked you to go, you've got to go," Moores told Faulkner.

With commitments at home during the summer, Faulkner didn't make the Nats camp in August 1965, but he arrived in the fall, his travel expenses partly covered by a thrilled Newfoundland government led by Premier Joey Smallwood. "I fitted right in—the first practice even," he said.

Faulkner was a defenceman by training, sometimes playing 60 minutes for the CeeBees. With the Nats, he also played forward, usually on the left side. He definitely was an odd duck. "They were all young guys, most of them were 11, 12 years younger than me. Fran Huck and Billy MacMillan and Morris Mott, those guys. Barry MacKenzie and Terry

O'Malley, they'd been there before, Gary Begg, a few more of them. I got in there pretty good."

Mott said Faulkner brought multiple skills to the team. "He was only with us the one year and you know it turned out that he was not only a good hockey player but he was also a good guitar player, so that made our road trips for that year." Faulkner still lugs his guitar to various events, including the reunions of the national team.

The newcomers to the Nats had a variety of backgrounds. The top name was Fran Huck, a 160-pound centreman, who had been lighting it up for his hometown Regina Pats, with more than 200 goals. The team came up short in the 1965 Memorial Cup semifinals, but Huck knew where he was going—university in the summer, and the Nats in the fall. "I've always wanted to play in the Olympics," Huck said in May 1965. "A lot of people don't realize the good talent the team has and the difficulties it has to get ready for overseas competition. After 1968 will be soon enough to think about pro. Too many players jump into pro ranks before they are ready." A few feathers were out of joint, but not from the NHL; Huck had left before his junior eligibility was up, as did Morris Mott. Montreal Canadiens' property, he was watched carefully, and eventually Huck suited up a few games for the Habs after the Nats closed up shop. "Montreal has been good to me," said Huck in 1970. "They have left me alone after I became too old for junior." The diminutive Huck, five foot seven at best, was great fun to watch on the ice, said long-time international hockey photographer Bruce Jessup. "I liked the way he played. He wasn't that big. Sort of a digger, and intense guy," said Jessup. "Huck had a lot of pit bull in him." Later, Huck played in St. Louis, and then five years in the WHA with the Winnipeg Jets and Minnesota Fighting Saints. Post-hockey, he became a lawyer.

Morris Kenneth Mott was only a little bigger at five foot eight. The native of Creelman, Saskatchewan, was playing with the Weyburn Red Wings in the provincial junior league, and was selected by the Regina Pats to bolster its lineup in the western side of the Memorial Cup playdowns against the Edmonton Oil Kings. There Mott befriend Huck, who had already committed to the Nats, so he too asked about joining, turning down a couple of offers from American universities. Coach

McLeod's familiarity with the juniors in Saskatchewan certainly helped. Mott, who would later become a professor at the University of Brandon, liked the balance of hockey and school, if not the financial aspect of the deal. By his recollection, he managed to get by on the $2,000 stipend from the Nats, which, broken down, was roughly $500 for tuition and books, and $75 for a month of room and board. Mott didn't declare a major until his third year, getting a feel for the workload in general arts. "If you were going to school you pretty well had to stay away from courses that had a lot of lab work because you couldn't guarantee that you would be there," he said. "We always went to Europe for a month in the spring and it was too difficult. You had to be able to do your work in hotels and airports. You had an assignment due and you had to be able to do some reading in your spare time, so things like science were kind of out." When the Nats folded, Mott went back to school—Queen's in Kingston—and then spent a couple of seasons in the colourful uniforms of the NHL's California Golden Seals, and a year in Sweden.

Prince Edward Island's Billy MacMillan was a Bauer Boy dating to St. Mike's, and was a 1961 Memorial Cup winner. A Maple Leafs prospect, the right winger stuck around after the school dropped out of the OHA, playing for the Neil McNeil Maroons before heading back home and enrolling at Saint Dunstan's University (now part of UPEI). He didn't think the money Punch Imlach and the Leafs were offering was worth sacrificing an education. In 1965, after playing university hockey, MacMillan accidentally bumped into Father Bauer in Moncton. "We had a great chat. I was wanting more as far as hockey was concerned, and going to university. He got in touch with me and invited me to go to Winnipeg and play for the national team," he said. When the Nats folded in 1970, MacMillan embarked on a solid NHL career, where his brother, Bobby, would follow a couple of years later. After playing with the Leafs, Atlanta Flames, and New York Islanders, he went into coaching.

For much of the Nats' existence, Jean Cusson was the representative of *la belle province*. Born in Verdun, he was 1962 Athlete of the Year in Quebec. While Cusson was enrolled at Collège Sainte-Marie, the affiliation with the University of Montreal allowed him to play in the more competitive Canadian Interuniversity Athletic Union. He quickly realized he had a lot to learn with the Nats. "I found that my speed was okay but my hockey thinking wasn't there," he said. "It was fast for me. I wasn't used to playing in a fast league. In other words, it took me a year to figure it out, what was going on." He'd go home from the rink exhausted, and not just from the action on the ice. "I used to come home very tired because I had to speak English every day. Even on the staff, there was nobody I could mainly speak French with." The French, however, did come in handy after he completed his teaching degree and taught the language during the day, and played hockey at night. Speedy and with scoring ability, Cusson was nicknamed "Eddie" by teammates, as his goal celebration reminded them of Eddie "the Entertainer" Shack. That speed would come in handy in his post-Nat life, playing hockey for years in Europe. There, he learned the secrets of sausage-making; upon returning home to Quebec, he teamed with his brother, Paul, to form William J. Walter Saucissier, which now has more than 30 locations and is run by Jean's sons.

Ted Hargreaves was another westerner new to the team. Originally from Weyburn, Saskatchewan, he played a season with Brigham Young University before transferring north to the Nats. After Canada closed up shop, Hargreaves bounced around hockey's high minors, including time as a player-coach with the Nelson (BC) Maple Leafs. He spent the 1973–74 campaign in the WHA with the Winnipeg Jets. He died in 2005. Others added to the system in 1966 were Rick McCann, a 21-year-old playmaking centre originally from Hamilton, Ontario, who'd been a top scorer at Michigan Tech, and Harvey Schmidt, who'd played defence with the Melville Millionaires of Saskatchewan's junior league.

At the top of McLeod's wish list was a veteran defenceman, and the team went after Lorne Davis. He had played professionally in the NHL, AHL, and WHL, until being reinstated as an amateur in 1961. In January 1966, Father Bauer went to court Davis in Regina, where he was playing senior hockey for the Caps. "The word is Father Bauer won't have to do much talking to bend the ear of Mr. Davis, because he's sold on the idea," wrote Jack Bennett in the *Winnipeg Free Press*. "But a 35-year-old man can't leave his family and a secure job behind for the sake of upholding his country's honor in hockey." After just a couple of games with the

Nats, McLeod was direct with his praise of Davis: "He doesn't give the puck away." The decision to join the Canadian team would pay off for Davis, too, who was a part of Team Canada's coaching squad at the 1980 Olympics.

A goalie was a must since Ken Broderick was finishing a degree course in psychology at UBC. Wayne Stephenson had tended net for his hometown Winnipeg Braves, and was signed from the junior Edmonton Oil Kings. He turned down an offer from the Boston Bruins. "Hockey is much the same as university in that one never stops learning," Stephenson said in 1967. With his quick hands, Stephenson was a mainstay of the Nats until the program was discontinued. He seamlessly entered the NHL, and played in two All-Star games during a career with St. Louis, Philadelphia, and Washington. With the loosening of the rules governing ex-pros playing amateur hockey, Stephenson returned to Father Bauer's side in 1980 for the post-Olympic Swedish Cup. The goalie died in June 2010.

Mott is quick to credit the veterans for being so open to newcomers, knowing that success would only be possible with some new legs. "They really took ownership of our development. Marshall Johnston was really good at that and all these guys, we were not only playing hockey together, a lot of them I was going to school with," said Mott. "Terry O'Malley, Paul Conlin, and we would talk in the cafeteria about defensive positioning and forechecking. We'd have it all laid out on a napkin or something. I've said this before—I thought those first couple years I spent with the national team were the best years of my life from a hockey point of view. I knew I was improving. I was getting so much better all the time."

With Winnipeg as its base, the national team played a number of NHL and minor-league teams during training camps, holding its own. Central Pro and Western Hockey League teams made up the bulk of games during the winter. When a regular player was injured or had a family or school conflict, there were still the Maroons to fall back on for a call-up here or there.

But for all their success against North American opponents—unbeaten in 15 exhibition games—the Nats still couldn't deal with the

Russians. A tired Soviet squad straggled into the 'Peg on December 16, having just lost to a reinforced Montreal Junior Canadiens team, 2–1. It was no contest, the USSR winning 4–0 and 8–6.

Just after Christmas came the debut of the Walter A. Brown Memorial Tournament in Colorado Springs, Colorado, featuring Canada, Russia, Sweden, and Czechoslovakia. The man behind it was William Thayer Tutt, who ran the multi-million dollar Broadmoor Hotel in the Rocky Mountains. He'd been heavily involved with American college hockey, and became vice-president of the IIHF. Walter Brown was the recently-deceased owner of the NHL Bruins.

Games were played in the quirky Broadmoor World Arena, 10 feet shorter and five feet narrower than the Winnipeg Arena, with barely enough seating, roughly 5,000, for the tournament to break even—but it was an ad for his hotel in the long run. "It was a tough tournament, because we played in a rink designed for figure skating, so it was very small," recalled Broderick. "Put 10 players out there and two goalies, it was just shoulder to shoulder."

Given that McLeod suited up and potted a few goals for good measure, Father Bauer was behind the bench again. Still, it was a familiar story—Russia winning all three of its games. Canada, on the strength of a win over Czechoslovakia, was second, and the Czechs third. McLeod made note of the altitude: "Obviously, you need to come here four or five days ahead of time to get accustomed to this altitude. It takes that long to get your skating legs." The Swedish and Czech teams would swing through Winnipeg for an exhibition tilt before heading home.

It was a decent showing, and gave the Nats confidence before heading to Ljubljana, Yugoslavia, for the World Championships at the beginning of March. Just prior to leaving for Europe in February, Winnipeg TV station CBWT aired a short film about the club. The footage was mainly shot in Colorado Springs. "It wasn't the kind of film that would make you get up out of your arm chair and start cheering for the Maple Leaf. In fact, we thought it fell a little flat," reviewed *Winnipeg Free Press* sports editor Maurice Smith. "An earnest attempt was made to point out how much some of the players on the team are sacrificing in order to represent their country in international puck competition. It was a good try, but it didn't bring a lump to your throat or tears to your eyes. Neither did the scene of the team's departure for Colorado Springs, when no one showed up at the airport to see the boys take off."

Just before the games in Ljubljana, McLeod talked with assurance. "Officially we came here feeling we had nothing to lose. But the players seem to have the idea that they can win," said the coach. "They have marvellous spirit and that can carry you a long way." Father Bauer, coaching while Shakey played, stood behind him. "I think McLeod has backing for his confidence," the Roman Catholic clergyman said.

The pleasant surprise of a not-so-pleasant tournament for the Nats ended up being George Faulkner, his veteran legs finding new life. He led the team with six goals, and tied in points with Fran Huck (each with eight). "We first planned to use George on defence, but when Lorne Davis became available we were able to put him on the wing, which is his best position," said McLeod in Yugoslavia. "At first he had a lot of bad habits, which is understandable after seven years at Harbour Grace. But he's worked hard and now I can't find much wrong with his play. And he gives so much, he's a good example for the other fellows."

The rejuvenated Newfoundlander wasn't enough. Another old pair of legs—and pads—made a difference, as Seth Martin returned to the net for Canada. Father Bauer specifically chose him to play against Czechoslovakia. "The Czechs have a phobia about Martin and I think we should take advantage of it," he said of the top goalie of the tournament.

It ended with Russia winning the World Championship, Czechoslovakia finishing second. Canada was third. It was its first medal since coming second to Sweden in 1962 at Colorado Springs—a tournament the Soviets and Czechs skipped.

Terry O'Malley was captain of the '66 team. "We almost withdrew because the refereeing was so bad," he said, recalling a March 10 epic against the Czechs, a 2–1 loss that lives on in infamy. The villains were refs Gennaro Olivieri of Switzerland and Andrei Chojnacki of Poland. Jim Proudfoot of the *Toronto Star* reported that 11 penalties were called against Canada, and "eight were impossible to justify." Then there were two disallowed goals by the Nats, one waved off in favour of a penalty and the other in a goalmouth scramble where the net came off and the goal judge never turned on the light.

It's comical reading about the penalties now, but it wasn't then for the players. Fran Huck got a slashing penalty when he collided with a Czech player. While on his way to the penalty box, O'Malley got a second minor for slashing when a Czech player nearby fell down as the Canadian skated by. The kicker, though, was a tripping penalty assessed to Seth Martin when a Czech stepped on his hand while skating through the crease.

Bourbonnais—known as "the Little Red Devil" overseas—tied the score in the third, making it 1–1. But it's tough fighting six opponents and two referees. "We were three people short in the last five minutes of the game, and they ended up scoring and beating us 2–1. Well, we were furious," recalled O'Malley.

In the dressing room, there was talk of walking away. An impromptu vote was taken and only two players wanted to stay in Yugoslavia. "Most of the guys have had it," Gary Begg said after the game. "We get abused back home and we get shafted here. It's nothing new. It started at the Olympics in 1964 and it's happened to us every time. Every man on this team gives up a lot to play because he thinks the Canadian national team means something. But how much can we take? Nobody cares about what we're doing and over here it seems they simply won't let us win. So what's the use of continuing?"

Coach McLeod wanted to leave. "I think we should stand up for our rights and walk out of here," he said. "But this is all for me. I am through with international hockey."

The debate went on throughout the evening, emotions rising and falling. At one point, Father Bauer brought in two members of the Canadian press, Jim Proudfoot and George Gross, to hear the arguments; they sided with the players. "When we walked into the dressing room, team captain Barry MacKenzie told us that no matter what we had to say, the team was going home. I tried to inject a bit of humor into a serious situation by suggesting that I'd join them on the flight home if they gave me the flight number," wrote Gross years later. "Father Dave didn't think it was funny and hustled us out of the dressing room. He then chased after the Canadian ambassador to get some support. The career diplomat explained the ramifications of a walkout to the players and the boys eventually settled down."

At another meeting, the team doctor, Dr. Jack Waugh, spoke up and suggested the club had a responsibility to Canada and Winnipeg to compete in spite of the circumstances. If not, it would possibly never again represent Canada. Diplomacy prevailed, much to Father Bauer's relief. "If you quit now, all the players that come after you won't have this opportunity that you had," he urged.

The Canadians had one game left, and Martin went in net, despite his swollen, bruised hand. The emotionally and physically spent Nats lost 3–0 to Russia. Proudfoot wrote that the loss "reflected nothing but credit on them. . . . It was a tremendous effort, anchored by the incredible goaltending of Seth Martin."

In the end, Russia took the gold, the Czechs silver, and Canada bronze. Martin was voted the tourney's top goalie, with Soviets Alexander Ragulin the top defenceman and Konstantin Loktev the best forward.

At the end-of-tournament banquet, O'Malley was seated beside IIHF president Bunny Ahearne. "I remember him saying to me over dinner, 'You know, you Canadians, you have no right to complain. You have no history.' There was smoke coming out of my ears with that one."

O'Malley swung back: "We might be young, but we know what's fair and not fair, and we have soldiers lying all over Europe that demonstrate that."

Chapter 16

CARL BREWER AND THE CENTENNIAL CELEBRATION

Upon returning from the World Championships in Yugoslavia, Father Bauer was asked how close his Nats were to converting their bronze medals into something shinier. "A defenceman, an offensive-minded defenceman, and a forward who could score goals," was the priest's appeal. God works in mysterious ways, as they say, and his prayer was answered, at least in part.

The return of high-scoring forward Gary Dineen, out of action to concentrate on his studies for a year, certainly fit one request. On August 30, 1966, Dineen wrote to Toronto Maple Leafs GM Punch Imlach:

> Dear Sir,
>
> Many thanks for your invitation to Leaf camp, which was forwarded to me out here at U.B.C. After due consideration I have finally decided to remain amateur for another year and a half, and only after the completion of the '68 Olympics will I consider turning professional. I have been offered a position with a national investment house, and I feel the practical education I'll receive at this firm will be a great asset to me in the future.

> May I express my sincere best wishes for an enjoyable and successful campaign for the Leafs next year. I remain,
>
> Yours sincerely,
> Gary Dineen

Imlach replied a week later, September 6, 1966, and was his typically acerbic self:

> Dear Gary,
>
> I am very sorry to hear that you are not considering attending our training camp. I think you are making a mistake, as next year the expansion can probably use you and I feel that playing touch hockey is not going to develop you along the professional lines.
>
> I also realize that I am competing against the National Hockey team as far as money is concerned and that your affiliations run in another direction.
>
> Yours very truly,
> G. Imlach

Dineen wasn't the only one having issues with Imlach.

Carl Brewer, the cerebral, high-strung defenceman, frustrated into a frenzy by the general manager's dictatorial bearing, sat out the 1965–66 NHL season rather than wearing the blue and white. He enrolled at the University of Toronto and worked on a bachelor of arts degree.

On September 6, 1966, at a private luncheon in Toronto's Albany Club hosted by Alan Eagleson, Brewer's lawyer and a Progressive Conservative member of the Ontario legislature, Brewer expressed a desire to have his amateur status reinstated so he could suit up for Canada's national team. Also at the luncheon were Danny O'Shea, who would suit up for the Nats, and Bobby Orr, who used the Nats as a brief negotiating tool while "the Eagle" worked out a deal with Boston Bruins

GM Hap Emms. Even *Sports Illustrated* noted that the Nats were a possibility for Orr in a feature story. "I'd have to say the chances of Bobby playing for the national team were probably 20 percent at best, but it would have been 100 percent if Hap had continued to be stubborn," said Eagleson in 2015.

Coach Jackie McLeod was hoping that the heavenly gift of Brewer was indeed going to happen. "I don't see how they (Toronto) can deny him of his rights," McLeod said from his Swift Current home. "He has definitely retired from professional hockey, having sat out last year. Toronto has his professional rights but what good is it when the guy won't play pro."

So began a battle that pitted the Canadian national team against the mighty NHL and foreshadowed Brewer's fight against Eagleson and his corrupt practices with the National Hockey League Players' Association.

The New York Rangers wanted him, for one. "We have been trying to get Brewer for the past year," said Emile Francis, GM of the Blueshirts. "I can't see us waiving him out of the league." Brewer was on the suspended list and then the NHL's student inactive list, so it was impossible for another team to draft him. For amateur reinstatement, even before he was approved by the Canadian Amateur Hockey Association and the International Ice Hockey Federation, Brewer would have to clear waivers, all other professional teams passing on him.

Brewer had been a star with the junior Toronto Marlboros, before joining the Leafs for the 1958–59 season. Four campaigns later, he was a second-team NHL All-Star, and then a first-teamer for 1962–63. The five-foot-nine, 190-pound Brewer was rough and tough, but also adept at moving the puck, racking up assists in the pre-Orr era of stay-at-home defencemen.

National columnist Jim Coleman waved the flag and challenged the powers that be to make Brewer's reinstatement happen. "I wish to make it perfectly clear that I am on the side of Canada's national hockey team, Father David Bauer, and Carl Brewer or any other hockey player who can assist in restoring Canada's international hockey prestige," wrote Coleman. "Ordinarily, I would be opposed to the practice of reinstating shopworn professionals as amateurs, to represent Canada in international competitions. But, Carl Brewer is no shopworn professional—Carl Brewer won't be 28 until next month; he is one of the two or three best defencemen in the entire world of hockey and he would be an invaluable addition to the national team."

The first domino to fall was expected; Bunny Ahearne reinstated three former pros, Carl Brewer, Bill Hay, and Jack "Red" Bownass, making them eligible for IIHF events. Brewer's challenge of the system brought national attention to the reinstatement issue for the first time, as well as the CAHA's cozy relationship with the NHL. Before, reinstatement had been for old pros, settling down post-NHL into career and family, playing hockey as a hobby rather than a job, as with the players on the Winnipeg Maroons.

The hypocrisy of the NHL brass was also evident, and its disdain for the national team program came to bear. "We're delighted to have Brewer play for Canada if he doesn't want to play professional," said John Bassett of the Leafs. "I've talked this over with my partners at the Gardens, and in a few days Stafford Smythe will outline our position in a letter to Clarence Campbell. . . . Our view is to say good luck to him, and what the hell. If Brewer plays for Canada, he'll still be wearing the maple leaf."

Globe and Mail columnist and all-around curmudgeon Dick Beddoes delivered a shot: "The normal approach of the NHL moguls is to dismiss the national team as a pleasant little amateur project run by that nice little priest, Father David Bauer, but don't bother us with its problems. Then, after the Canadians habitually lose the world championship, the moguls horsewhip the national team through the country's sports pages. We are a perverse people, always handy with a rope to lynch losers." But Brewer was no loser.

While awaiting his severance from the NHL, Brewer headed to Winnipeg, and, unable to legally suit up, got to know the team, acting as an assistant coach, selling tickets, and going on a couple of goodwill missions with Nats public relations man Phil Reimer. He was careful to not say anything in the press that further upset the apple cart. He also worked for the Indian Affairs Department in Kenora, Ontario. Brewer penned a piece in the October 8 issue of the *Winnipeg Free Press*, showing great humility:

> To date these Nationals have not been victors in world competition, but they have shown to people of Eastern and Western Europe that Canada's young men are astute and cultured individuals who have a conscious desire to elevate the image of Canada abroad.
>
> For my own part, as a hockey player and a Canadian citizen who is proud to be such, I would be privileged to join in representing Canada along with so many fine young men—lawyers, teachers, chartered accountants, university students et al.—in world competition.
>
> Yet, one major problem remains after tonight's exhibition—can I make the team?
>
> To stem the tide of the Nationals, perhaps the NHL might see fit to reinstate me and weaken the Nationals defence.

It took until December 16, but Brewer was finally okayed, the news relayed via telegram by CAHA president Fred Page to Jackie McLeod. "This is the kind of player we need—one with lots of experience," said Shakey.

The Nats were over the moon. "Man it's about time!" said Roger Bourbonnais.

"He is going to be a fine teacher. We'll learn a lot from him," said Gary Begg.

Terry O'Malley figured having Brewer as a fellow rearguard would mean one less goal a game.

Armed with techniques he'd learned from other NHLers, Brewer did indeed make his teammates better. "Carl showed me a whole bunch of drills, and we skated a lot," said Herb Pinder. "I got bending my knees more, and lengthening my stride. That year was a huge development year for me, and I gained confidence."

After 18 months on the sidelines, Brewer was eager to get back into the game, and played just days after the announcement, in Vancouver and Victoria, BC, against a second-rate Russian touring team.

While Brewer wanted to be a Nat, Serge Savard was the one that got away. "Serge was all for playing with us when he attended our summer rookie camp in Montreal, but as I see it, another source convinced him not to play for us," McLeod told the press in September. There had even been a plane ticket in his name to Winnipeg, unused. It was Canadiens GM Sam Pollock who inked the rearguard to a two-year deal.

There was new blood in the Nats again, some young, some considerably older. The top recruit was Toronto's "Dapper" Danny O'Shea. He'd led the Oshawa Generals in scoring in a losing cause, as his squad fell to the Edmonton Oil Kings in the 1966 Memorial Cup final. The six-foot-one centre was a key part of the Nats until the team closed up shop. Seven years in the NHL and WHA followed; his brother, Kevin, also made the bigs. Brian Harper was the "little" brother of NHL veteran Terry; at over 200 pounds on a six-foot frame, he was among the biggest of the Nats, lining up at right wing. The Regina native had played two years of junior with the Brandon Wheat Kings before starring with the University of Alberta.

There was little doubt how Adolph "Addie" Tambellini from Trail, BC, got invited to play with the Nats. He'd been a teammate of Shakey McLeod's with the Trail Smoke Eaters, world champions in 1961. He was 30 when he arrived in Winnipeg, his experience a decade of senior hockey, a short stint in the Western League, and a couple of seasons in Austria. After his single season with the Nats, Addie returned to Trail. He died in February 2004. Even more senior than Tambellini was Jack "Red" Bownass. The Winnipegger had been playing pro hockey since 1950, on teams across the continent. He played parts of four seasons in the NHL with Montreal and the Rangers, but never stuck. He'd been coaching for two years before suiting up for Canada, making the amateur reinstatement relatively painless—especially compared to Brewer—for the six-foot-one, 190-pound defenceman. His bigger contribution would come after the 1967 World Championships, when he was tasked as the boss of the second national team in Ottawa.

The other difference for the national team heading towards the 1967 World Championships was maturity. The six-foot-one Gary Begg had put on 10 pounds of muscle, earning his "Moose" nickname for more than just his Moosomin, Saskatchewan, upbringing. Marshall Johnston's accuracy improved. Fran Huck learned how to use his great skills to control play.

On Christmas Day in Winnipeg, with the Centennial tournament just around the corner, the Nats beat Russia's B team, 6–1. "The Canadians have caught up with our best," Russian coach Anatoley Kostrukov said after the game, praising Brewer. "There is nothing to choose between our best and your Nationals."

The now-annual Walter Brown Memorial event in Colorado Springs started the next day, and it didn't begin well for Canada. The Nats were surprised by a "bunch of Raggedy Anns" from the Western International Hockey League—the thrown-together team held them to a 5–5 draw. Just a three-team tournament, the Canadians beat the Americans, and then faced the thrown-together team again with an old friend in the opposing net—Seth Martin. "Holy Moses," said Father Bauer after the game, praising Martin for nearly stealing the game from his former teammates. Canada won 3–2, and took the tourney as well.

It was a precursor to the greatest moment of the Nats—the Centennial hockey tournament in Winnipeg. From the first game on New Year's Day 1967, with the Cameron Highlander cadet corps pipe band and legion flag bearers leading the players onto the ice, to the last, with Canadian Prime Minister Lester B. Pearson presenting the tournament trophy to team captain Roger Bourbonnais, it was a memorable event.

The Centennial featured Canada, the United States, Russia, and Czechoslovakia. It was designed as a showcase for Winnipeg, hoping to secure the 1970 World Championship. Given the frenzy created by 51,000 passionate fans over six games—packed into the decked-out and polished Winnipeg Arena—it was a precursor to the Jets of the WHA.

For Guy Maddin, the Centennial tournament was thrilling because it was actually broadcast live on local television. "For some reason, I wasn't at that game. Maybe it was such a hot ticket that I got pushed off my seat by some adults or something like that," said Maddin. "But I was happy to watch on TV anyway. . . . It might have been the first time for a live hockey of that magnitude [to be] broadcast in Winnipeg."

The final standings don't tell the whole story, because the game that everyone wanted to see was Canada versus USSR on January 6.

	GP	W	L	T	GF	GA	Pts
CAN	3	3	0	0	17	8	6
CZE	3	2	1	0	16	9	4
USSR	3	1	2	0	13	11	2
USA	3	0	3	0	4	22	0

Jan. 1—CAN 5, CZE 3;
Jan. 2—USSR 7, USA 1;
Jan. 3—CAN 7, USA 1;
Jan. 4—CZE 5, USSR 2;
Jan. 5—CZE 8, USA 2;
Jan. 6—CAN 5, USSR 4.
MVP: Václav Nedomansky, C, CZE

With Russia unable to top the standings, having lost to the Czechs, it still put on a heck of an effort. In a tight-checking affair, the penalties called by referees Hal Trumbull of the United States and Zdenek Korinek of Czechoslovakia proved the difference—Canada scored three of its five goals with a Soviet in the box, and the Russians counted three with the man advantage.

Billy MacMillan was the hero, teaming with centre Gary Dineen and Jean Cusson. Just 14 seconds after the Russians tied it 4–4 on the power play, MacMillan took a pass from Cusson—who tied for the goal-scoring lead (six) in the tourney with Václav Nedomansky—and slid the puck into the net past Viktor Konovalenko.

The calm Brewer was a difference-maker, scoring on a deflected blast from the blue line, and frustrating Russians into penalties. "We saw the Czechs coax several Russian players into penalties Wednesday night so we decided to try the same thing. It seems Carl did a good job at it," said McLeod. The high-scoring Soviet ace Vyacheslav Starshinov, in particular, was "bewildered and bothered" by Brewer and was kept off the scoresheet. Asked to pick the top players, Father Bauer was diplomatic:

"There [weren't] three stars out there, there were twenty."

It was the first time since 1963 that Canada won a tournament involving Russia and Czechoslovakia.

Things seemed to be going the right way for once, and *Free Press* sports editor Maurice Smith caught Father Bauer in an upbeat mood. "You know," he said, "if I had to make a choice of going to the Olympic Games in 1968 or the world tournament in Vienna, I'd choose the latter, because I'm sure this team has such a good chance to bring the world title back to Canada."

The fever was starting to grow outside of Winnipeg as well, the oft-ignored Nats suddenly a hot ticket. Just two days after winning the Centennial, they were at the Montreal Forum, tying the Russians 3–3 in front of 15,000. At the end of January, 16,000 turned out at Maple Leaf Gardens to see the Soviets and Canadians tie again, 2–2. Letters started to come in to the team on a regular basis, and when the team got to Vienna, a 30,000-name-strong note was waiting, along with a gem of a poem:

Russians are red
Czechs are blue
If you'd win the championships
We'd appreciate it.

With winning came more ticket sales, which eased the financial pressures; as did the Canadian Hockey Foundation. The CHF was established by a collection of Canadian business leaders, with John J. Wintermeyer at the front. The plan was to set up two funds, a scholarship and a general fund, to offer financial assistance to national team prospects. "We must at once create this non-profit organization to help support our national team financially," Wintermeyer said. "This is our opportunity to tell young Canadians we believe in them—and that we are willing to do something about it."

Scott Young played up the team in a *Globe and Mail* column at the end of January. Young had run into Father Bauer in the Edmonton airport, and they travelled to Toronto. They talked hockey, naturally, and Young, who had been in the Nats' corner all along, was a cheerleader. "If it weren't that the word might embarrass Father David Bauer, due to his calling, I would call it a miracle," wrote Young, adding that the Nats were gaining momentum, and that a "line of applicants was forming" and a second team was in the planning stage.

"I feel the team has improved considerably from last year—remember we had six new players then," explained McLeod. "Our biggest asset now is experience. All the players have been together on the same team for some time now and it is starting to show up."

Vienna beckoned, and the Nats were on a roll, with 33 wins, 2 losses and 4 ties in 39 prep games. "Winning in Winnipeg has given this club its biggest boost yet. We have work to do, but I honestly think we'll be better prepared this trip than ever before," said McLeod.

Health issues, however, shook the team. The flu had been going around, and O'Malley had been suffering from mononucleosis since the Centennial tournament, but did play in Vienna. Coach McLeod was confined to Ottawa Civic Hospital with stomach issues just before the team left for Europe, forcing Father Bauer to adjust his plans and take over. McLeod missed a couple of exhibition games in Czechoslovakia (a tie and a win) and Sweden (two losses), arriving "looking drawn and weak from his five days in hospital" according to a CBC TV report. Then there was a game on a Canadian army base in Germany. "Tours before tournaments such as this, they are tiring. And for us to come on a tour before a big match, I think this takes away from our game in the tournament," said Father Bauer.

But there was money to be made from those exhibition games, and ambassadorial duties too. Many Czechoslovakians, in particular, were passionate fans of Canadian hockey. The Prague arena was always joyously loud, whistles shrieking, bells clanging. At the the Nats' hotel it was common to see dozens of hockey enthusiasts hoping for a glimpse of the team, or better yet, an autograph, a team postcard, or, the Holy Grail, a Team Canada pin.

"The whistles were boos," said Marshall Johnston. "The thing I remember about the Czechs, especially, was Seth Martin, who had been over there previously with Trail Smoke Eaters in World Championships and so on. He was fantastic. The Czech crowds, especially the Czech crowds, they just really loved him. When we came on the ice, everybody was, 'What's this all about?'" The rinks were also interesting, sometimes open-air with stands, sometimes with a roof but no side walls. The fans would follow their team too, and in Vienna, just 35 miles from the Czech border, the Russian national anthem was jeered.

In a 1967 CBC feature, *Summit on Ice*, O'Malley talked about the trips to the barnstorming tour: "Carl Brewer described it as every one being a Stanley Cup playoff. I believe sometimes you get a little tired of travelling. Like tonight, we weren't up for that game. . . . It's very tough, but you have to go through these games. You can't make a mistake because there is no second chance. Each individual hamlet, village or town that you come into, they're expecting you to do your part for their country. . . . There's pressure that way, as far as in respect to a 70-some schedule, where you might get another shot at the fella come Sunday night or Saturday night."

A price was paid for the extra travel and McLeod was always against the extra games. "We had to go to Europe with a bunch of sick guys," said McLeod from Canada, his charges away. "I was going to use the tour to make up my mind which 17 of my 21 guys to use for the tournament. Now I'll have to do a bit of guessing." Last-minute cuts included Lorne Davis, Duane MacPhail, Ken Broderick, and Danny O'Shea. Broderick expressed his disappointment to the CBC: "It was a bitter pill to swallow when Jackie told me the news. Naturally, I was disappointed but I still feel that Jackie made the decision on what he based would be best for the team."

The first bump in the road was March 21 against West Germany, coached by a Canadian, Ed Reigle of Winnipeg. Though the Nats won going away, 13–1, they didn't exactly play Catholic-priest-approved hockey. "I picked Canada to win the world championship this year," said Reigle. "I still think they can do it. But they'll have to act a lot differently on the ice than the way they did against my team Tuesday night, particularly in the last 10 minutes. If they play that way against the Russians, they'll get their pants shot full of buckshot." The Canadians had been responding, they said, to West German spears throughout the game and battled back.

The next fight came, once again, with referees—Ted Daily of the United States, and Ova Dahlberg of Sweden. The opponents, again, were the Czechs. In the first period, Dineen made a baseball-like pass to Cusson but it was waved off. Confusion reigned. Ref Daily told Dineen: "Your stick was over your shoulder and, anyway, I blew the whistle." After the game, Gordon Juckes of the CAHA was livid. "The puck was not even shoulder high. There was nothing wrong with the goal. It was a bad call like so many others we've had in Europe over the years."

It wasn't even the worst call. There was photographic proof from the Swedish newspaper *Aftenbladet* of the other blunder. Canada was up 1–0 in the third, on a goal by MacMillan. Jack Bownass made a pass from behind the net to MacMillan, who popped it in. The official, Dahlberg, said no goal, because Jean Cusson was in the crease, and perhaps because the Russian goaler, Viktor Konovalenko, made a scene. "When Bownass was behind the net I was definitely in the crease," said Cusson at the time. "I thought he would pass to me, but when he passed to Billy I skated out and was about three feet from the net when the goal was scored." The photo of the goal proved Cusson to be right. Cusson said the same thing in 2014: "The mistake I made was going in and going out."

The normally placid Roger Bourbonnais screamed in frustration: "Why does it always have to happen to us? What do you have to do to win over here?"

With almost 50 years to absorb the slight, Cusson doesn't think that the referees were totally to blame. "It's like in soccer, it's the players, especially the Czechs, they were the worst ones. They were faking. You touch them a little bit and they go down. You know what I mean? They fell on the ice. The referee sometimes got influenced by that. That's what I blame the European referees for, not because they favoured . . . but especially for penalties, the guys used to get mad on our team. It got worse after that."

For all the noise and controversy, it ended in a one-all draw. The *Globe and Mail*'s cantankerous columnist Dick Beddoes summed it up pretty well: "The word masochism, in any case, fits our annual vain attempt to win hockey decisions in Europe. The folly of trying to win in your opponent's home town has long been established, but we persist in sending our people across wild waters to strive for country 'tis of thee, home, mother and other chauvinistic claptrap."

The key game, as per usual, came against the USSR two days later, a 2–1 heartbreaking loss for Canada. This time it was a missed offside call on Boris Mayorov that frustrated the Canadians. Future international hockey photographer Bruce Jessup was in Vienna as a fan. "The Russians got a goal to go ahead 2–1. It was offside by about 10 feet, and they never called it." Martin made the initial save on Mayorov but Vyacheslav Starshinov converted the rebound.

Equally catastrophic was an injury to Brewer. O'Malley said that Brewer and Starshinov had been battling all game, including some less-than-legal stickwork. "Starshinov gave the stick back to him, and cut the top of his eyelid," recalled O'Malley. Brewer's cye swelled shut, and the trainer, Bill Bozak, did what he could, taping the eye open with adhesive tape. "We lost him for 10 minutes of that period and they got one goal," said O'Malley. "It was just a lucky goal, (Anatoli) Firsov got it. I still remember, he was changing and he flipped the puck up in the air and our defenceman came to knock it down and Seth Martin, who was our goalie—great goalie—went into a butterfly to take it into his body and just as the defenceman came across to knock it down, it tipped on his fingers and then went in over Seth Martin's shoulder. That tied up the game. That's all it takes. It changed the momentum."

Back home after the tournament, Seth Martin told Don Pilling of the Lethbridge newspaper how close the Nats were. "With a break," he said, "we could have been ahead by three or four goals in the first period. We dominated the game that much. But as the game wore on we ran out of gas. That was the story."

Maurice Smith caught up with Father Bauer at 3 a.m. in the Intercontinental Hotel, unable to sleep, and described the priest as "all wound up inside—as tight as a violin string." Bauer shared his thinking: "I think our boys gave one of the most courageous displays against Russia last night of any team I've ever been associated with. They were hurting badly from injuries. I'm sure had the Russians played any other team in similar condition it would have been close to a rout. What makes me feel so upset is that the boys sacrificed such a great deal in order to play for Canada. To lose a world's championship by a goal is bad enough but when that goal was offside it's hard to take. Then there was the Czech debacle too. But I guess the heartache will wear away. It usually does."

Playing for silver, the Canadians were spanked by the Swedes 6–0, with goalie Seth Martin giving way to Wayne Stephenson in the second period after surrendering five goals; the Swedes scored on the new keeper just 10 seconds in. "What can you say about a game like that?" sighed McLeod.

Once again, Canada claimed bronze. The Soviets took gold, their fifth straight, on the strength of the brilliant Anatoli Firsov with 12 goals and 11 assists. By comparison, Canada had difficulty scoring in the games that mattered; setting aside the 13–1 romp over West Germany, the Nats only scored 15 other goals, and gave up 15, five more than in 1966. Sweden took silver. Brewer was named a tournament all-star, and American goaltender Carl Wetzel was the only other non-Soviet on the list.

McLeod talked about a second national team after the medal presentation. "Our national team system is all right. I know that against Russia, it tends to look like boys against men. But we are not far behind any European club at the moment," he said. "I'm not knocking these players here, but I think we would get better results if there was more competition for every place on the club from two to three teams operating at once."

After the success of the Centennial tournament and the attention that team (finally) garnered, it was time to face the music upon returning to Canada. "For the first time in the four years I've been with the team I feel embarrassed to come back to Canada," said assistant captain Marshall Johnston during a stopover in Montreal on the way to Winnipeg. "I've never felt worse about a game. We were aiming for first place and the fact that we lost it subconsciously affected us. I'm not saying that we didn't try or do our best. What can you say without it sounding like an alibi? Canada was really behind us this year. We didn't live up to what the people had built us up to be. The people and the press were right—we should have won."

The delicate balance of studying and playing hockey came up again.

"It's difficult to study over there," said Morris Mott. "I got most of my reports done before leaving and tried to do some reading overseas. But I probably only had about three days altogether." Marshall Johnston, Ken Broderick, and Barry MacKenzie were all employed as teachers and took exam papers to grade. A few months after the tournament in Vienna, Brewer admitted to being in awe of the work ethic of his teammates: "I don't know how they do it. They work or go to school until five o'clock and then they play. Some of them were writing exams. Imagine, writing exams on Friday before the game."

Around 3,000 fans came out to the Winnipeg airport, with a band and many banners. The players were surprised. There was always next year, the Olympic Games in Grenoble, for a rematch with the Russians. "I want to beat those guys so bad I can hardly wait to play them," said Huck.

Father Bauer stayed in Europe to preview the facilities in Grenoble, while Brewer left on a vacation to Greece. He wouldn't be allowed to play in the Olympics, his days as a professional damning him in the views of the IOC.

Brewer made an impact, even if he never quite felt at home with the Nats. "He couldn't sleep at night," recalled O'Malley. "During the games, when we were playing those games in Vienna, we'd look out the window, and there he was—he'd go for a walk, and he'd be sleeping on a park bench outside the apartment building, just because he was so wound up." Compared to the other Nats, Carl Brewer was a "superstar," said O'Malley, who roomed with him on the road. "He might have relished the limelight, but it wasn't an easy experience for him because he knew he was under the spotlight."

The legacy of Carl Brewer, who died in 2001, went well beyond the ice. His widow, Susan Foster, finished their memoir *The Power of Two: Carl Brewer's Battle With Hockey's Power Brokers*. It detailed how Brewer's relentless questioning of the NHLPA and Alan Eagleson led to an investigation and his admission of guilt. The book doesn't delve too deeply into Brewer's time as one of Bauer's Boys, but it's clear "his time with the national team was a big disappointment for him personally," wrote Foster. "Carl was wrestling with his religion and had hoped to find some support and direction working with Father." Instead, Father Bauer's schedule prevented him from finding time for Brewer and his questions. Foster also said that McLeod felt that Brewer was a threat, a potential replacement as a coach. "All in all, his time with the national team and Father Bauer was a deep disappointment for Carl and caused Carl to be even more upset and confused. The one good result from this adventure was that Carl was hired by the Finnish Ice Hockey League to coach in Helsinki which was very satisfying for him."

Brewer and Foster attended a reunion of the Nats in 1980 in Vancouver. Rick Noonan said that Brewer told him he always felt disappointment in the fact he didn't deliver as he should have while with the Nats. "I remember Marshall Johnston coming to me and saying, 'Get Carl to deliver the closing salutations,'" said Noonan. "I did so and Carl gave a very emotional goodbye. Susan Foster later sent me a card thanking [me] for having Carl give the goodbye to that reunion and [saying] that it was very important to him."

Federal Health Minister Allan MacEachen saluted the Nats with a telegram, and Johnston read it to the team on the plane: "I had the opportunity of being in Vienna last weekend and saw at first hand how well this team, as gentlemen and as a group of talented players, acquitted themselves as representatives of this country." MacEachen didn't agree with the premise that the Canadians could not win in Europe. "I cannot subscribe to this theory. Nor, in spite of our disappointment, do I feel that we should be discouraged. Instead, let us learn from our experience and prepare for another year."

Chapter 17

END OF THE CRUSADES

To say the road to Grenoble was a little bumpy would be to say that Noah only faced a little drizzle. It was all on the line at the Olympics. Again.

And at the 1967 World Championships, Terry O'Malley summed up quite succinctly his four years in the Canadian Olympic program for a CBC special. "When I first came on, I wasn't aware what I was getting into. I wasn't aware of European competition. I knew that this was a chance for me to get my education and play hockey," said O'Malley. "Now, it's almost turned into a crusade. I'm not sure that I feel like I have to. You play for yourself first of all, and then this way you feel like you're making your contribution to the rest of the team and to Canada."

There would be even more players suiting up for Canada in the fall of 1967, thanks to the establishment of a B team, located in Ottawa.

Beyond that, on the A team in Winnipeg, there was a necessary youth movement, since reinstated professionals, like Carl Brewer and Red Bownass (now coaching the Ottawa Nats), would not be allowed into the Olympics. NHL expansion had arrived, meaning more jobs, at better wages, in hockey. The Nats, committed to the Olympic program, stayed true, for the most part. One departure was trainer Bill Bozak, who left in the summer to join the San Diego Gulls of the Western League.

Replacing Bozak was Scotty Clark of Saskatoon, a friend of Jackie McLeod's from his Saskatoon Quakers days. "He was my first choice after Bill resigned," McLeod said. Ken Esdale would later walk in off the street looking for work and land a part-time gig as a trainer—and he'd also serve as an occasional goalie, both in practices and less important games.

At six foot one and 200 pounds, defenceman Brian Glennie immediately became one of the biggest Nats. He'd been in the Toronto Maple Leafs system playing for the Marlboros, winner of the 1967 Memorial Cup. Leafs GM Punch Imlach assumed, wrongly, that Glennie would take the offer put in front of him. Glennie's father had wanted him to play on the national team, and respecting his wishes after his passing that summer, Brian signed up. "Let's just put it that Punch and I didn't get along. I wasn't the only one," said Glennie. "He didn't think that I had anywhere to go, but I did." It was a welcome relief from grief. "I was a pretty big mess after my dad died, because I didn't know if I was supposed to sign with the Leafs, stay home and look after my mom and my brother, who was 10, or go out west to Winnipeg and play for the Olympic team. It was my mom that probably made the decision for me. She said, 'Dad always wanted you to go to the Olympics.'"

Glennie enrolled at the University of Manitoba and got to work, eventually moving in with Barry and Diane MacKenzie. They were close to campus, though it required snowshoes to walk across a snowy golf course to school.

Through the years, Imlach had many run-ins with players that chose the Nats over the Leafs. No doubt frustrated, he dealt the options on eight separate players in the national program to the expansion Minnesota North Stars, run by Wren Blair. With his own international experience, Blair was patient, knowing he wouldn't get a crack at Barry MacKenzie, Gary Dineen, Danny O'Shea, Gary Begg, Terry O'Malley, Marshall Johnston, Paul Conlin, and Ken Broderick until after Grenoble.

He gave it a half-hearted effort before the debut 1967–68 season. "I don't think I did a good job of selling pro hockey to those guys last summer," Blair said at the time. "My heart wasn't in it. I felt they had obligations to the national team until after the Olympics. I know how much that means and I really didn't put a lot of pressure on them. After the Olympics, some of them certainly will turn pro. It's possible that most of them will be interested."

Steve Monteith, a right winger with speed out of Stratford, Ontario, came to Winnipeg from the University of Toronto. In school, he did degrees in commerce and law, and on the ice, he set scoring records for the Varsity Blues—102 goals, 147 assists, and 249 total points during the 1962–67 and 1969 seasons.

Herb and Gerry Pinder were brothers from Saskatoon. They'd been lighting it up with the Saskatoon Blades of Saskatchewan's junior circuit—Gerry, two years younger, led the league in goals and points, and Herb in assists. After they were eliminated from the playoffs by the powerful Estevan Bruins, Coach McLeod invited them to camp. For Herb, his junior eligibility up, it was an easy decision; Gerry had to weigh the options between going back to Saskatoon and the powerhouse Edmonton Oil Kings, which included a decent paycheque.

"I wanted to go and make the team," said Gerry Pinder. "I think there was pretty long odds that we'd make it, but we didn't think that. I was only 18 at the time." He worked hard in the summer, knowing he'd be playing hockey against men.

When the Pinder brothers moved to Winnipeg, they had to find a place to live. They stayed at the Viscount Gort Hotel for a time, and on the campus of St. John's-Ravenscourt. They also lived with the Maddin family, first on a temporary basis, then a year living above Mrs. Maddin's hair salon (alas, no free haircuts, confirmed Gerry). "The Pinder brothers boarded at our place, and slept in the very same bedroom that Father Bauer did," said Guy Maddin, launching into a story of the supernatural.

Sometimes young Guy would be booted out of his room so Father Bauer could stay over. Other times, they'd share the room and the bed. "I felt very important," said the award-winning director, who loved to collect toys from films such as *Frankenstein* and *Dracula*. "I had all these Frankenstein and Dracula models in my room. . . . He made me feel very important by pretending to be scared of them, of their unholiness. He made me put them in the closet when we slept."

The place to stay, however, for hockey players in Winnipeg was with Mrs. Bridgette Burke. Like Ma Byers at the Hockey House on the UBC campus, she was a wonderful character. "The old girl, we used to call her. She was part of the whole group, with the Winnipeg team. This group had all kinds of contacts, because they worked with the junior hockey players," said O'Malley. "She took us in. We had the right names, O'Malley and Conlin, both as Irish as Paddy's pig. She took us in. Her husband had just passed away, and it just so happened that she was having cataracts removed, and with a nervous disorder, she lost all her hair. 'I look a mess,' she'd say."

Gerry Pinder was with Mrs. Burke for a year. "She was about 75. My brother and I stayed. She had a small house and we had small rooms upstairs. The second year, the two of us were going to be a little bit too much for her," he said. "She was hilarious. She used to call Trudeau a tortured little rat. She had sayings and she had a delightful sense of humour. She was quite a bit older. So we ended up, really, the first year, second half of the first year, we ended up cooking on our own and so on. She was getting on, but always a tremendous amount of fun."

O'Malley also recalled the food, and learning to say no. "She used to cook these meals for us. Of course, being taught to eat everything on the plate, we'd eat everything she put in front of us. We were hungry as well after practice. Then she'd put more on there, and we'd eat it up. Then she'd put more on there." It was a test to see what they needed. "Well, I just had to find out what your appetite was!" she said.

A devout Catholic, Mrs. Burke would sprinkle the players with holy water, their hands, their feet, and the back of their heads. She even did it to a good Protestant like Marshall Johnston, saying, "Marshall, if it doesn't do you any good, it won't be doing you any harm!"

Gerry Pinder studied business at the University of Manitoba, and described his routine. "Our typical day in Winnipeg was, you're up at about seven and you're off to university. Practice was at five, so you'd leave the university at 3:30–3:45, go to practice. We'd get off the ice, our practices were usually longer than an hour, so 6:15 you'd get off the ice. You'd go home, get some dinner and go straight to the library until 10 or 11:00 every day, in order to pass your classes. Most of the guys were in university. The ones that weren't had already gotten their degree and were working."

Post-Olympics, Herb Pinder smashed up his ankle while skiing and never had a pro career; instead, he got his law degree, and the hockey contacts paid off, with 30 years as a part-time agent to the likes of Dave "Tiger" Williams. Gerry played almost a decade in the NHL and WHA, sticking it out through a tough eye injury. "I couldn't see out of my left eye. . . . But you didn't want to say anything, because nobody wants you if you can't see," he said. Then he went back to university and got a commerce degree, majoring in finance; that led to a career in real estate and development. Together with other family members, they owned the WHL's Regina Pats for a time.

The support for the Nats continued to grow, and tour organizers got on board, arranging for travel packages to the Olympics:

> Join Canada's National Team at the 1968 Olympic Hockey Championships.
>
> 14 action-packed days in the Alps.
>
> Be there! Grenoble, France, for the opening of the '68 Hockey Olympics on February 6th. You can do it—with this terrific Lufthansa Tour that leaves Toronto on February 4th, 1968. Tour escorts are Harry Watson, ex-NHL great, and John Russell, ex-member of Canada's national hockey team (a man who knows many of the competing players and officials). For one low price, you get: return flight via Lufthansa jet, accommodation in a charming Alpine hotel, delicious meals, a Series #2 Hockey Pass good for all the big games, and more. Prices start at just $607.00 . . . based on a 14–21 day economy class GIT fare for 15 people travelling together.

John Russell remembers: "I was asked to conduct a tour from Winnipeg to the Grenoble Olympics," said the "celebrity" who'd played with the Nats in 1965. "I looked after some of the stuff for the travel agency. [They] wanted somebody that had some connection with the team to be the leader of the fans that were going over there." A separate ad promoted the famed Maurice "Rocket" Richard as the tour leader.

Just a day after the Toronto Maple Leafs won the Stanley Cup in Toronto, beating the Montreal Canadiens in six games, the city of Winnipeg held a dinner to honour its Nats. Prominent sports figure Cactus Jack Wells was the emcee of the "rib-tickling civic banquet." Only four of the Nats missed the event. Many notable politicians were there. Alderman Mark Danzker said that it took the Centennial tournament to reveal what "the Nationals meant to Winnipeg" and that "the rest of Canada got the message."

Monsignor Athol Murray, 76 and still passionate and unpolished, was the keynote speaker. "Monsignor Murray loves Canada with a fiery zeal," reported Maurice Smith in the *Winnipeg Free Press*. "It is his firm belief that the National team can and is, playing a major role in making us not French Canadians, English Canadian, or Polish Canadians, but simply Canadians."

The dishevelled priest with a penchant for salty words begged the players to ignore professional offers and continue to suit up for their country. "If Brian Conacher, an also-ran with this team four years ago, can make it big with Toronto, can you imagine what those damn commercialists of the NHL are going to offer these (current Nats) fellows," Pere Murray said. "This team is the greatest project of 1967 because it's making us think Canadian." He also praised the city's fans for embracing the team. "You Winnipeggers have been given the extraordinary privilege of being custodians of the team. Look at their names—Cusson, Cadieux, Johnston, O'Malley, MacKenzie, Huck—and they tell you the Nationals are comprised of various races. And they come from every province."

Murray came to Winnipeg again in September, as the Nats faced off in two exhibition games against the NHL's Detroit Red Wings. He was not the only hockey royalty in town.

"Hockey Weekend in Winnipeg" included the opening of a new home base for the Nats—the Dutton Memorial Arena on the campus of St. John's-Ravenscourt School For Boys in Fort Garry. The $450,000 facility was built to international rink dimensions to better accommodate training for Winnipeg's favourite amateur team, though the Nats never did use it much. Two of the donors behind the Nats, Calgary industrialist Max Bell and Winnipeg financier James Richardson, were alumni of the school and heavily involved in the fundraising. The arena was named in honour of Joe and Alex Dutton, sons of former NHL player, referee, and president Mervyn "Red" Dutton, who were killed in action while with the RCAF during the Second World War.

Father Bauer blessed the arena, already home to a who's who of visitors. NHL President Clarence Campbell was there, all the Red Wings—including Gordie Howe, and management Sid Abel and Jack Adams—as well as all the Nats. Other hockey names included King Clancy, Babe Pratt, Sweeney Schriner, Eddie Shore, Frank Boucher, Foster Hewitt, Bill Mosienko, and Frank McCool. Syndicated columnist Jim Coleman was the master of ceremonies and read out telegrams from the likes of Conn Smythe of the Leafs.

During his speech, Red Dutton spoke at length about what Canada meant to him. "What a feeling it is to be a Canadian. We have the greatest country in the world and hockey unifies it more than any other sport. We can well be proud of our national game and the men who play it."

President Campbell attended one of the Red Wing-National team games, a win for the Detroiters at the Winnipeg Arena. He was at his diplomatic best: "I'm glad Canada's national hockey team is so popular in Winnipeg, not only for the sake of the team, but also for the building in which they play. . . . It is a fine arena and deserves the support of all hockey fans."

After a preparatory tournament in Grenoble at the new Stade de Glace in October, and many games against Western Canada Senior League opponents and touring teams from Russia, Romania, Italy, the United States, and Finland, it was time for a second international tournament in Winnipeg. This time, it was just a three-team affair, with Russia and Sweden battling Canada.

For a change of pace, it was the Russians complaining about the refereeing, even if they won 5–1. That night 10,134 fans braved 33-below-zero weather with a wind chill of –61 degrees to head to Winnipeg Arena. "I must confess," said Anatoli Tarasov, "our coaches and players didn't know which rules we were playing. But the worst of it was neither did the referees." There were 20 penalties called during the game. The Russian master called for a smoothing out of the differences between international and North American hockey rules. "The Canadian people invented the game of hockey," said Tarasov. "Therefore I think they should be the ones to stabilize rules for both professional and amateur hockey. I believe they (the rules) are too much different."

When the Swedes upset the USSR, 6–4, in a wide-open affair, it left Canada and Russia tied at two wins and one loss, and their rematch drew the biggest crowd to date, 10,743 fans, to Winnipeg Arena. The *Winnipeg Free Press* reported fans were crying "blue murder" and turned into a "frustrated sea of garbage-throwing zealots" due to the refereeing.

The main culprit was Russian referee Anatoli Seglin, though Canada's Gordie Kerr was the other official, and there isn't any record of which referee called which penalty. In total, Canada had 15 penalties, and the Russians scored on three power plays; Russia had eight minors. "It could have been coincidence, but it appeared a team was always penalized by the rival country's referee," wrote Bob Hainstock in the *Winnipeg Free Press*.

The highlight of the 4–2 loss for Canada was a penalty shot midway through the first period, the Soviets up 1–0. Gary Begg had interfered with a Russian breakaway. In net for Canada was Wayne Stephenson, and Russia sent out famed marksman Anatoli Firsov. The attacker went in a little too close and the puck limply rolled to Stephenson. "Suddenly the puck was there and I grabbed it," Stephenson grinned after the game.

After the USSR was presented with the Donald Bain Memorial Trophy, Coach McLeod went to his usual bailiwick and lambasted the officiating. "I thought," he said, "in our first game against the Russians which we lost 5–1, the officiating was fair to both sides. But it certainly wasn't that way tonight. Twice we had a three on one and a two on one break, but each time we were called offside by the Russian referee. When that happens to a hockey club it hurts and hurts badly. I can't see why, when we are playing in Canada, that we need a Russian referee. When we play in Europe, we know what to expect from the officials, but we shouldn't have to put up with it in our own country. Our own officials are capable."

Jim Proudfoot of the *Toronto Star* was in Winnipeg for the three-team tourney and called a spade a spade:

> Because of their many problems, Nats have become an alibi team. They always have some very logical excuse for failure. Players were worrying about exams, or were studying, or were unable to train properly because of their studies. Or the refereeing was bad. That's one you can always use in world hockey. Another old story is the one about how the Russians are really professionals and spend all their time on hockey and how can Canadians be expected to compete? Sometimes, Nats lose because they don't have the patriotic backing of all Canadian citizens and other times they lose because they have so much support they're nervous.

The influential Proudfoot closed the column calling for Father Bauer's return to the bench:

> The ultimate criticism of the national team is this: it's never been as good as it was in its very first season, back in 1964, and that's allowing for today's stronger opposition. . . . There is only one way the current club can succeed next month and that's with Father Dave Bauer, its founder and original coach, behind the bench. He can persuade players to surpass their own capacities and he can make the personnel switches it takes to defeat a superior opponent. But that would be a backward step, too, because this is Jackie McLeod's team and will be even more so in years to come, when he becomes a wiser strategist. For every member of Father Bauer's basic nucleus, left over from 1964, there's a player that McLeod has brought along. Confusion over leadership, a problem even last season, must be avoided even though it might conceivably produce temporary triumph.

The Grenoble Olympics immediately loomed, and it was suddenly time to head back to Europe. Local businesses paid for a full-page ad in the *Free Press* that wished the team well. It read: "GOOD LUCK NATS. THE FOLLOWING FIRMS WISH CANADA'S NATIONAL HOCKEY TEAM SUCCESS AT THE 1968 WINTER OLYMPICS IN GRENOBLE, FRANCE . . ."

The prognosticating began. "Frankly, the present Olympic squad of that country doesn't look so formidable as the team which played in the last world championships. Probably one of the reasons is the absence of Canadian guards of the calibre of (Carl) Brewer and (Red) Bownass," said Arkady Chernyshov, forever in the shadow of Tarasov in Russian coaching ranks. "In all these years of games and rivalry with the Canadians, I've grown accustomed to something changing among them at the last minute—and for the better; a new, gifted and experienced man is inserted unexpectedly in the lineup or else the trainers spring an original tactical surprise at the decisive moment."

Looking back, Paul Conlin admitted he felt pressure. "The public's expectations and our expectations as players were that we would do better than we did in '64," he said. "But at the same time we recognized that we were underdogs. The Russians had a fabulous team, and the Czechs and the Swedes weren't that far behind. But we felt we were able to cope with them."

Father Bauer, while in Prague for a couple of pre-Olympic games, said the team was more experienced—hardly the case, given that the Pinder brothers, Glennie, and Monteith were all new, Gary Begg was home injured, and such veterans from the 1967 World Championship team as Brewer and Bownass were ineligible.

The Canadian Olympic team marched into the stadium in Grenoble wearing white fur hats and Hudson Bay coats, ringed with bands of black, yellow, red, and green—the Olympic colours. Skier Nancy Greene carried the flag. Prime Minister Lester B. Pearson sent along a message: "All Canadians will be watching your competition with keen attention and wishing you well." But the hockey players weren't there—they had a game to prepare for on February 6. They were there for the duration, as the final matchup, against the USSR, was on February 17, the last day of the Olympics, and the medal presentation was set for the closing ceremonies. (In fact, three qualifying hockey games took place before the

Olympics opened, Finland, East Germany, and West Germany playing their way in over Yugoslavia, Norway, and Romania, respectively. The consolation round also featured Japan, France, and Austria.)

It started off a bit chaotic for Canada. At a February 5 meeting of the various management and coaching staffs, everyone was told to present proper documentation for their players. No one had told the Canadians to bring their players' passports. That lead to an IIHF official madly checking documents at rinkside just before the first game on February 7.

Canada's first game, a 6–1 win over West Germany, unfolded as planned. The second game, against Finland, did not. Wearing an orange face mask and leaping about like an acrobat, 24-year-old Finnish goalie Urpo Ylönen rebounded from an 8–0 loss to Russia and helped his country to its first-ever win over Canada in Olympic or World Championship competition. The 5–2 loss dimmed Canada's gold medal chances in just the second game. "The harder we tried, the worse we got," said McLeod. The Finns were definitely an up-and-coming hockey power, and nearly knocked off the Czechs as well. Also surprising were the Americans. Though they only won two games in the tournament over the two Germanys, and tied Finland, they put major scares into Sweden (4–3 loss) and Canada (3–2 loss).

Against Czechoslovakia, Huck, Bourbonnais, and Cadieux scored goals within 11 minutes in the second, but the Czechs came storming back in the third, with two goals, when it all fell apart. Well, the rink, anyway. At 14:40 of the period, the door to the Canadian bench fell off its hinges onto the ice. Repairmen were summoned. The seven-minute forced time out helped calm down the Nats and they held on for the first win over Czechoslovakia at the Olympics since 1960. "We're past a big obstacle," said Broderick. "Czechoslovakia has always been the one that slowed us down." Perhaps the Nats were fired up by the presence of skier Nancy Greene of Rossland, BC, who had just won Canada's first medal in Grenoble, a silver in slalom. She'd be back, this time showing the Nats her gold medal in giant slalom, after their next game against Sweden.

As great as the Nats played against Sweden—and they were really great, with a 3–0 Broderick shutout—the real gift came from the Czechs, who knocked off the Soviets, 5–4, the first loss for the Russians in world or Olympic hockey since 1963. All of a sudden, gold was a real possibility. Canada, Russia, and Czechoslovakia were tied with one loss atop the standings. Canada would take gold with a win over Russia, a silver medal with a tie, and a bronze with a loss.

All the dreaming and scheming had come down to a single game. The Canadian Broadcasting Corporation announced it would show Canada-USSR live via satellite on the national network, with Ernie Afaganis and Fred Sgambati at the microphones, proving that the Nats had finally cracked the national consciousness.

"Now we settle it on the ice," said Ray Cadieux in the post-game dressing room. The rules were clear on who could claim a medal, and no amount of behind-the-scenes shenanigans would change that.

As for Father Bauer, he hadn't changed his tune in Grenoble: "This is our year. I feel it my bones. It's our turn."

The earlier game, a 2–2 tie between the Czechs and Swedes, had clarified the medal picture—the winner would take gold.

It began with promise as the Canadians killed off two Russian penalties to start the first period. It was a Soviet penalty that killed them. With Yevgeni Zimin in the box, Anatoli Firsov tipped the puck into the open side for a short-handed marker to give the USSR the lead. Poised and confident, the Big Red Machine began rolling on all cylinders, and according to Father Bauer, the heart of the team was ripped out when Evgeny Mishakov's breakaway goal at 12:44 of the second period made it 2–0. Viktor Konovalenko played great in the Russian net. After his team cruised to a 5–0 victory and another Olympic gold medal, his comrades jovially tossed the husky keeper in the air three times. "The months and months of constant training and conditioning, during which they developed speed, superb positional play, letter-perfect passing, machine-like teamwork, and did nothing else but think hockey, brought the Soviets the gold medal they wanted," wrote Maurice Smith.

"Once we got down 2–0, we had to open up and that is tough to do against the Russians who handle the puck so well," said McLeod at the time.

Reporters noted the mood in the Canadian dressing room. "They had been beaten badly on paper although it was their finest game of the

Olympic hockey tournament," reported the *Montreal Gazette*. "They had nothing to be ashamed of but it was no consolation. Nothing could fill the flat dead void in each man's stomach, the hollow emptiness where tense hope and determination had stormed scant hours before."

The mercurial Dineen, with so much talent, yet so emotionally unstable, was spotlighted. The *Free Press* noted his error that resulted in the first Soviet goal: "Centre Gary Dineen, whose play has been a major disappointment, was slow in covering a Soviet break on a loose puck. The Soviets put Firsov in the clear and the mighty Russian sniper picked the low left corner at 14.51 with what turned out to be the winner." He was Bauer's special project in many ways, and Dineen wouldn't face his mentor. "Gary, try to believe me. I'm proud of you. I'm not disappointed," comforted the priest.

"His pet was Gary Dineen. Gary was this incredibly talented player," recalled Herb Pinder. "This incredible talent, he's gone now, but probably a little immature and a little full of himself. He was never in very good shape. He relied on his talent. He seemed to be a bit above it all. Good guy. His nickname was Crazy. I remember the first time we met him, we got talking about Europe, and he said, 'Oh yeah, the girls in Europe, they're very mundane.' I'm going, 'I don't know what the fuck that means . . .' But I guess I was impressed, I don't know. He was always trying to impress. But as a player, wow. I took his spot, so he became the extra guy. He basically played himself out of the spot, even though he was this incredible talent. Part of it was the emergence of our line."

But Father Bauer still had some pull. Herb Pinder sat for the last couple of games in Grenoble and Dineen played. At the subdued after-party for the Nats, Dineen was inconsolable.

Ross Morrison had been around Dineen in those early years of the Nats. "He was a little wacky. He was not the normal product of normal hockey. He had a different perspective on things," said Morrison. "He had a questioning mentality. He wouldn't agree with Bauer on a bunch of things."

Everyone expected Dineen to turn professional after the Games, which he did. It's maybe the biggest mystery to evolve from the Great Experiment—why didn't Dineen become a star? He had all the talent in the world, a marksman who could skate. His cousin, Bill, had succeeded, playing with the Detroit Red Wings. In 2015, all Shakey McLeod could do was shake his head. "There was a guy with some talent." Dineen played all of four games in the NHL for the North Stars, and bounced around the minors. He won a Calder Cup with the AHL's Springfield Kings in 1971, and then retired at age 27 to spend a year as coach and general manager of the team.

"No, I'm not going to regret the fact I never made it in the NHL, not at all," Dineen told the *Toronto Star*'s Jim Proudfoot in 1972. "I was never obsessed with pro sport's ranking system as a means of measuring success or failure. Maybe I'm wrong, but it was never especially important to me. Now if you were to apply other yardsticks, I might concede that my career was a disappointment. Perhaps I failed to do what I set out after, but I don't use the normal criteria."

Springfield, Massachusetts, would become his home and Dineen's legacy became New England junior hockey. Through his youth teams, Dineen sent more than 300 boys on to college hockey. "Dineen found his niche there," said Morrison. His most notable grad was Bill Guerin (and closing the loop, former Nat teammate Marshall Johnston was in charge of scouting when the New Jersey Devils drafted Guerin), but 35 others were drafted by the NHL. He battled cancer for 10 years until his death on April 1, 2006. "I've never seen a man endure what he has endured with such perseverance. He never once talked about what he was going through," said Eastern Junior Hockey League commissioner Dan Esdale in a newspaper story.

For the rest of the Nats, time has offered good perspective on their accomplishments in Grenoble. Broderick had a special table custom-made where all his medals, pennants, pins and other trinkets from his Bauer days are shown off. Others, like Gerry Pinder, have given some thought to it. "I would argue, and this wouldn't be popular, but I would argue that our bronze medal was a better performance by Canadian hockey than the pros and their gold medals, because we were true amateurs playing against true pros."

Reverend Bauer sadly considered the future for both the national team program and the Games themselves as pro sports grew. "I wonder what will happen to the Olympics," Bauer said. "I wonder. There's isn't an amateur within 100 miles of this place."

Unlike previous tournaments, there was little bellyaching by any of the teams about the refereeing at the 1968 Olympics. Just two penalties were called in the Czech-Canada game. But Coach McLeod, perhaps a creature of habit, filed a protest after Canada's 3–0 win over the Swedes, as six of the eight penalties had been called against the Nats. Of the top four teams, going into the final, Canada was actually the *least* penalized.

Captain Marshall Johnston was designated as the man to head up to the podium on behalf of the team. A black-and-white photo of the ceremony still hangs in his office in Minnesota. A sullen Johnston is wearing his Hudson Bay coat. To one side is Jozef Golonka with a silver medal and to the other, Boris Mayorov of the USSR, with the gold.

"I'm not smiling," explained Johnston. "When I got off there and I walked over there was somebody from the Canadian Olympic team just tore a strip off me up and down. They said, well you weren't smiling and you weren't this and that. And I said, well no, I wasn't smiling. We got the bronze. In Canada, for hockey, you want the gold, you don't want the bronze."

The newspaper commentary was pretty matter-of-fact. The Soviets were too good.

"There is an attitude of 'so what' about our side getting shellacked by the big bear in Grenoble, but nearly everybody is full of gratuitous advice and ready to spank the Nats for their failure," wrote Hal Walker in the *Calgary Herald*.

He could have been talking about Dick Beddoes in the *Globe and Mail*: "Canada's national team made the Olympic competition lively while it lasted. Now we can feel cozy again; we are back in the old groove. We are clearly represented before the world by losers."

Sports editor Milt Dunnell of the *Toronto Star* was a little more diplomatic. "Certainly, our national team was sneezing against thunder when it tried to get the job done," wrote Dunnell. "This is the stark fact that will cause the Canadian Amateur Hockey Association some sleepless nights. The gap between Canada and the comrades has widened instead of closing."

Even the trip home was bumpy. France to Montreal went okay, but Air Canada Flight 909 was delayed three hours in Toronto by mechanical issues. With Winnipeg media hyping the return of the city's team, and encouraging fans to head to the airport where mayor Stephen Juba was scheduled to meet to the sounds of a Shriners' pipe band, it was a bigger issue than perhaps it might have been.

Jack Matheson of *Winnipeg Tribune* foretold the future, and the formation of Hockey Canada: "I don't know if we really felt we had a chance against the Russians. The whole concept of the national team is . . . wrong. But sending a junior team isn't the answer and we've tried the seniors before. I'd say we need a council of war with the National Hockey League. We have to lay it on the line, especially to the teams in Montreal and Toronto, and ask for help."

Huge changes were ahead for the Canadian national team program—and its founder.

Some new friends that Father Bauer made in Grenoble offered him a chance to build a completely different national team. Japan needed to up its game for the 1972 Olympic Games in Sapporo, and it found its man.

Chapter 18

MAN OF THE WORLD

Hokkē arrived in Japan in the 1920s, and the All Japan Championships have been around since 1930. The Japan Ice Hockey League started in 1966, and lasted until 2004. Its heyday was the 1970s and 1980s, coinciding with the arrival of Father David Bauer and his many disciples.

It began with a meeting at the 1968 Olympic Games in Grenoble. Japan had a team in the 1936 Winter Olympics, but was idle until 1960, when it finished eighth. In 1964, it was 11th, and it was 10th in Grenoble. In the World Championships, Japan only played in 1930 (6th), 1957 (8th), 1962 (9th in Pool B), and 1967 (first in Pool C). But with the 1972 Games coming to Sapporo, on the northern Japanese island of Hokkaido, the idea was to offer up better coaching for its players. Enter Father Bauer. "He was the mentor that they were looking for to reinvigorate their program," said Barry MacKenzie.

At the centre of Japan's hockey history were other men of the cloth. The Scarboro Missionaries from Canada were founded in 1918 to train and send priests to China. Following the Second World War, the Catholic missionaries went to Japan to help the country rebuild its educational system. In 1965, Father Bob Moran, who had gone to St. Michael's College and played with the Junior B Buzzers, headed over.

Noticing the Seibu Tetsudo team playing hockey in an arena near his Tokyo church, Father Moran went down to check things out. His Japanese was pretty good, so he asked to join the practices. Soon, he was asked to join the team, as the rule was that two *gaijin* were allowed per team. "He did so for a couple of years, even flying in weekly from the island of Kyushu, a thousand miles away, to make practices and tournaments once his priestly duties were complete," wrote Terry O'Malley in a personal essay on his own history with Father Bauer. "But more importantly, he recruited two outstanding Canadians of Japanese descent from Chatham, Ontario, Mel and Herb Wakabayashi." Reassigned to the United States, where he'd next play hockey for St. Lawrence University, Father Moran was asked who might be able to fill a similar mentoring role with the Japanese hockey system.

He suggested Father Bauer, and given his success with the Wakabayashi boys, his advice was heeded. Not only were the Wakabayashis great hockey players, but they also excelled at baseball. One of their Chatham teammates was future Baseball Hall of Famer Ferguson Jenkins. They took different routes to university, though. Hitoshi—Mel—went to the University of Michigan, where he was league MVP in 1966, and took a crack at the pros, briefly playing in the minors. Osamu—Herb—went to Boston University, where he was a two-time all-American, and later named one of the 50 greatest hockey players in Eastern Collegiate Athletic Conference history, a list which features the likes of Ken Dryden, Joe Nieuwendyk, Adam Oates, and Martin St. Louis. Mel first went off to Japan in 1967, and Herb followed two years later. They both represented Japan at the 1972 Olympics (Herb played in 1976, too). Eight years later, in Lake Placid, Mel was the Japanese coach. Herb played, and carried the flag into the stadium for the opening ceremonies.

Other Canadians had some influence on Japanese hockey. Art Potter of the Canadian Amateur Hockey Association went there for 10 days after the 1964 Olympics, when hockey was still under the auspices of the Japan Skating Association. Len Corriveau spent time in the country in the mid-1960s; he'd been a coach in Quebec and would later become a referee.

O'Malley recalled watching the Japanese practice in Grenoble, along with Father Bauer, and thinking they were good skaters. "[Father Bauer] said, 'Here, I want you to see this.' So he brought me down. I remember looking through the window and watching the Japanese national team practice. They had their drills," said O'Malley. "They had their catcalls, their musical kind of intonation when they're doing their exercises so they don't feel the pain. . . . They could really skate well."

At the time, O'Malley didn't understand why Father was showing him the Japanese team. "Only later did I find out that a member of the Japanese hockey delegation had asked Father Bauer if he would be interested in coming to Japan to assist with the Seibu Tetsudo (Railway) Hockey Club. He agreed." Little did he know how his own life would be affected by the decision.

Yoshiaki Tsutsumi was the chairman of the Japanese Ice Hockey Federation, and the owner of Seibu. At one point in the 1980s, he was reportedly the richest man in the world, worth an estimated $21 billion before a scandal cost him his fortune.

In October 1968, Father Bauer flew to Japan to take charge of a month-long, country-wide series of hockey clinics. He would continue to travel to Japan twice a year, usually for six weeks at a time, until committing to helping the 1980 Canadian Olympic program, but he never distanced himself from his Japanese friends. "Father Bauer did not receive any remuneration for his advice," wrote O'Malley in a personal essay. "However, the company was always generous, with first class lodging. It also provided for many of Father Bauer's nieces, nephews and family whom Bauer felt would receive a widened education from experiencing Japan."

The trips were reciprocated; Japanese players and teams made their way to Canada for exhibition games, particularly at UBC. Bob Hindmarch at the Vancouver-based university is held in high regard in Asian hockey circles. "More than 30 years ago, Bob Hindmarch brought Father Bauer to Japan. Until then, we didn't know real Canadian hockey," said Shoichi Tomita, the vice-president of the International Ice Hockey Federation, in the Hindmarch biography *Catch On and Run With It*. "The image of Canadian hockey was they just fight! All we knew was that they played a very rough game. But Bob Hindmarch's philosophy was completely different. It was about education: physical education and psychological education. He saw hockey as combining the person and athletics. Therefore, we really respect Bob Hindmarch, and also Father Bauer."

Maurice Smith of the *Winnipeg Free Press* asked Father Bauer about Japanese hockey in the winter of 1970. The priest said they had improved considerably. "Their positional play, technique and skating is much better than it was," Bauer said.

A number of "Hockey in Japan" stories appeared in the 1970s, all of them addressing the uniqueness of company loyalty that was central to the game. Hockey grew out of employer-offered after-hour activities. The Seibu Corporation of Tokyo led the movement, and when other large companies followed, a six-team Industrial Hockey League was born. Players on the team held other positions within the company, not all that different than the Trail Smoke Eaters senior teams in British Columbia.

Seniority is key as well, said O'Malley in 1975. After a year with Seibu, where the team was commonly known as the Bears, he became a player-coach of the spinoff Kokudo Keikaku—the Bunnies—in 1972, a secondary team owned by different divisions of the same company. O'Malley learned to not embarrass older players; no one wanted to lose face in front of lower-ranking colleagues. "If a senior player makes a mistake, everyone just waits for a younger player to foul up and then redirects their frustrations onto him," O'Malley said. "Consequently, the youngest player takes most of the flak."

As Father Bauer worked with the Seibu Corporation, the play changed for teams based near Tokyo. "The style of play is a cross between Canadian and European, but here in the south it's more Canadian than European, mostly because of Father Bauer's influence," said Dave McDowall of Toronto in 1979. "There's more hitting, as in Canada, more play up and down the wing."

According to MacKenzie, there were two factions in Japanese hockey at the time. Hokkaido, the northern island, had allied with Russia, and the Oji Seishi team brought over famed Russian captain Vyacheslav Starshinov. The southern teams, controlled by Tsutsumi, had Bauer and his allies. "It was really a battle to see who controlled Japanese amateur hockey," said MacKenzie. "It was really Tsutsumi trying to control all of Japanese hockey. It was really a battle that more players from the south, main island would be on the national team."

Away from the rink, Yoshiaki Tsutsumi and Father Bauer became great friends. Tsutsumi tried convincing him to stay in Japan permanently, knowing that a chapel run by a famous Canadian priest would have plenty of weddings to officiate, as younger Japanese liked a traditional and a Western ceremony. When the subject was broached, Father giggled, not realizing that Tsutsumi was serious; he suggested O'Malley might be a better choice for permanent residence in Japan. Later, Tsutsumi put Father Bauer on the board of the Toronto Prince Hotel, owned by his company.

The priest liked to tell a story that proved the trust Tsutsumi had in him and illustrated the cultural differences they faced. A Seibu employee was stealing designs for golf courses from the company and reselling them. He was discovered, since his choice of car had overstepped his salary. The company froze him out, stopping his phone calls from going through to his desk and no longer delivering tea to him; realizing the jig was up, he resigned, and the company threw him a goodbye party. Tsutsumi asked Bauer what he'd have done, and Father responded, "I would have fired him on the spot and made and example of him." Tsutsumi responded by saying that wasn't a "very, very Christian thing to do."

Tsutsumi and Father Bauer eventually had a falling out when the Bauer-lead Seibu team did not win in a five-game championship series against Oji. In the deciding game, the goalie from Seibu was injured. The substitute coming in cold was in tough, and the team lost 5–0. "Now in Japan, if the boss was embarrassed the whole company blushed. But Japan has a different way of showing its disapproval," wrote O'Malley. "It ignored Father Bauer—no more private audiences with the president."

Many of "Bauer's Boys" became hockey *gaijins*, and more than a couple parlayed the chance to learn a new culture into business opportunities.

Doug Buchanan is Exhibit A. He played at the University of British Columbia, after Father Bauer's time there. But he was an excellent player, and Father still loved the game, heading to see the Thunderbirds practice and play when his priestly duties allowed. With a group of Japanese players coming to UBC during the summer, Bauer needed helpers to run the training program he had in mind.

"Dougie, can you come and help me train and coach these Japanese kids?" asked Bauer. Just 23, Buchanan figured the extra ice time would be good for him. Following that camp, Father Bauer asked Buchanan to join him in Japan. "North American hockey has lost its heart and lost its soul. Come to Japan, it'll be the best thing that's happened in your life."

With the World Hockey Association in full swing, there were plenty of places to play in North America, and his hometown Vancouver Canucks held Buchanan's NHL rights. Father Bauer convinced Buchanan to have dinner at the fancy Trader Vic's restaurant at the Westin Bayshore in Vancouver with representatives from a Japanese company. They made him an offer; Buchanan hemmed and hawed and decided to call Phil Maloney, GM of the Canucks, one last time. He told him of the offer, and Maloney responded, "What? They play hockey in Japan? I've heard a lot of lines from a lot of players, but this is the first time I've heard this one. Tell me what they're going to pay you and I'll see what I can do about matching." Buchanan told Maloney the sum. There was a long pause and Maloney answered, "Well, enjoy Japan."

Buchanan spent five years in Japan, until Father Bauer said, "Dougie, we're going back to Canada. The Olympic team is starting up again and I'm kind of in charge."

In 1994, Buchanan co-founded Miura Golf Inc., based in Vancouver and Japan, with the late Herb Wakabayashi and Rick Noonan, who hosted the company in his garage in the early years. Now a top lawyer in New York City, Buchanan is still president of Miura, but another Thunderbird who went to Japan, Bill Holowaty, runs the day-to-day operations.

Father Bauer, teamed with Dr. Bob Hindmarch, was very selective of the type of person he suggested to the Japanese, and Holowaty is indebted. "To this day, I owe my business career to the fact that he believed that I would be able to have success there," he said. Other names that went to Japan were a part of Bauer's Olympic teams, such as

Barry MacKenzie and Randy Gregg, and some were seeking adventure, such as NHL veterans Garry Monahan and Ted McAneeley.

Barry Wilcox was not among those recommended by the priest to go to Japan, but knows that Father Bauer, Hindmarch, and their charges paved the way for him to play a season with Kushiro's Jujo Seishi. "Because he had such [a] significant impact on international hockey in general, he was a person that was quite revered, quite respected, so therefore when he made recommendations for players to go to Japan, they knew that he'd select players that would fit in, that would work out there. That's why . . . they respected him as well, it wasn't just that he had former players that he would send over there that [were] going to be sort of true representatives of Canadian hockey and Canadian society, he made sure that these players that were going over there were well-rounded."

Father Bauer's worldly influence extended to Austria as well. Nine years after the Games in Innsbruck, Father Bauer was behind the bench for the Austrians, coaching the Group B World Championships, which it hosted in Graz. The team finished with two wins and five losses, good for fifth in Group B, and eleventh overall.

If circumstances were different, Father Bauer might have gotten a chance to coach in China too. Following the 1980 Olympics, the opportunity came up for clinics in China. There had already been interaction between the People's Republic and UBC, with Dr. Bob Hindmarch taking the Thunderbirds on a brief tour of China in 1970.

Buchanan and Father Bauer were approached about helping the Chinese national team improve, so that it would be a respectable host in the upcoming Pool C of the World Championships. It took some convincing for Buchanan to get on board, but he saw business opportunities apart from the hockey.

But Father Bauer would not join him. He developed shingles and couldn't travel. Hindmarch contacted another BC coach, Cam Kerr, and he took Father's spot. "Politically speaking, it was quite interesting," recalled Kerr. "The first experience, as anyone would understand, is as you get off the airplane, walk down the ramp and there's a guy with an AK-47 standing at the bottom of the stairs to welcome you, an army guy.

Of course, we were followed around, we couldn't go anywhere. Our interpreter was interrogated after each night. I was an educator and Doug was involved in the lumber business a little, so he wanted to know a little bit about those industries." The Chinese government was careful about what the visitors saw, trotting out child singers and showcasing specialty schools rather than the day-to-day life of the average citizen. "The hockey was interesting. The whole experience was certainly worthwhile," said Kerr.

George Gross, the Czechoslovakian-born *Toronto Telegram* and *Toronto Sun* sportswriter, was interested in the world sporting scene in a way that many of his colleagues were not. He kept tight friendships with key figures around the globe, Father Bauer included. "He fascinated me with some of his ideals and philosophies. Most of them offered even the biggest cynic food for thought," wrote Gross in 1988. "They admired him in Russia and loved him in Japan. They called him the Hockey Father and kept inviting him back. Not only for his hockey knowledge, but also for his beneficial influence on young people, a trait so rare and yet so vital in today's society." Gross compared Bauer to an American president: "He inspired young men in John Kennedy fashion, to do something for their country, not to wait for their country to do something for them."

It was all part of the bigger picture that Father Bauer consistently preached: "I echo Pope Pius XII, who said athletes have an obligation to world and to country, but first they have an obligation to world peace."

Chapter 19

AND THEN THERE WERE TWO

In the lead-up to the 1968 Grenoble Games, Father Bauer, Jackie McLeod and the CAHA set up a second team, based in Ottawa, to complement the squad in Winnipeg. Looking back, the extra team attracted some truly great players who went on to long NHL careers; of course, part of the reason that so many went to the pros is that the Olympic program was suddenly axed at the beginning of January 1970, ending the education/hockey dream.

The idea of a B team was hardly new. Russia, Czechoslovakia, and Sweden all had secondary teams that toured extensively, seeing the world, the competition, and acclimatizing themselves to the rigours of the game on the road. Those teams may not have stayed together the whole year, but it allowed more players to polish their games internationally. The *Report on Amateur Hockey in Canada* had recommended a second team in January 1967.

Maurice Smith, the *Winnipeg Free Press* columnist who knew the Nats perhaps better than any other ink-stained wretch, urged the CAHA to consider the idea of two teams immediately following Canada's win in the Centennial tournament. Smith's premise was that, because of the victory, Canada "will not lack for financial support in the future." He foresaw mass departures after the 1968 Games, which is essentially what happened.

"After 1968 at Grenoble, where the Olympics will take place, a number of the players on the present national team will surely succumb to professional offers. There's no reason why they shouldn't because by that time they will have done their bit for Canada," Smith wrote. "Thus it will be necessary to have fitting replacements available who are ready to take up where those they replace left off. And to do this effectively, they should be trained to play hockey the same way the Nationals have been."

Smith was right. After Grenoble, Ken Broderick, defensive aces Marshall Johnston and Barry MacKenzie, star forwards Gary Dineen and Danny O'Shea, and others left the program. But many stayed loyal, too.

Having two teams meant that Canada could venture more abroad, with a deeper talent pool allowing for greater balance between work and school.

At the CAHA annual meeting in May 1967, Gordon Juckes addressed the complications of being polite versus preparing for the Olympics. Canada had always been more than willing to head abroad and spread the gospel of hockey. Senior teams went on barnstorming tours through Europe, and the national team played exhibition games before major tournaments for both the money and the experience. (The two-team Nats would end up short $107,000 over the 1967–68 operation.) With teams such as the USSR, Czechoslovakia, and Sweden having caught up to—and surpassed—the skill level of the Canadians, Juckes saw it as necessary to occasionally say no.

"Last year it was felt by the players and the management committee that we were still playing too many games prior to the tournament in Europe, and this year it has been pretty well agreed that we will not accept any more than three games prior to the [Olympic] tournament," he said, with two games planned for Prague and one in Sweden.

There were plenty of other invitations, including the opening of the hockey rink in Grenoble in October 1967—a single round-robin with Canada, Russia, Czechoslovakia, and the United States. "It has been agreed that in view of the fact that the team will not be going overseas and playing a long schedule prior to the Olympics that the Winnipeg-based team will represent Canada at this tournament at Grenoble in October," reported Juckes.

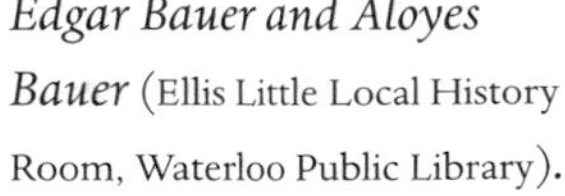

Edgar Bauer and Aloyes Bauer (Ellis Little Local History Room, Waterloo Public Library).

Dave Bauer was #1 on the St. Michael's football team (Courtesy St. Michael's College School).

Studying at the University of Toronto (LEFT Courtesy St. Michael's College School). *Bobby Bauer was coach, general manager, and president of the Kitchener-Waterloo Dutchmen when this photo was taken before the 1950–51 season* (RIGHT Imperial Oil – Turofsky/Hockey Hall of Fame).

Dave Bauer with the University of Toronto Varsity Blues (OPPOSITE Imperial Oil – Turofsky/Hockey Hall of Fame).

Milt Schmidt, Bobby Bauer, and Woody Dumart prepare to board a train at Windsor Station on October 11, 1945, in Montreal, a week after their discharge from the Canadian military (TOP Le Studio du Hockey / Hockey Hall of Fame). *Herb Cain, Bruins coach and general manager Art Ross, and Bobby Bauer in the dressing room after Game 6 of the Stanley Cup semifinal on April 1, 1941, at Maple Leaf Gardens* (BOTTOM Imperial Oil – Turofsky / Hockey Hall of Fame).

Members of the UBC Thunderbirds in the 1963 Totem yearbook. From left: Bob Parker, assistant coach Dave Hindmarch, Mike Smith, Pete Kelly, head coach Father Bauer, and Denny Selder (TOP Courtesy UBC Alma Mater Society Archives). *Posing as coach of the St. Michael's Majors* (RIGHT Courtesy St. Michael's College School). *Toronto mayor Nathan Phillips, Father David Bauer, and Jim Gregory of Toronto's St. Michael's College Majors after the 1961 Memorial Cup win* (BOTTOM Imperial Oil – Turofsky / Hockey Hall of Fame).

Father Bauer coaches the Nats in a February 1965 exhibition game against NHL Oldtimers at Toronto's Maple Leaf Gardens (Graphic Artists/Hockey Hall of Fame).

Team Canada at the 1964 Winter Olympics (TOP Courtesy Hockey Canada). *Ken Broderick played goal for the Nats from 1963 to 1968* (LEFT Courtesy Ken Broderick). *Newcomers to the Olympic program in 1965 included Winnipeg Maroons Al Johnson, coach Gord Simpson, and Gary Aldcorn* (RIGHT International Hockey Archives).

Coach Jackie McLeod and some of the Nats informally pose for a photo in Winnipeg (TOP Courtesy Guy Maddin). *Jean Cusson breaks in against Sweden* (BOTTOM Courtesy Rick Noonan).

Carl Brewer made a major difference for the Nats in the short time he was there (RIGHT Courtesy Terry O'Malley). *Roger Bourbonnais lifts the Centennial Cup in 1967* (OPPOSITE University of Manitoba Archives & Special Collections, Winnipeg Tribune fonds, PC 18-862-013). *Canadian Prime Minister Lester B. Pearson congratulates Roger Bourbonnais on the Centennial Cup victory* (BOTTOM University of Manitoba Archives & Special Collections, Winnipeg Tribune fonds, PC 18-862-009).

A concerned Father Bauer watches Team Canada at the 1968 Olympic Games (TOP). *Jackie McLeod was coach of Canada's National Team from 1966 to 1970* (OPPOSITE). *Canadian captain Marshall Johnston, right, appears sullen beside Czechoslovakia's Jozef Golonka with a silver medal and the USSR's Boris Mayorov with the gold* (BOTTOM).

(ALL PHOTOS International Hockey Archives)

Bunny Ahearne with Gordon Juckes of the Canadian Amateur Hockey Association (TOP Hockey Hall of Fame).

Terry O'Malley, Father Bauer, and Trent Yawney during the 1988 Winter Olympics (OPPOSITE Courtesy Hockey Canada).

CANADA
CANADA

Having fun at a St. Michael's College fundraising dinner in April 1988 (TOP Courtesy St. Michael's College School). *The Canadian National Team from Father Bauer's years reunites in September 2015 on Manitoulin Island in Ontario* (BOTTOM Photo by Greg Oliver).

It was almost a *nyet* to the Russians, though.

"The Russians are celebrating a big anniversary in their country and they wanted our national team to go to their country in December and they had every right to expect we would accept their invitation because they have been very good at sending their teams here. However, it would be just impossible for our national team to go over to Grenoble in October, over to Russia in December, and then back in February for the Olympics, so we turned them down," said Juckes. "Since then plans for the second squad in Ottawa have progressed so well that I was instructed to write them and tell them that we would be glad to send our second squad of the national team over there if they still wished us to do so."

The Russians weren't always easy to deal with. The Grenoble tournament was informed only days before its opening game that the Soviet Union wouldn't be coming, leaving it a three-team derby, with Czechoslovakia, the U.S., and Canada. It had done the same with the Walter Brown Memorial Tournament in 1966, reminded the CAHA's Gordon Juckes. "They've done it again," Juckes said, "and undoubtedly they'll go unpunished." Then there was a change of heart, and Dynamo Moscow, a club team in third place in the fight for supremacy in its home league, headed to the brand spanking new arena in Grenoble, which held 10,000 for hockey.

With four players from the 1967 World Championship team, Dynamo took the honours in Grenoble, going unbeaten. The Americans, with future pros Larry Pleau and Lou Nanne shining, were second, downing Canada and a weak Czech team, loser of all its games, that international hockey correspondent Herman Pedergnana labelled a "motley collection of second division players." (Nanne could have played for Canada, but he was turned away by Father Bauer in September 1963, after vetoing a contract offer from the Chicago Black Hawks. A special act by the U.S. Congress would later make him an American citizen in time to play for the red, white, and blue in 1967. Nanne, who played and managed in the NHL, admits he held a grudge: "[Father Bauer] calls me in '67, and he says, 'You're not an American yet. I've got a good deal for you. You can fly over tomorrow and play in the '67 World Championships with us, and I've got a job for you with Pillsbury, we'll move your family to

Winnipeg.' I said, 'Father, do you remember who I am?' He said, 'What do you mean?' I said, 'I'm the same guy you wouldn't give a tryout to in '63. I'm never playing for you.' So I didn't.")

A second period free-for-all of stick swinging between Canada and Dynamo made news. Upon returning home, Coach McLeod discredited news reports out of Grenoble. It wasn't, as reported by Ted Hargreaves, charging the Russian goalkeeper and the Dynamo team rallying to his defence, said McLeod. It was Dynamo captain Vitaly Davydov cross-checking Terry O'Malley at centre ice that drew Hargreaves to the scene, and the Russian goaler skated out to even the odds and chopped Hargreaves on the back of his neck. In either version, the benches emptied, things settled down, and Canada still lost 3–0, saved only by its heroic goaltender, Wayne Stephenson.

The club sent to Grenoble was an excellent example of why a second team was a must. An October tournament meant that Nats regulars Gary Begg, Barry MacKenzie, Gary Dineen, Roger Bourbonnais, Fran Huck, and goalie Ken Broderick stayed home. In their stead went the likes of Penticton Bronco Jack Taggart, just 17 years of age, and brothers Gerry and Herb Pinder, not much older. Backing up Stephenson was Bobby Taylor from the Calgary Spurs senior team.

Former pro Jack "Red" Bownass was put in charge of the eastern squad, made up of very young players who were seen as the nucleus of the 1972 Olympic team. Like McLeod, he was a veteran hockey player, with a long list of minor-league teams and a brief NHL stint, and still young enough at 37 to step into the lineup when needed to anchor the defence.

Starting in the fall of 1967, the eastern Nats played as the sixth team in the Quebec Provincial Senior Hockey League, based out of the Hull Arena. That season was a 40-game schedule, 10 less than the loop's other teams, so some games were worth four points instead of two. It was established right from the start that the team couldn't compete for the Allan Cup, even if it won the QPSHL title. The western Nats played a partial schedule in the Western Canada Senior Hockey League, and had a deal with the league to store a few players on scholarship.

Father Bauer and McLeod made sure to repeatedly mention that the

Ottawa squad wasn't a B team. "Essentially, Canada has one National Team but split into two sections," Bauer told the *Ottawa Citizen* in August 1967. "Neither can be considered first or second except in point of establishment. We expect our Winnipeg squad to have an edge since almost all last year's team will be returning. But there's nothing to say that the Eastern squad can't develop into the nucleus of our international competitive unit."

The initial training camp was in late August in Kingston, and a second camp, with prospects winnowed out, took place in Hull. New faces came and went in Ottawa, pro contracts dangled in the faces of such names as Butch Goring, eventual Conn Smythe winner with the Islanders, and Bob Berry, who played and coached in the NHL for years. Old faces popped up too, like Jean Cusson, once called "Montreal's gift to Canada's national hockey team," who was teaching nearby.

"This is just the next step in Father Bauer's plan. Expansion for us means east and west and not south. We hope some day to have a network of national amateur clubs across Canada," said the CAHA's Lionel Fleury.

Father Bauer's plan continued to emphasize education and hockey, though the latest recruits wouldn't prove quite as determined to seek out higher degrees. For one, many of them were younger than the original Bauer Boys of 1963.

Terry Caffery was 19 years old when he agreed to join the Ottawa-based program in the fall of 1968. "I remember saying to Father Bauer, 'I'm approaching this like a four-year plan to play in the '72 Olympics, and turn pro after that,'" recalled Caffery.

Chuck Lefley and his brother, Brian, natives of tiny Grosse Isle, Manitoba, thought they had scholarships to Denver University, only to see them rescinded when junior hockey brokers in Winnipeg blocked their move to Colorado. They refused to play junior for the local Jets in the Western Canada Hockey League, instead practising with the Nats. "They gave a kid a home that didn't have one, really," said Lefley. "My dad just happened to give Father Bauer and Jackie McLeod a call and ask them if it was okay if I just practiced with them." The next season, he signed up for the national team program. With a few 18-year-olds, such as Lefley, Jack Taggart, and Steve Carlyle, mixed in with the veteran student-athletes, it was a chance to learn. "We were all first-year university guys. They were veterans of it, so they taught us the ropes on how to mix studying with playing and travelling. We'd be away for weeks at a time sometimes."

Ab DeMarco was one of the non-students, unless you count those couple of days at an Ottawa high school. After returning from a hockey trip, he drove around, couldn't find the school, and gave up. In a way, it was a throwback to his father's era, when an educated hockey player was a danger to the established system. Ab DeMarco Sr. had been a pro centreman from the late 1930s into the 1950s. DeMarco Jr. was playing with the OHL's Kitchener Rangers when Father Bauer approached him and teammate Denis Dupere about signing. Father made the pitch in the Bauer home. Ab Junior recalled the offer being $3,500 a year, tax-free, a far cry from the $9,000 or so the New York Rangers were offering. "My dad says, 'What the hell, you get to go to Europe a couple of times. It'll be an experience.' I said okay," recalled DeMarco Jr., who later finished high school in his hometown of North Bay, Ontario.

An entire line from the Toronto Marlboros was recruited too: Terry Caffery, Steven King, and Richie Bayes. That certainly got the notice of the NHL, which wasn't pleased with the expanding national team program.

"It was a chance to study and play for Canada," said Caffery. "I remember that summer of July '68, I was either going to go play for the national team or I was going to go to Boston University on a scholarship. That was the decision. I wasn't going to turn pro, I knew that." He was at Ottawa's Carleton University on a general bachelor of arts degree, but ended up finishing his degree later from the University of Ottawa.

In principle, it made sense to have a greater selection of candidates from which to construct a team, but it generated a divide between east and west. Some of the players never even met until overseas at a tournament. With time, that changed, but the rivalry between the two teams never disappeared.

The veteran presence in The 'Peg made a big difference in the strength of the teams, especially since it had an established goaltender in Broderick. "They were a first-year team. They were younger," said Gerry Pinder. "We had the Dineens and O'Malleys and MacKenzies, and Gary Begg, Conlin, Ray Cadieux. We had the guys that had been around a long time."

But as the veteran squad with the names that the public—and the opposition—were familiar with, the Winnipeg team was called upon more often for higher profile games, the roster sprinkled with a few additions from the east. There were the usual issues with schooling; after finishing his law degree in Winnipeg, Roger Bourbonnais went to Edmonton to article, and suited up for the Edmonton Nuggets of the Western Canada Senior League, even playing his old mates a couple of times, but then joining them for trips abroad.

The loyalty of the original Bauer Boys went both ways, said DeMarco, choosing his words carefully. "There was really—and I can see why—Father Bauer, who was in charge, he really idolized the boys from Winnipeg. Those were his boys, they'd been there. . . . They were his buddies. I'm sorry, but we had some real nice players on our team, you know what I mean? And youth. We had guys like Denis Dupere who was playing in the All-Star game in the NHL and they didn't even bring him when on the World Championship tour, because they had to bring some of their favourites, guys that had been there the year before, because the year before was an Olympic year."

That 1969 World Championship in Stockholm would be the last involving a Canadian team for eight years (and it was the first year to see separate tournaments for the A, B, and C pools). With the strict rules on professionals lessened, the 1969 team was somewhat fluid, indicating the difficulty in managing a greater pool of potential players. It foreshadowed the modern World Championships, held in late April, where new players arrive to support their country as their teams are eliminated from the NHL playoffs.

Mainstays such as Begg, Terry O'Malley, Huck, Bourbonnais, Mott, and Hargreaves were thrown into a blender with a sort-of-demoted Bownass—McLeod would coach in Stockholm—and youngsters like Carlyle, Ken Stephanson, DeMarco, and Bob Murdoch, and the Marlies line of Caffery-Bayes-King.

In net it was initially Wayne Stephenson from the west and Steve Rexe from the east, but the staff made it known from the start that if Seth Martin's Trail senior team was eliminated from its playoffs, the hope was he'd ride his white horse across the Atlantic and further bolster his international reputation. Instead, a future Hockey Hall of Famer and federal politician, Ken Dryden, finished his commitment at Cornell and came over for two games, with Rexe pushed to the stands, feigning a broken leg.

The political side of Dryden wouldn't emerge until 2004, when he was elected as a Liberal Party candidate in the Toronto riding of York Centre, but there was plenty of politics going on behind the scenes with Team Canada.

Hockey Canada, a partnership between the Government of Canada, the NHL, amateur hockey, and the business community, had just been formed. While the CAHA still existed, and ran the Nats, its future was uncertain, and it was beholden to the feds and their $200,000 contribution that helped keep the program running.

Just before the team left for Europe, it was announced that Leighton "Hap" Emms, the 64-year-old owner and general manager of the defending Memorial Cup–champion Niagara Falls Flyers, would be taking over the national team the following year. McLeod, caught before boarding the plane, was incensed. "This is a ridiculous time to release information about Emms being approached for the general manager's job," McLeod said. "Our kids are trying to get ready for the tournament and now they're mixed up wondering what's going to happen next year."

They should have worried about what was happening on the ice.

With the top six teams participating, it was a double round-robin tournament. The Americans didn't win a game, and Finland only took two. Canada came fourth, with four wins, unable to deal with the powers of Russia (gold), Sweden (silver), and Czechoslovakia (bronze).

The worst was a 7–1 loss to the Soviet Union on March 19, where Canada gave up five goals in the first period. The Nats were outshot 35–20 in the country's 14th meeting with Russia in Olympic and World Championship play. Only worse was an 8–0 drubbing at the hands of the Czechs at the 1965 tournament.

Near the end of the championships, emotions boiled over. In a 4–2 loss to Sweden, with Dryden starting for the second time after blanking the U.S. 1–0 in his spectacular debut, right winger Kevin O'Shea lost it, punching Bert-Ola Nordlander behind the Canadian net. He drew a five-minute penalty, and fans threw coins at him as he left the ice. "We're only humans," said McLeod. "We like to play hard and we do play hard. We are never out to injure anyone. Occasionally, there is a loss of composure."

The true story of the 1969 tournament was far more dramatic than a punch, though. The World Championship was originally scheduled for Prague, but when the Soviet Union invaded Czechoslovakia in August 1968, it was decided to go to the safety of Stockholm. The political tensions between the two countries were played out on the ice at the Johanneshov arena on March 21 and 28. Bolstered by hundreds of telegrams from back home, and banners that read "Tonight, even tanks won't help" and "In August you, tonight we," the Czechs gave it their all. "You talk about passion in games, they played each other twice, double round robin, and the Czechs won both times—they won 2–0 and they won 4–3," recalled Dryden.

That set off celebrations in Prague with crowds hitting the street and the glass windows of Aeroflot smashed, and a bonfire made from office furniture lighting up St. Wenceslas Square. Cries of "Ivan go home" and "For August" rang out from the estimated crowd of 100,000.

As for Canada, even in the darkest moments of the poor finish in Stockholm, there was something to look forward to—the World Championship was coming to hockey's birthplace for the first time in the spring of 1970. Montreal would host early games and Winnipeg the rest. Like the Centennial tournament, the Nats were expected to rise to the occasion and, finally, win. But they didn't even get on the ice.

Chapter 20

CANADA SHUNS THE WORLD

The January 4, 1970, decision to drop out of world competition at the amateur level was a surprise to many people, especially those who did not follow hockey closely. But to those who were familiar with the backroom shenanigans of the IIHF and its Napoleonic leader, Bunny Ahearne, the strategic retreat was most welcome.

The seeds of international discontent had been sown years earlier by Ahearne and the last-minute change of rules that cost Canada a medal at the 1964 Olympics. A little more than a year later, Canada received another slap in the face when it was denied a chance to host the 1967 World Championships.

The scene was Tampere, Finland, and the representative countries of the IIHF met at the World Championships in March 1965 to decide who would host in two years' time. Canada had never before requested the World Championships, and Gordon Juckes, secretary-manager of the Canadian Amateur Hockey Association, made the pitch for the Dominion, focusing on the hundredth anniversary of Canada's independence from Great Britain as a natural tie-in. Also applying were Austria and Switzerland, though few gave Austria any shot, since it had just held the Olympics in Innsbruck.

Before the tournament—and the vote—Ahearne dismissed a

Canadian reporter who argued the president's point that the Russians or Czechs would beat an NHL team with ease in a game under international rules. "You people seem to think the game of hockey is your exclusive property and that you shouldn't lose. Well, look what happened in Britain. We developed soccer football, golf, tennis, and boxing but we're not number one in those sports anymore. The same thing is now happening to you in hockey."

Maybe that should have been a sign, but Ahearne was one of five that voted *for* Canada to host the 1967 event; another was William Thayer Tutt, the rep from the United States that hosted the annual Walter A. Brown Memorial Tournaments in Colorado Springs. In the end, 35 European and Asian delegates voted against Canada.

Maurice Smith, sports editor of the *Winnipeg Free Press* reported that Lionel Fleury, president of the Canadian Amateur Hockey Association, was in tears following the verdict. Juckes was angry, and talked about wanting to get out of hockey altogether. "As for Father Bauer, the popular priest who inspired the formation of Canada's national hockey team and has devoted so much time to it—the look on his face said more than any words," wrote Smith, who tried to make sense of it for his readers. "It turns out now that Canada was the victim of a double cross. At first, Gordon Juckes had very little comment to make but later in the day he revealed that both Russia and Sweden had advised the Canadian representatives in pre-meeting talks, that if they requested a title series involving the top three European teams in the 1966 championships plus the USA and Canada, they would go along with it." Russia backed out of the idea, citing political issues with East Germany, but Sweden bailing was out of the blue. Juckes stormed that he would quit his position in the CAHA if Canada sent any team to Sweden in the next three years for any international match.

Later in 1965, Tutt blamed Canada for its arrogance and dismissal of the minnows of the hockey world. "The Canadian newspapers blamed the Communist [bloc] for swinging the votes against Canada but that wasn't the case," Tutt said. "The Canadian delegation made it clear that it wanted only the 'A' pool of the series. That's all it could afford. Other countries in the bidding were willing to take all three pools, A, B and C.

This is what killed Canada's chances."

Bauer hoped that *losing* the bid would lead to greater things for Canada. "I hope," he said, "the people and the government of Canada will get behind us more than ever. Our national pride is at stake now more than it ever was."

The next pitch, made in March 1967 in Vienna, was successful. For the first time, Canada would host the World Championships. This one was also tied into another centenary—1970 would mark 100 years since Manitoba joined Confederation, and, since many IIHF members at least *knew* of Winnipeg, capital city and host of the wildly successful Centennial Cup, it made sense. But the Winnipeg Arena couldn't host all 30 games (just the six big teams in the A Pool), so a second city would be needed. Vancouver and Ottawa were considered, but Montreal won out.

Harold Martin, past president of Winnipeg Enterprises, was tournament chairman for the Winnipeg segment of the tournament, and tickets went on sale—"package-deal tickets at the outlandishly low price of $75!" (And payment was allowed by installment.) By December 1968, 4,000 tickets had been sold to individuals, with a corporate buy still to come. "Our plans for the 1970 tournament in both Winnipeg and Montreal are already well ahead of those for Stockholm in 1969," said Martin. "We intend to make this a memorable undertaking indeed and we are well on our way toward attaining that objective."

The *Report on Amateur Hockey in Canada* had been tabled in the House of Commons in January 1967. Among its recommendations was a second national team for a deeper talent pool, better pay for coaches and management of the Nats, and a Canadian Hockey Foundation, which would oversee the national team, removing financial onus from the CAHA. "It'll be a change to be on the giving end of the beefs, and watch someone else try to skate around them," said Juckes in September 1969, puffing on a cigar.

Following that report came the boldly named Task Force on Sports for Canadians. It had been commissioned by the Honourable John Munro, the Minister for the Department of National Health and Welfare in the Liberal government, shortly after Canada's poor showing—just five medals—at the 1968 Summer Olympics in Mexico City. A look into sports in the country had actually been part of the Liberal campaign by Prime Minister Pierre Elliott Trudeau for the June 1968 federal election. Trudeau was a sports fan and avid canoeist, and was a familiar sight at important games, especially hockey and the CFL, during his lengthy time in office. When he talked about hockey, he didn't sound like a politician, but a fan. "Hockey is considered our national sport and yet, in the world hockey championships, we have not been able as amateurs to perform as well as we know we can," he told a crowd at Selkirk College in British Columbia in June 1968.

The task force chairman was W. Harold Rea, a Toronto business consultant who had been involved with the YMCA across Canada. Its two main members were Dr. Paul Wintle Desruisseaux of Quebec City, a former competitive swimmer, and gold-medal-winning downhill skier Nancy Greene, the native of Rossland, BC, who had become a national sensation. Chris Lang acted as director-administrator, and the polling company Douglas D. Maxwell Limited was charged with research and public relations.

At its core, the *Task Force on Sports for Canadians*, written by Douglas Fisher and Sydney Wise, looked at the professional-amateur divide:

> Probably the most important and entrancing question before us on the professional-amateur matter deserves a sociological treatise because such a study could tell us so much about the Canadian mind. Why is the Canadian public so upset when inferior teams represent Canada abroad? Why are such teams cursed as "amateur" and "shamateur"? Why does the demand surge up that we get professionals to represent us? Our judgement is that Canadians have come to expect a good showing by any sporting team which wears a Canada crest in international play. They want somebody to do something about it, and more and more the responsibility is being fastened on, and accepted by, the federal government, at least to take part in the leadership and to sustain our emblem-bearers. We must be frank and ask Canadians to recognize that the level of excellence in most international competition is so high, and is

> likely to go so much higher, that our response to the challenge in many sports, and specifically hockey, must be a considered and thorough one requiring co-operation from all elements in each sport, including the professionals. In other words, to achieve and maintain international repute, there must be some redressing in the old and continuing antithesis between the professionals and amateurs.

While the *Task Force on Sports* addressed far more than hockey in its myriad of pages, it is on hockey that it had the most impact. The result was Hockey Canada—an organization that's still going strong today as the controlling force of the various levels of men's and women's national teams.

"That's the watershed," said Chris Lang. "Out of the *Task Force on Sports* came Hockey Canada. So I wrote the *Task Force on Sports*, came up with the idea of Hockey Canada, incorporated Hockey Canada, and I was the secretary of Hockey Canada for 30 years."

The Canadian Hockey Foundation, established in 1966, was the forefather of Hockey Canada, the lessons learned in its ineffectiveness helping future plans. In 1971, Father Bauer wrote about the CHF. "The Foundation, not being explicitly connected with the CAHA, enabled the national team to bypass the limitations which the agreement of that body with the NHL would have placed upon its recruitment of players. It suffered, however, from the fact that it was really without authority and that it could not gain recognition from the federal government as a tax-exempt corporation able to accept donations. From the realization of these limitations came the idea of a Hockey Canada Corporation."

The ice had melted under the skates of the traditional powers of amateur hockey, the CAHA; broke as it may have been, the CAHA had steered the ship for decades and was left in the stands a cheering parent.

"It was in essence a partnership to bring everybody around the table—the NHL, CAHA, colleges, Bauer, citizens, community, whatever," recalled Lang. "We decided at the first board meeting for Hockey Canada, the big thing that we were getting screwed with was the eligibility of pros at the IIHF World Championships."

Hockey Canada's first decision proved comical. On April 23, 1969, Hap Emms, former NHL general manager with the Boston Bruins, and a junior hockey power with the Niagara Falls Flyers of the OHA, was named managing director. He planned to operate out of Maple Leaf Gardens but still run his junior team—and direct still-eligible talent to his Flyers rather than the Nats.

From the beginning of his Toronto press conference, it was clear all Emms had in mind was getting more pros to represent Canada. He claimed that Stafford Smythe of the Toronto Maple Leafs had promised him players, and Emms dreamed out loud of having Dave Keon and Norm Ullman suiting up. (It was news to Leafs GM Jim Gregory: "There's another question: are they on loan for two weeks or a year?") It was Emms who started pushing for the World Championships to get moved back in the calendar year so that players not participating in the Stanley Cup playoffs could get in the game. Less than four months later, by early August, Emms had quit. He claimed that the travel expectations were too much.

"It is our belief that the 64-year-old Emms discovered he had bitten off a little more than he could chew and at his age didn't want the aggravation and indigestion," opined Maurice Smith in the *Free Press*. "When he was in Winnipeg a couple of months ago, Emms did not particularly impress the majority of local newsmen when interviewed at the Fort Garry Hotel. At that time he did not seem to know in which direction he was going and gave only vague answers to the majority of questions fired at him. Even then, you got the impression that Emms felt he was caught up in a whirlpool and was not strong or young enough to swim his way out." It was surmised that one of the other breaking points was Emms' desire to install Eddie Bush, a notorious believer in rough-and-tumble, fight-'em-in-the-alley junior hockey, as the national team coach. The drastic change from the fair and diplomatic Jackie McLeod and Father Bauer was too much for Emms' Hockey Canada bosses.

Enter A.J. "Buck" Houle, who was well-liked, and for the true power brokers of hockey in Canada, the NHL, he was perfect. Houle had played left wing for the junior Toronto Marlboros, but his pro career was derailed by the Second World War. He served his country overseas with Conn Smythe's sportsmen's battery, and gained a new boss. Upon returning home, he worked in Smythe's gravel pit and coached the Weston Dukes at the Junior B level in the Leafs organization. Next, he was promoted to look after the Marlies, and went full-time into hockey in 1960, helping the Leafs as a scout and running the Marlies, who won the 1964 Memorial Cup. Dutifully loyal to Smythe and the Buds, he went west to manage the Victoria Maple Leafs of the Western Hockey League.

"Mr. Houle was strongly recommended to Hockey Canada by the two professional clubs—Toronto Maple Leafs and Montreal Canadiens—who are represented on our board," said Hockey Canada's Charles Hay. "He was also recommended by Clarence Campbell, president of the National Hockey League."

Houle's first task was to find a new coach for the Nats, and Red Kelly, just released as coach of the Los Angeles Kings, was in the running until he chose to take over the Pittsburgh Penguins. In the end, McLeod remained in charge.

Shakey recognized that the job had changed. "It's getting tougher all the time. The pro clubs pay big money and there is a terrible temptation to reach for it," he said in 1969 upon returning from the World Championships. Gary Aldcorn a former NHLer who had played for Canada in the Nats-Maroons season, was named assistant coach; he'd later work in player development for Hockey Canada.

It was a "composite team," said Houle. "We are thinking long-range, you must remember, of the '72 Olympics for instance, or the '71 world tournament in Geneva. We'll have the best of the 18 players left from last year's team, plus the best pros and amateurs that I can beg, borrow or steal from Montreal and Toronto. We're working on it right now."

There had been off-and-on noise about trouble with the Winnipeg-Montreal tournament all through 1969, with key players like Martin and Juckes attempting to ease concern. A Swedish newspaper, dated November 3rd, even reported that the tourney would be in Sweden.

IIHF president Ahearne had his own concerns, and, as usual, wasn't scared of mentioning them to anyone with a pen and paper. He told John Robertson of the *Winnipeg Free Press* of his reservations:

> 1. There will be no 1970 world tournament in Canada unless the Canadian government supplies him with written proof that it will allow East Germany into the country to complete;
> 2. The International Ice Hockey Federation will never . . . repeat never . . . open its door to allow National Hockey League to represent Canada;
> 3. The new Hockey Canada organization "is a lot of nonsense," and that he will make an announcement on Monday which will put an end to the whole concept;
> 4. Unless Canada goes along with his ideas it will not win another tournament "for a thousand years" more and there seems to be no question that he can back up his dictates. Ahearne is listed officially as the president of the European Hockey Federation but his power base consists of controlling the votes of more than half the 29 member countries through proxies and as one delegate put it: "If Ahearne decided next year that the world championship would be played on Swiss cheese instead of ice—and with bagels instead of pucks—then it would happen."

Ahearne was particularly leery of Hockey Canada and the string-pullers behind it. "I don't trust politicians," Ahearne said. "That Hockey Canada organization is just a waste of time and money. . . . Let your politicians stick to the job of making a mess running your country."

The issue over the Russian-controlled East Germany was beyond his scope, said Martin. The North Atlantic Treaty Organization didn't recognize East Germany as a state, and since Canada was in NATO, that was official policy. "But where world politics are involved you never know. I'll sleep better when we do get written assurance," he said.

Ultimately, Ahearne's threat—"I have the power to move the tournament"—proved to be true.

To most, it was a fight over who got to play; Canada wanted professionals to be allowed, and the rest of the world, meaning the European countries, did not. In the United States the game still was not the powerhouse it would become when a "Miracle on Ice" put it into the spotlight.

The key meeting took place in Crans-sur-Sierre, Switzerland, in July

1969. Fresh off the 1969 World Championships, there was much talk about the pros in the game. Canada went in with high hopes—a truly open tournament, where anyone could represent their country in the World Championships. Examples from other sports were trucked out during the argument; soccer, tennis and skiing had all found ways to live with amateurs and professionals. Shot down, the next vote was for 12 professionals—defeated 35 to 15—and the next ended in a 25–25 tie over nine professionals. Ahearne cast the deciding vote . . . in favour of Canada.

"We are disappointed that we did not get support for our proposal of an open tournament," Charles Hay said. "But under the circumstances this is success in a sense."

Canada left Crans-sur-Sierre believing everything was set for the World Championships at home for the first time. Nine pro hockey players *who had not played in the NHL that season* would be permitted, meaning that they would be strong minor-league veterans or promising youngsters unable to make the big clubs.

Of course, Canada had used a few reinstated pros, like Red Bownass and Brian Conacher, already and had shown progress against the dominant Russians. Carl Brewer, a rebel with a cause, had been an exception, still at the height of his skills. But the 250 best professionals, in their prime and not in the twilight of their careers, were playing professionally in the NHL.

Two trips overseas indicated that the pendulum was starting to swing back Canada's way. The first true professional hockey players to suit up in Russia arrived at the end of August 1969. There were 10 players from the farm system of the Leafs and Canadiens, thrown together in a brief training camp in Winnipeg before heading over. Past and future NHL mainstays such as Phil Roberto, Jim McKenny, Al MacNeil, and Wayne Carleton were among the loaners, mixed in with Nats like Bob Berry, Fran Huck, Chuck Lefley, and goalie Wayne Stephenson. The competition was club teams: Khimik Voskresensk, Wings of the Soviets, Dynamo Leningrad, and Jokerit from Finland.

With bodychecking allowed all over the ice for the first time internationally, Canada won three times, and lost only to the Wings, to sit atop the tourney. "On the whole I am satisfied with the team's performance in this tournament, with the exception of the game against Wings of the Soviet when my boys were simply unrecognizable," McLeod was quoted as saying. When he got home, he warned the press to not get overly excited about it, because these weren't the top teams in Russia, or even Finland.

Lefley has given some thought to how the triumph in Leningrad might have been perceived. "My guess is it opened everybody's eyes over there, and they thought, 'My God, they've got quite a nice hockey team here. The championships are being held in Winnipeg. We'd better maybe think about doing something about this.'"

Then in December, at the eight-day Izvestia Cup at Moscow's Lenin Central Stadium, Canada tied the Soviets 2–2, and finished second, behind Russia, but ahead of Czechoslovakia (which handed Canada its only loss), Sweden, Finland, and East Germany. (Had Sweden beaten the Russians in the last game, Canada would have won.) Harkening to the stewardship of Father Bauer, the players sat through a 20-minute briefing by the Department of External Affairs at the Toronto airport before departure, reminding them they were Canadian representatives abroad, and while things, like the food, might be unappealing, it was important to not make a scene. The team had 700 pounds of baggage, including chocolate bars, orange juice, powdered milk and even toilet paper.

A key to the excellent showing in Russia was the play of veteran Billy Harris, said Rick Noonan. "Billy was very humble and very aware of how difficult [things were that] the national teams had gone through. He and I became pretty close friends. In the end, he said that was his greatest thrill in hockey, was playing with that national team. He'd won three Stanley Cups."

Following the Izvestia tourney, a Russian squad toured Canada, and the Nats prevailed, winning three games, tying twice and losing once. Until that point, the USSR had been somewhat agreeable to open competition—perhaps out of curiosity. But how would they save face before losing it? Turn to the old Olympic credo on amateurism. IOC boss Avery Brundage confirmed that any player who had played against a professional player, knowingly or not, put his amateur status at risk. The European countries met in November, without inviting Canada, to talk about professionalism. Russia was in pursuit of the 1976 Summer Games at the time, so upsetting Brundage was a big *nyet-nyet*. (Ironically, Canada would get those games—and Russia would be awarded the 1980 Olympics.)

Brundage's warning to Ahearne in a letter dated December 11 was blunt:

> The fact the IIHF has opened its World Championships as well as other tournaments to professional players, will no doubt affect the Olympic eligibility of all participating teams.
>
> While the IOC has not passed officially on this situation since it has only now been informed officially, you should know that all teams participating in the Soccer Football World Cup in which professionals are [permitted] are ineligible for Olympic competition.
>
> It can be expected that a similar decision will be reached in the case of ice hockey.

In late December, the CAHA, Hockey Canada, and Munro sat around the table and talked money. The CAHA was worried about any debt incurred over the World Championships in Montreal and Winnipeg, and Hockey Canada agreed to foot the bill.

If anything, men like Houle were overconfident, full of hubris about Canada's role in world hockey. "Who needs whom the most? Does hockey need the Olympics or do the Olympics need hockey? Does Canada need world hockey or does world hockey need Canada?" Houle said in December 1969. "In Japan they're building a new arena to look after the Olympic hockey for 1972. If there's no hockey somebody will commit hari kari. Hockey is a big money maker and it carries the Winter Olympics. Last year Brundage had to back down on the South Africa [apartheid] issue in the Olympics and he's fouled up the skiing picture too."

The Canadian hockey powers, including NHL President Clarence Campbell as an observer, headed off to Geneva for a meeting with the IIHF, determined to make a stand for an open tournament. As it turned out, they were a little late.

"We showed up at the meeting January 4, except it all had gotten moved to January 3. They had a meeting and they agreed to take the tournament away from Canada and put it into Sweden," recalled Lang. "Everybody thinks we withdrew. Bullshit. . . . Everybody thinks we quit. They took the tournament away. People miss the detail."

Though it sounds like children fighting in the schoolyard ("like a little boy who's lost his toffee apple," quipped Ahearne), Canada stood up to the IIHF, took its puck and went home. Sweden won the right to host the tournament and the estimated half-a-million in profit it would generate (until it realized that Canada was a major draw). Russia strengthened its grasp on the gold medal. The press reported that there wasn't an on-the-record vote, but that Sweden, Czechoslovakia, East Germany, Finland, and Russia all said they wouldn't play in further World Championships if professionals were allowed.

The decision to drop out of international hockey was front-page news in Canada. "We quit," said CAHA president Earl Dawson, in a widely circulated Canadian Press story by Bruce Levett. "We will not return until the rules permit us to enter a team that is truly representative of Canadian hockey, so we can play our best players as all other countries do."

The *Ottawa Citizen* quickly penned an editorial under the title "The Hockey Charade":

> Canada's withdrawal from this year's World Championship tournament will help bring to a head the whole issue of amateurism. The hypocrisy and evasion practised by many countries have long been scandalous. Their teams have been amateur in name only. Now the entire question is being brought into the open. . . .
>
> Canada has played patsy to Europe's professional hockey teams for long enough. These teams call themselves amateur, and Canada has gone along until this year, when it sought agreement to include professionals on its team for world hockey purposes. Otherwise, the competition is too unfair. Because of the Olympic rule against professionalism, European teams wouldn't play along.

> Canada then had no choice. Either this country is given a fair shake in world hockey, or it must pull out of the whole charade.

Ahearne shed crocodile tears. "I have done everything I could on behalf of Canada," he said. "I am quite happy to put myself in the hands of the other 28 nations in the IIHF. I am sorry to say that, in my opinion, the CAHA no longer controls hockey in Canada so far as the IIHF is concerned." Brundage avoided the issue: "I have no comment," Brundage told a Chicago paper. "That is an exclusively hockey matter and we, the IOC, have nothing to do with it."

Left in the lurch was the national team, united into a single program once again based in Winnipeg—coincidentally playing in Ottawa. That meant Munro was in the stands at the Civic Centre, watching the Nats beat a touring Czechoslovakian team, 2–1, the last goal scored by Bill Heindl on goalie Vladimir Dzurilla. "I can't see playing any longer in light of Canada's withdrawal from the world tournament," said Fran Huck after the game.

The press also cornered Munro at the arena. "We feel, rightly or wrongly, that Canada should be allowed the use of professionals in view of the practices in other countries involved," said the cabinet minister. "Our plans were formulated several months ago and we could not back down."

The next day, January 5, a press conference was held in room 1950 of Ottawa's Skyline Hotel, with Minister Munro and Hockey Canada's Charles Hay, wrung dry from the flight from Geneva to Montreal to Ottawa. The elephant was not in the room, though its presence was felt.

"The NHL has been completely genuine in its support for our international aims," said Hay. "If I thought I had been a pawn, I would not be here tonight."

For those who lived through those times, there is little doubt the NHL had a hand in the pullout from international hockey and the dissolution of the national team concept, which had been a thorn in its side since 1963, stealing potential skaters from its grasp.

"The NHL were not very happy with the way the team was set up, because we took some of the players that the NHL wanted—or held them for a while," said McLeod. "That didn't sit very well with some of the clubs in the NHL, but some of the clubs were very good to us. They'd come play exhibition games with us in Winnipeg, Calgary, some of those towns. They were very good to us. But they weren't that happy with us."

Alan Eagleson swears that the NHL didn't have it out for the Nats. "The NHL was never anti–Father Bauer or anti-national team," he said. "I very much disliked terminating the national team. I think that was a major error . . . because even though it wasn't a powerhouse, it was competitive." It also gave "players the opportunity to play for their country, even though many of them didn't make the NHL. On the other hand, a significant number did."

A laughable column by former Leafs GM Punch Imlach in the *Toronto Telegram* seems to indicate that the curmudgeon had had a change of heart concerning the Nats. "The national team has come a long way, and it would be folly to discontinue just because the tournament has been changed, and especially silly to use as an excuse the fact that we didn't get our way," he wrote, forgetting his battles with Father Bauer and such players as Gary Dineen and Brian Conacher, who shunned the Leafs, at least for a time. "Our players get a university education if they desire. To my way of thinking, it is a hockey scholarship, and I would like to see this enlarged with Hockey Canada leading the way and with all universities in Canada being brought into the program. The universities could use the same approach to hockey as they do to football."

The final nail was put in the coffin on February 19, in private dining room number eight at Toronto's Royal York Hotel. NHL President Clarence Campbell and Hockey Canada's Charles Hay presided. *Toronto Telegram* columnist Scott Young was there and wrote:

> Campbell admitted that the NHL has always opposed the national team-in-being concept. And why not? It was the only competition the NHL had for the minds and bodies of young hockey players in Canada.
>
> And Charles Hay agreed, with a sort of sad logic, that it was just not reasonable for Hockey Canada to compete with the

> NHL for players and still have to count on the NHL for general co-operation and support.
>
> It was after these admissions had been made, accompanied by their flawless balance-sheet type logic, that I turned in the room and saw, at the back, Father David Bauer.
>
> He was staring at the row of big wheels in the front of the room, the professional morticians officiating at the death of the good idea he had borne and nurtured. He said nothing, but his face was not exactly expressionless. . . .
>
> No eulogy was spoken. But I know a lot of the players who were part of this idea that carried the puck for Canada in international competition through most of the 1960s.
>
> I think the eulogy exists, if only in men's minds.

For the record, the initial games of the round-robin World Hockey Championships were scheduled for Montreal, March 12–20, 1970, and the rest in Winnipeg, March 22–29. It wasn't exactly a hot ticket in Montreal, but in Winnipeg, it was something else. The Nats called the city home and the team was loved. The *Winnipeg Tribune* spoke for its readers in an editorial after the World Championships were taken away from Canada and returned to Stockholm: "Here in Winnipeg, though, there is a feeling that the CAHA turned on us the way European hockey men turned on them. . . . Don't worry about the money the tournament planning had cost so far, because Ottawa seems to have an endless supply and the government has offered to pick up whatever tab there is. But how can they pay Winnipeggers for five years of hoping, dreaming, and perspiring as they planned the best world tournament anybody ever saw?"

There was bellyaching about money. In all the initial stories, Munro vowed that the federal government would cover up to $150,000 in losses relating to the tournament in Montreal and Winnipeg. "We'll have to refund around $75,000 in sold tickets and figure out how much money we've invested in promotion, advertising, travel, etc.," whined David Molson, president of the Montreal Canadiens, who, as a member of the Hockey Canada board, supported the decision. Television rights in Canada for the championships, sure to be a ratings hit, were held by

CTV. "We paid $125,000 for the rights. In the past, the Canadian rights were worth only $5,000," said CTV sports director Johnny Esaw. "We are still holding back a cheque for $50,000, because I don't think we'll televise the tournament from Stockholm without a Canadian entry. It will depend on Ahearne how much money we'll lose. He might say that last year's tournament in Stockholm was worth $10,000, in which case he'll give us back $65,000. But he may say that it was worth $75,000 and we won't get anything back." Championship rings were commissioned, and former Nats trainer Ken Esdale has in his possession the one and only prototype that was made.

The tournament in Stockholm was won by Russia, for the eighth straight year, with the hometown Swedes second and the Czechs third. Aside from Finland and East Germany, the sixth team in the tourney was Poland, as the United States turned down an invitation.

There was talk of a replacement tournament in Winnipeg, maybe the best university teams or a collection of wide-ranging senior teams taking on the Nats, but nothing ever came of the ideas.

Winnipeg mayor Stephen Juba even jumped into the fray, sending a telegram to Munro: "I often wondered how long Canada would tolerate the international ice hockey situation. . . . If any awards are to be made sir, you should be the recipient of a gold medal because your statement will bring about fair play and consideration to our Canadian athletes in the future." And another to Ahearne, whom he had met with in Winnipeg: "I didn't realize at the time you were putting the cheese in the trap. . . . It appears now your hockey philosophy is politically oriented. To say the least, I'm utterly disgusted."

The Nats limped along for a short while, as many of the players were still in university and opted to not drop out and pursue a professional hockey career.

"Once the national team folded, the NHL basically was . . . 'Take this offer or leave it,'" said Terry Caffery. "The only option for guys was the national team. Once there was no national team, then it was back to the old days of, 'Okay, here's your $5,000 bonus. Sign here.'" So he did, playing with Chicago and Minnesota in the NHL, and New England and Calgary in the WHA.

Gerry Pinder also signed and became a veteran of nine NHL and WHA seasons. "It's too bad, because we had all dedicated ourselves to the '70 tournament in Winnipeg. Franny Huck was going to stay, Herb and I were going to stay. Everybody had opportunities to turn pro. The NHL was pretty happy with the breakup of the team in '70 because there were so many of us that they wanted in the National Hockey League."

The Winnipeg Jets held a Jackie McLeod appreciation night on December 11, 1970. The Jets were facing the Saskatoon Blades in a Western Canada Hockey League game. The coach of the Blades? Shakey McLeod. A crowd of 3,169 turned out for Shakey, as his Blades lost 5–3. Phil Reimer was master of ceremonies, and Father Bauer was there, flying in from Sapporo, where he'd been working with the Japanese national team.

Those who weren't there sent in telegrams, including Russian coach Anatoli Tarasov, Ken Broderick, Marshall Johnston, Billy Heindl, Lorne Davis, Red Bownass, Barry MacKenzie, Mike Poirier, Bob Murdoch, Ken Dryden, Chuck Lefley, Fran Huck, Ted Hargreaves, Gary Begg, Gerry and Herb Pinder, Terry O'Malley, and Paul Conlin. There were also notes from Murray Williamson, coach of the U.S. Nationals; former Nats trainer Bill Bozak; and Bill Hunter, owner of the Edmonton Oil Kings, who would be a key factor in the World Hockey Association two years later.

"Jack was a good friend of Canadian and European hockey—and especially of the people of Winnipeg," said Father Bauer. "He had, and still has, tremendous dedication, loyalty, honesty, and integrity to everyone with whom he works. His efforts toward international participation by Canada kindled a flame that still burns brightly. There is still hope that those efforts haven't been wasted."

Surrounded by his wife, son, and daughter, McLeod tried to draw attention away from himself. "There's a lot of other people who should be standing up here instead of me," he said.

While he never won a gold medal leading Canada, McLeod was presented with one by the Manitoba Sportswriters and Sportscasters Association. As well, there were two replica Red River carts, an honorary citizenship award from the City of Winnipeg, a colour television set from the fans, and two round-trip tickets to Hawaii for he and his wife, Bev.

After the Nats were shut down by Hockey Canada, McLeod coached mainly junior hockey, and never got a big-league job. "Jackie McLeod was certainly qualified to coach in the National Hockey League. I think that there was some prejudice against him after the team folded, because he stayed with the Olympic team for those years and didn't go coach in the American League or NHL or wherever," said Gerry Pinder.

One of Shakey's old buddies from the ball diamonds of Saskatchewan was Emile "the Cat" Francis, a goalie-turned-NHL-coach and general manager with the New York Rangers. They'd faced each other on the ice too, the sniper versus the keeper. Loyal to his friend, Francis was one of the few NHL power brokers who arranged for exhibition games with the Nats. "That was because of Father Murray, Father Bauer, and Jackie McLeod, who was the coach," said Francis. "Hell, those three guys were friends of mine, and I really respected the program that they were running. So that's why I played against them all the time."

Francis considered the question of why McLeod never coached in the NHL. "You know, that's a good question. I don't know, because I thought he did a great job with Team Canada," said Francis. "He had a great reputation. Christ, he knew all [the] hockey players in Europe. Whenever he'd go over to Europe to play, he'd be the first guy to call me when he came back. I'd say, 'Jack, did you see any prospects over there?' He knew who could play and who couldn't."

While McLeod got his thank you, many who gave their lives to the national team, working behind the scenes and not on the ice, were forgotten.

Guy Maddin eulogized the Nats in his book *My Winnipeg* and his father's role as secretary and jack of all trades with the team. "When the national team was disbanded by a federal bureaucrat's stroke of a pen in 1970, my father died," he wrote. "With nothing left to do, he died. I'd like to say he spontaneously combusted right on the ice of the arena—that would have been great—but it was quieter than that. He shrank into a puff of cigarette smoke, and was gone."

Chapter 21

THE SUMMIT SERIES: 'WE TOLD YOU SO'

With the 1972 Summit Series, Canada returned to international hockey in a big, professional way, pitting a selection of National Hockey League stars against the best of the USSR. And while history tells us that Canada eked out a victory over the course of the eight-game series, winning four games, losing three, and tying one, for the players who had donned the red and white of Canada during the previous decade, there was a real element of satisfaction—vindication even—now that the entire country finally understood how truly powerful the Big Red Machine was.

Overconfident and arrogant at first, the 1972 squad realized quickly that this would be no cakewalk. Almost all of the former Nats have a story about warning others what the NHLers were up against.

Tall, creative centreman Peter Mahovlich broke out of the shadow of his brother, Frank, during the Summit Series. He potted a key goal in the second game, where he zipped around three Soviets while Canada was shorthanded; in the final game, he came to the rescue of Alan Eagleson in the Moscow stands. What Mahovlich didn't do was heed the words of his brother-in-law . . .

Paul Conlin and Peter Mahovlich had married sisters. In the early summer of '72, Conlin recalled sounding the alarm. "They didn't think the Russians were going to score a goal let alone win a game," Conlin said. "I tried to impress on him, 'They're a pretty good team, you'd better get prepared,' but it fell on deaf ears, until after the first game in Montreal. I went down to the game and actually flew back to Toronto with the team. Wow, you could hear a pin drop on the plane coming home. They were in utter shock at how good the Russians were."

Brothers Herb and Gerry Pinder played for the Nats, but only Gerry graduated to the NHL. One of the raps on the Soviets was that their goaltending wouldn't hold up. Herb Pinder scoffed at the notion: "I remember telling really close friends, 'Look guys, you have no idea. If the goaltending's that bad, why are they low-scoring games when they play each other? Talent isn't limited to Canada. These guys can skate, they're in better shape than we are, they can move the puck better, they're better coached. You're going to be shocked.'"

Like the rest of the country, Herb Pinder was plunked down in front of his television to watch the first game. After Phil Esposito scored two quick goals, a buddy called, teasing, "I told you so . . ." When the Russians roared back, Pinder tried to return the teasing, but his friend wouldn't take the call.

Billy MacMillan had also moved up to the NHL and sounded the alarm. "I told them before the goddamned thing started, anyone I met."

Rod Seiling and Brian Glennie were on the roster and had previously skated for Canada in the Olympics against the Russians: Seiling in '64 and Glennie in '68. Coach Harry Sinden had played in the 1960 Olympics as a part of the Kitchener-Waterloo Dutchmen, under the stewardship of Bobby Bauer. Looking back to the Soviets he saw, Sinden can only shake his head. "The Russians were so good in the '60s and '70s—they were so good. To come close, like Father Bauer did, is something. For a while, all we did was come close too."

If there was consultation with Father Bauer and Jackie McLeod, Sinden doesn't remember it.

During Game 3, in Winnipeg, Father Bauer was interviewed at rinkside for television by Bill Good Jr., with Good towering over the diminutive priest. He felt the results of the first two games—7–3 Russia and 4–1 Canada—brought "to the surface many problems which we had domestically and still have in our game of hockey. I think the point has been made, both on Saturday and on Monday evening, and also tonight, that we have a little bit of learning to do," said Bauer. "It was so difficult through those years for Jackie, myself, the players, or anyone else to point this out because there was no standard against which anyone in this country could judge our effort. I think these games more or less speak for themselves."

Good Jr. acknowledged as much, throwing back to play-by-play man Johnny Esaw. "Father Bauer, I think when we see the success of the Canadian team and the difficulty they have against the Soviets, it gives you an idea, John, that perhaps those national teams were being vastly underrated by Canadians when they went overseas a few years ago."

Esaw, one of the most influential men in the history of televised sports in Canada, concurred: "I think it's good that we should not forget the efforts of people like Father Bauer, Jackie McLeod and the gang that tried so hard for so long."

Father Bauer travelled to Russia for a few of the games, but was home for Game 8. He watched it on TV like millions of Canadians, at St. Mark's College with his pal, Rick Noonan, who had been given the task of being the aide-de-camp for the Soviets when they were in Canada. "They needed someone to eat, sleep and drink—well, not drink, though we had the odd vodka—eat, sleep and live with the Russians," Noonan told Tom Hawthorn of the *Globe and Mail* in 2012, celebrating 40 years of the Summit Series. "I was the first one on the tarmac in Montreal when the Aeroflot jet landed. From then on, I was always last on and first off the bus."

During one game in Moscow, Pat Marsden hosted an odd couple of Father Bauer and Punch Imlach, then GM of the Buffalo Sabres, during the first intermission. A trench coat draped over his arm, Father Bauer offered his thoughts on the games so far—and the support for Canada. "I think that the contingent here has the quality that the great Russian observer Tarasov said that he wished his team had, which is perhaps a little more enthusiasm, a little more desire, and when they get that he figured they'd be just about the best. These fans here have been tremendous in support of the Canadian team."

Always one to play the Canada card, Bauer added that he hoped the series would "serve as a point of unity at home and perhaps with a little bit of care, here, some good relationships abroad."

At the end of the grueling series, Canada had deeper respect for the skills of the Soviet players.

Herb Pinder said there were a number of phone calls between old Nat teammates. "We're all calling each other because it was a vindication," he said. The veterans of the international game knew all the issues the NHLers were going through, from the poor food to the questionable refereeing. "We were in awe of what they accomplished, because we knew exactly what they were going through and how good that Russian team was."

NHL players' union president and Hockey Canada director Alan Eagleson made the Summit Series his own in many ways, leaping to the forefront of international hockey even if he only had a bit part in organizing the actual event—it was far more bureaucratic and fraught with political tension behind the scenes than most fans will ever know. "The only way to do it is government to government," recalled Chris Lang, who worked with Hockey Canada and travelled to Moscow with Douglas Fisher, and hammered out the deal with Canadian ambassador Robert Ford and the Soviet reps.

The Eagle had an interesting relationship with Bauer. They enjoyed each other's company, yet butted heads constantly over players who chose an education and representing their country over the promised riches of the NHL. "I think Father Bauer enjoyed the tournament, but I think he was inclined to cheer for the Russians on occasion, more because of me than the team," Eagleson joked. "It proved that the Russians were good hockey players."

Sinden knows how close it really was. "We won in the last 34 seconds. Those Russian teams were spectacular."

Chapter 22

BACK IN THE GAME

Moscow's Izvestia Cup, the Rudé Právo Cup in Prague, the Spengler Cup in Switzerland, the Ahearne Cup in Sweden—there was lots of silverware to be won in international hockey. Aside from the incredibly successful Summit Series, Canada's first baby step back into the world of global shinny involved a team in the 1972 World University Games, held in Lake Placid, New York.

Sixteen countries took part in the World University Games, run by the International University Sports Federation, but only three in the hockey round-robin: Canada, Russia, and the United States. Predictably, USSR won gold, with five victories and a tie with Canada, which won three, lost two, and had the tie; the Americans didn't win a game.

"It was a funny tournament, because there were only three teams," said Jim Irving, who had been with the Canadian national team in 1969 and would later earn a medical degree. "It was a good team, a few guys from the national team, Steve Carlyle, me. But the Russians were better, there was no doubt."

It was an interesting collection of players for Canada, and definitely a glimpse into the future and the country's return to Olympic hockey at the 1980 Games, also in Lake Placid. Helming the university students was Clare Drake of the University of Alberta (with four of his Golden

Bears suiting up for their country). Tom Watt of the University of Toronto was the team's manager (six Varsity Blues were on the squad). They'd be co-coaches for Team Canada in '80.

Watt said that Father Bauer was supportive—"we had his help"—but it was a complicated event. "The CAHA was not allowed to compete internationally. You signed a CAHA card and senior teams were not allowed to play; but the colleges, we didn't sign CAHA cards," said Watt, who had taken his national champion U of T team to the World Student Games in Innsbruck, winning a bronze medal. Like the senior teams of the late 1950s and early 1960s, the Varsity Blues were in way over their heads against international talent. "Here was the University of Toronto competing against the best students in Russia, the best students in Czech Republic, the best students in Sweden. And here we are one university," said Watt. Drake and Watt sought advice from Bauer on fielding a better, united team, come 1972.

A few notable names were on that 1972 student team: Larry Carriere played seven NHL seasons with the Sabres, Flames, Canucks, Kings, and Leafs; Steve Carlyle had been with the Nats in 1969 before playing four seasons with the WHA's Oilers, where a teammate was Bob McAneeley; Gavin Kirk was also a WHA guy, following the franchise from Ottawa to Toronto to Birmingham before going west to the Oilers; John Wright skated with the Canucks, Blues, and Scouts; Jack Gibson played for the Toros in the WHA.

Rick Cunningham from Trent University in Peterborough, Ontario, is a great example of the inconsistencies over eligibility that made international hockey so maddening. He played 323 regular-season games in the WHA as a defenceman before heading to Austria, where he suited up for Salzburg and then Vienna. Cunningham settled down with a local gal, and ran a chain of sporting goods stores, exclusive distributor in the country for Bauer and Cooper products.

In 1984, just before the Games in Sarajevo, the International Olympic Committee tweaked its rule on professionals. Anyone who had played in the NHL was ineligible, but the WHA was okay. Five players were immediately toast: Mark Morrison and Don Dietrich of Canada, Jim Corsi (whom the statistic so loved by the analytics crowd is named after) and Rick Bragnalo of Italy, and Greg Holst of Austria. Canada's Mario Gosselin and Dan Wood had signed NHL deals but were allowed to stay. But Cunningham was okay.

Dave Anderson of the *New York Times* had a field day with the "Olympic joke" that made up Rule 26 of the Olympic charter. "Rick Cunningham should have been ineligible too. But since the WHA no longer exists, in the IOC's judgment it apparently never existed," he wrote, arguing for a true open Olympics, with professionals alongside the pros. There would be some pros allowed in 1988 in Calgary, but it wasn't until 1998 that the best in the world competed at the Olympics—and the IOC had been pushed that way, in hockey at least, by the success of other competitions that allowed professionals.

The 1974 Summit Series pitting the World Hockey Association players against the USSR didn't quite resonate with the public the way the '72 series had, but it kept alive the desire for true competition.

Father Bauer, quoted in Quebec City when the Team Canada '74 camp was underway, said the club didn't have the horses to compete with the Russians, which was a familiar line for him. "As even the most dedicated Team Canada supporters have agreed, this team has less pure talent than the 1972 entry," said Father Bauer. "But when I look at the players here and compare them with those we had, I can only be impressed."

Goaltender Gerry Cheevers, playing for the Cleveland Crusaders, recalled asking his old coach from St. Mike's about the upcoming foes. "He was well aware of how good the Russians were—in fact, we all were in '72. . . . We talked about them. I can remember asking him, 'My style of goal, does it fit playing the Russians?' And it really didn't. I was a blitzer or something. He sort of coached me by saying, 'If you stay on your feet, your skating will help you play against them.' Because they passed so well."

Cheevers played seven of the eight games against the Russians, in a losing cause. The USSR was too strong, winning four times, tying three games, and losing just once. Or maybe it was simply that the WHA players were not the best players to represent Canada. Quick, besides the big names—Gordie Howe, Bobby Hull, Frank Mahovlich, and Paul Henderson—who were all getting a little long in the tooth, can you name many others from that Team Canada? (For the record, the rest of the team included Rick Ley, Marty Howe, Mark Howe, Pat Stapleton, J.C. Tremblay, Mike Walton, Rejean Houle, Brad Selwood, Andre Lacroix, Tom Webster, Ralph Backstrom, Jim Harrison, Rick Smith, Paul Shmyr, Bruce McGregor, Serge Bernier, Marc Tardiff, John McKenzie, Al Hamilton, Barry Long, Pat Price, Wayne Dillon, Gavin Clark, Dennis Sobchuk, Ron Chipperfield, with Don McLeod the goalie on Cheevers' off day, and fellow keeper Gilles Gratton hardly getting out of the bar.)

The '72 and '74 friendship tournaments laid the groundwork for the first true tournament that featured the best players in the world—the 1976 Canada Cup. It was the brainchild of Alan Eagleson, who has always maintained the idea came to him while on a ladder painting his cottage, and soccer's World Cup playing on the radio. Eagleson, as the executive director of the NHL Players' Association, was able to slowly broker a remarkable peace between the IIHF, NHL, and even the WHA. The six-team round-robin tournament, played in September 1976, ended with a best-of-three final between Canada and Czechoslovakia, which had won the World Championship that spring. With a hobbling Bobby Orr playing the last great hockey of his legendary career, Team Canada easily won the first game of the final 6–0, but the second was a nail-biter, going to overtime, before Darryl Sittler scored the winner of the first truly international best-on-best hockey tournament. Captain Bobby Clarke was presented the Canada Cup by Canadian prime minister Pierre Trudeau.

Fittingly, the man who contributed the iconic shiny half-maple-leaf trophy had plenty of experience on the world stage. Winnipeg's Johnny McCreedy had won the Allan Cup, the Memorial Cup, the Stanley Cup, and the World Championship during his playing days, the first to have accomplished the feat. Post-hockey, he took a job with the Sudbury mining giant Inco, rising through the ranks of the massive company to become vice-chairman in 1979. "Inco, with John McCreedy's help, figured out how to get the nickel to make the Canada Cup," said Eagleson. "We were friends a little bit before that, but that really cemented our friendship." Teledyne Canada also contributed funds towards the $50,000 trophy.

To get all the other countries on board for the 1976 Canada Cup, Hockey Canada had to make a deal with the International Ice Hockey Federation to re-enter the World Championships, starting in April 1977 (so that NHL and WHA players eliminated from the playoffs could play), and the Olympics. "We had to," said Chris Lang, formerly of Hockey Canada. From that agreement, international hockey truly grew: powerful Russian teams competed against the NHL in what was known as Super Series; the first World Junior Championships (there had already been European junior tourneys) happened in 1977; Canada Cup tournaments were held in 1981, 1984, 1987, and 1991; the World Cup replaced the Canada Cup, and was held in 1996, 2004, and 2016.

The World Championships finally allowed professionals, eliminating the arguments over players who were paid by their country for such other jobs as military service. There were natural ties to the Bauer Boys, past and future. Derek Holmes managed the team in 1977 and 1978. Holmes had played on the Ottawa-based Nats before embarking on more hockey tourism, coaching the national team in Switzerland, a club team in Finland, and playing in Austria. He was assisted by player agent Bill Watters, who was the understudy/right-hand man to Eagleson. Given his international experience, Tom Watt's name came up again (as did Bauer's). "For anyone to say Tom Watt will be the coach is presumptuous to say the least," Watters said in February 1977. "We've got certain individuals in mind but, as yet, we have no idea who our man will be."

Veteran bench boss Johnny Wilson was named coach, since his Colorado Rockies weren't exactly playoff material. There would be none of the ambassadorial responsibility that Father Bauer preached to his flock. Instead, fans in Vienna, Austria, were treated to a veritable gong show. A short list of transgressions included Phil Russell of the Black Hawks decking a foe while heading to the Canadian bench during a stoppage of play; Phil Esposito of the Rangers punching Czechoslovakian coach Jan Starsi and later refusing to shake a referee's hand; and Carol Vadnais, also of the Rangers, spearing Sweden's Kent-Erik Andersson, sending him to the hospital. During a game against Russia, Eric Vail of the Atlanta Flames swung his stick at an opponent's head and was ejected.

The results of the games were nearly as ugly. Canada had some decent names, like Phil and Tony Esposito; forwards Rod Gilbert, Ron Ellis, Pierre Larouche, and Jean Pronovost; and rearguards Vadnais, Dallas Smith, and Russell. But Canada had been out of international hockey too long and the rough style of the NHL just didn't translate. Canada finished fourth, behind Czechoslovakia, Sweden, and Russia.

In 1978, Canada took a bronze in Prague, edging out the Swedes in the final game. It was Canada's first World Championship medal since 1967. The following year, the result was reversed, and the Swedes took third in Moscow. Of note, the Canadians were far better prepared for international hockey as Marshall Johnston, a Bauer Boy from 1964 to 1968, was on the coaching staff.

But the Olympics, with the "amateur" requirements, were something else, said Lang. So Hockey Canada returned to the past for the Games in Lake Placid. "Now we've got nobody to run it, so what we did is we put Bauer up to be the de facto head. Then we hired Rick Noonan, who was the men's athletics director at UBC, and made him general manager, so he ran it with Bauer—with Bauer up in the top of the building," recalled Lang. It was all official by February 1978: Canada was returning to the Olympics in 1980, 12 years after its last appearance.

Bauer had been away in Japan and Austria, but was always a part of the picture, whether an official board member of Hockey Canada or merely an advisor. He spoke before a special Commons-Senate committee studying Canada's role in international hockey in October 1977, one of many during three days of public hearings. The priest urged Canada to quickly decide on a plan for the 1980 Olympics or "we'll be setting our boys up for an embarrassment."

Compared to the budgets for Bauer's teams in 1964 and '68, the details of the 1980 financials would make an old priest blush. "Game Plan" was a federal funding agent for amateur athletes, and hockey qualified for the dough ($350,000) that was available through Sport Canada.

"We're gearing at those players who will not be offered the lucrative contracts. We want to enrol those players who will not make the National Hockey League until they are 24 or 25 years of age, if ever. With our alternative these players will compete for Canada in a top level brand of prestigious hockey, all the while getting their education at the college or university level," Hockey Canada governor Georges Larivière told the *Globe and Mail*. "When they finished a three- or four-year segment of the program they could then go to professional hockey, benefiting from what we had to offer."

Larivière saw the program continuing past 1980 and preached patience. "The program is new and it will be a slow process before it is fully operational," Larivière added. "In Canada we have elite hockey players but no elite hockey training program. This is what we want to install. Putting our best hockey players together does not necessarily mean we are going to win. We will be putting able hockey players together for a three- or four-year period and subjecting them to an elite training program. We should receive good results."

Holmes, with his experience abroad, was installed as the overseer of Canadian international hockey, a super scout of sorts, tasked with keeping track of Canadian talent across the globe. His title for the 1980 team was technical coordinator. In 1978, he addressed the difficulties he was facing with commitments. "In picking players for the Olympic team we would have to consider whether they are likely to remain amateurs until the Olympics in Lake Placid," he said. "We might petition the National Hockey League and World Hockey Association to let some of their draft choices stay with us instead of signing them to professional contracts and sending them to the minor leagues. I think the pros know that hockey in Europe is of the calibre that would help the development of these boys."

Father Bauer's noble experiment started up in August 1978, involving roughly 150 junior and college players with Olympian dreams at three tryout locations—Upper Canada College in Toronto, the University of Alberta in Edmonton, and Laval University in Quebec City. Writer Roy MacGregor talked to the priest about getting the program going again. "I remember thinking as the committee interviewed me, 'How can I adequately answer these questions?' Surely all the answers were to be found in how we'd put together that original team," Bauer told McGregor. "You know, I always hoped somewhere along the line what we were trying to do back then would surface again. . . . I hope that the philosophy would be needed again. I think we are now at that point."

"We have a tremendous amount of work to do on the skill levels of the players," Father Bauer told Donald Ramsay of the *Globe and Mail*, "because a lot of our players are not going to be first, second or third-round draft choices. To compensate we must stay together five or six months in a training-camp atmosphere and this is what we're planning prior to the Olympics. We will not dominate anyone in Lake Placid, and we must work on patterns to offset the strong points of the stronger teams. It's an exciting challenge and we will be ready when the time comes. We must stress the team approach and develop our systems on that basis. It's the only way we will be successful."

But it was the same old story—the NHL was not a fan of the Olympic program. Players who would have contributed to the success of the '80 team left both early and late in the process. When camp opened in August 1979 in Calgary, news stories talked about top-ranked junior players, Laurie Boschman of the Brandon Wheat Kings and Paul Reinhart of the Kitchener Rangers. "They're two of the top underagers in the country," said co-coach Lorne Davis at the time. "We're happy to have them here. When I was scouting I thought there may be only five underaged players who could make this team. They're two of the best."

Neither would suit up for Canada in the Games. The NHL draft occurred in August that year, because of the redistribution of WHA talent, and seven players from the Nats were taken. Three struck around: Kevin Maxwell of the University of North Dakota, chosen by the Minnesota North Stars; Glenn Anderson of Denver, who was picked by the Edmonton Oilers; and Tim Watters of Michigan Tech, a Winnipeg Jets pick. Vincent Tremblay of the Quebec Remparts was drafted by Toronto and bailed on the Olympic program, along with Boschman (to the Leafs) and Reinhart (to the Atlanta Flames). Dan Makuch of Ottawa was taken by the Rangers, but didn't make the Nats.

At least Boschman and Tremblay left early in the process, just three weeks in. Goaltending would prove to be an Achilles heel for the Canadians.

Reinhart was from Kitchener, and Father Bauer knew his family. He wavered a few times, and went with the team to the Rudé Právo Cup in Prague, and then wanted to come home. "It was a surprise to me. We knew that he was wavering at the beginning, but then when he went with us to the Rudé Právo tournament in Czechoslovakia, which is where he played with us first, then we thought he'd be there," said Clare Drake. "You could tell he was going to be a key part of our team. Then when he waffled around and talked to the pro people, they kept putting pressure on him." Watt was less diplomatic: "It was like Father got stabbed in the back. There was a big rift there. Paul then went to Atlanta."

Chapter 23

IN THE SHADOW OF A MIRACLE

Today, it's known as the Miracle on Ice. In 1980 a bunch of American college kids banded together to knock off the mighty Soviet Union, the powerhouse of international hockey at the Olympic Games in Lake Placid. ABC announcer Al Michaels is remembered for his unforgettable line at the conclusion of the 4–3 win, "Do you believe in miracles? Yes!"

It wasn't even the gold medal game. That occurred two days later, when the Americans beat Finland, 4–2, to claim hockey supremacy—well, amateur anyway—for the first time since the 1960 Games in Squaw Valley, where the red, white, and blue rode a hot goalie, Jack McCartan, to victory. The 1980 golden game drew 32.8 million fans, a U.S. viewership record that stood until the 2010 Olympic hockey final with USA versus Canada in Vancouver.

Like the United States, Canada had sent a collection of college kids to the Olympics, to face the grizzled men from Russia, Sweden, and Czechoslovakia.

But for a very, very bad bounce, it could have been the Canadians atop the podium. *Really.* The Canadians, with a team put together by Father Bauer and his Holy Trinity of coaches—Clare Drake, four-time Canadian collegiate championship coach with the University of Alberta Golden Bears; Tom Watt, with eight Canadian titles at the University of Toronto; and Lorne Davis, with his NHL experience and 30 years of hockey lessons—came awfully close to beating the Russians. But, as they say, close only counts in horsehoes and hand grenades.

The players from the 1980 Canadian Olympic team have come to terms with the Miracle that wasn't theirs. They've had to. "I hear about it all the time," said Tim Watters, who lives in Arizona. "I don't think there could be a better thing for hockey in North America at the time. . . . Hockey was thrown to the forefront and it really brought along so much growth of the game. That's one of the reasons that I'm in the U.S. I still help coach down here."

A number of the U.S. players turned pro, and a handful enjoyed long-lasting NHL success: Ken Morrow, a New York Islanders draft pick as the team came of age, Neal Broten, Mike Ramsey, Mark Johnson, and Dave Christian. Only their coach, Herb Brooks, who had played for the U.S. in the 1964 and 1968 Olympics, is in the Hockey Hall of Fame (though assistant coach/GM Craig Patrick will probably go in one day as well).

The Canadian squad, however, can boast of far more professional success: Glenn Anderson is in the Hockey Hall of Fame as one of the greatest goal scorers of his generation; Dr. Randy Gregg has five Stanley Cup rings and a medical degree; Jim Nill played nine years in the NHL and is the general manager of the Dallas Stars after apprenticing for years in Detroit; Paul MacLean potted 324 NHL goals before moving into coaching, being nominated once for the Jack Adams Award as coach of the year before winning it in 2013; and Tim Watters lined up on D for the Jets and Kings over 14 years. Other NHL careers were less impressive, but still notable: Don Spring (259 games), Dave Hindmarch (99), Kevin Maxwell (66), Ken Berry (55). A few, like Kevin Primeau and the goalies, Bob Dupuis and Paul Pageau, had just a cup of coffee in the bigs. From the coaching staff, Father Bauer is in the Hockey Hall of Fame, while Clare Drake and Tom Watt are definitive examples of the Hall's ignorance towards university hockey. (Think about basketball, can you imagine Dean Smith and John Wooden on the outside, looking in to the Naismith Basketball Hall of Fame?) Ultimately, three members of the 1980 Canadian squad, Warren Anderson, Gregg, and Watters, would again represent Canada in the Olympics, after the amateur rules had been loosened.

Dr. Gregg has given a lot of thought to the "what ifs." Had Canada prevailed in Lake Placid—despite a sixth-place finish, it's not all that far-fetched—what would have happened to the players? "Would we have all signed professional contracts? Would most of us not made the profession? Would we have given up opportunities to go back to school and do things?" mused Gregg. "The Miracle on Ice for the Americans was a miracle because they hosted it, they had struggled being a team throughout the whole year, they weren't particularly friendly with each other. There were a lot of miracles, not necessarily just positive ones, that brought them through. To give them credit, of course, they came up big in the time they had to."

American goaltender Jim Craig might have been the most famous player at the time, but he played only 30 NHL games. Like many of his teammates, he found a calling after the Games, preaching teamwork at seminars and business conferences.

"I'm not sure many of us would want to be public speakers about a game that we won in the 1980s for the rest of our life," said Gregg. "There were many things that we wanted to do . . . and maybe part of that was Father Bauer's idea that you can get more out of life than if you're simply a hockey player."

The fact is, despite the disappointing finish, members of Team Canada 1980 remain steadfast in their belief that it was a great experience, and for some who didn't go pro, it remains the pinnacle of their hockey days.

The lasting bonds, were formed in Rig 80—named for the Olympic quest. It was collection of 10-by-24-foot Atco trailers that had housed a drilling crew on an Arctic oil rig in the MacKenzie River Valley and donated by Nabors Drilling Co., of Edmonton. The trailers were plunked down at the back door of the Calgary Stampede Corral, in the heart of the city. For the players and staff, they could roll out of bed and go to work.

"It really brought the team together," said Gregg, the captain. There was a rec-room trailer, a wash-up trailer, a sleeping trailer. "When you live together, there's not much else that you can do than become a real team, a family."

Brad Pirie agreed. "You either had to love everybody or you'd have World War III going on. When I look back, it was probably one of the most memorable parts of the experience, was living there, because we were all just so close."

Aches and pains could be heard through the thin walls. Particularly achy was defenceman Terry O'Malley, the ultimate Bauer Boy, who'd played with him since St. Michael's College, right through the Nats and Japan. He'd been summoned from Notre Dame College in Wilcox, where he was teaching, as a last-minute replacement for the departed Paul Reinhart. The 39-year-old O'Malley hadn't played competitive hockey in a year and worked his butt off to get in shape for his third Olympic Games—12 years after his second.

"He was a pretty motivating character because, I mean, we were all in our early 20s . . . and he was friggin' old, that's all we knew!" said Pirie (the average age on that team was 22). "He was a motivating guy because you're looking at him, he'd come in at night for practice and he'd just be hurting like you wouldn't believe. Because it's not easy to compete at that level after you've been off for a couple of years. . . . He could hardly walk at night."

There was a ritual that helped the team come together. When they went to Czechoslovakia, the participants got beautiful crystal snifters as presents from their hosts. The fragile snifters that survived the trip home were around the trailer. O'Malley was partial to drink before bed. "In the evening to help him mellow out, he'd pour a big shot of brandy into the snifter, and he'd circle it around, and he'd hold court," said Pirie. Technically, O'Malley wasn't the oldest in the trailer, because co-coach Lorne Davis, the first hired, also lived there, as did team doctor Dr. Geoff Thomas and trainer Dave Bodnar.

Though Father Bauer didn't arrange the accommodations, they fit into his philosophy, said Tom Watt. "Father wasn't one to spoil the players," he said. "We were fed out of the Round-Up Centre. Clare and I had apartments. I didn't bring my wife or my kids. I had an apartment within walking distance of the Stampede grounds, and so did Clare." Watt and Drake had taken leaves from their respective universities, Toronto and Alberta, and a brewery, Molson, stepped in with cash to subsidize Drake's sabbatical.

The three-headed coaching trio had issues, said Barry MacKenzie, a retired defenceman brought in as a guest coach. For example, he describes a teaching session about properly receiving the puck off the boards.

"When I played, it was, 'Here's what you do. Period.' There's no options," recalled MacKenzie. "So Tom would get out there and say, 'No, no, coming around, the puck comes around the boards, you take it off your skate, and you pick the puck up over here.' Clare would say, 'No, no, no, you turn like this here.' And then Davis would say, 'No, no, no, here.' So the three of them were telling you how to do something and none of them would agree on anything." MacKenzie says he remembers thinking, "Holy shit, this team is in trouble."

Father Bauer had taken a leave from St. Mark's College as well, and stayed at a nearby Basilian House, where the Bow and Elbow rivers meet in town. Bill Hay, a Hockey Canada director with business interests in Calgary, often drove him to the arena. Perched up high, looking down on the action, the priest was a familiar sight. "The man haunts the practice sessions like some inquisitive, presbyter rink rat," wrote Wayne Skene in his lengthy feature on the team, "The Unpaid Boys of Winter," that ran in the Southam newspaper chain. "Dressed in his familiar, dark blue parka, complete with fur trim, Father David Bauer cruises among the vacant arena seats, appearing for a moment behind the players' bench, watching his team struggle through its drills. A few minutes later he emerges high up in the dimly lit stands, pausing to write his thoughts in the ever-present notebook—recording personal tendencies, plots for future strategies."

Watt and Drake said that Bauer let the coaches to do the coaching—for the most part. But he was still an educator. Father would assign readings. "We used to meet in the Basilian House and he would give us things to read and we would discuss the players," said Watt. "One I remember was Solzhenitsyn's address to the graduating class at Harvard about freedom."

For the 1978–79 year, there were many players on Olympic scholarships at various Canadian universities. They'd get together regularly for camps in different parts of the country, and then be tossed together as a touring national team, competing across Canada, drumming up interest. The summer camp, however, helped the coaches figure out who would be the perfect fit for the 1980 Games. Injuries made some cuts easier than others.

Rather than playing for Canada, Larry Riggin, who had injured his knee, ended up back at the University of Alberta, and led the Golden Bears to another CIAU title as the captain. "Frankly, I had a better year than they did, because they did very poorly," he said.

It was after the Golden Bears won the CIAU championship, in 1979, that Father Bauer made the decision to make Randy Gregg—the CIAU Player of the Year, and at six foot four and 215 pounds, the biggest player on the team—the captain, a year in advance of the Olympics. It didn't sit well with everyone, since Gregg was often away with his medical training. Gregg was seen as the exemplar for the priest who preached a balance between hockey and education. "Being the captain doesn't necessarily mean it's a popularity contest," said Tim Watters. "Randy, in my eyes, he was the right person to wear the 'C.'" The CIAU, under its current name of U Sports, now presents the Dr. Randy Gregg Award to reward excellence as a student-athlete.

Following two years of camps and tryouts, the team was whittled down to 23 core players. Having seen the difficulties earlier Bauer Boys had balancing school and hockey, those in university—17 of them—were encouraged to take a break. Seven others already had degrees, with a few pursuing advanced degrees, like the future Dr. Gregg.

"We thought at first that the players would be able to continue their college careers while preparing for the Olympics but we didn't have the time on our hands we thought we would," Davis told the *Toronto Sun* in October 1979. "Besides all the tournaments and exhibition games, we're doing extensive testing both on and off the ice. We test for weaknesses on the ice and for physical deficiencies off the ice."

Advancements in the understanding of athletics and the human body made for a much better-conditioned Canadian team than their 1960s brothers—the University of Alberta's department of physical education made sure of it. Still, they constantly played catch-up to the Russians, the undisputed czars of physical fitness.

The touring teams—the Canada Reds and Canada Whites—were a surprising moneymaker, playing across the country against WHA and NHL franchises, junior teams, or touring squads like Dynamo Moscow.

As with Winnipeg and the Nats from 1965–1969, the Olympians were the only big-league team in Calgary, and support from the fans was undoubtedly a factor in the Flames uprooting from Atlanta after the Lake Placid Games. For many games, the Corral would be packed with 6,000 people—and when the Maple Leafs played the Nats, 7,300 were shoehorned in. A big part of the success came from the support of local business. Doug Mitchell, a former CFL player (and future league commissioner) turned lawyer, was in charge of the board of directors of the Canadian Olympic hockey team.

"Community interest in the games was terrific," Mitchell told syndicated columnist Jim Coleman in January 1979. "We attracted fans who hadn't attended a hockey game in Calgary in many years. They were coming out of the woodwork."

The total budget for the Olympic hockey program between 1979 and 1980 was $1.1 million, with the federal government kicking in about $400,000. "Our philosophy is to keep within the hockey community without going to the government trough," said Chris Lang, Hockey Canada's full-time secretary-treasurer at the time. Corporate donations made up over $100,000, and Hockey Canada was, for the first time, proactive with its image, garnering another $100,000 from 16 licensees. The WHA, while it existed, and the NHL, contributed money. Alan Eagleson, executive director of the National Hockey League Players' Association, was also on board, and made sure the NHL players were, too. "I told Father (David) Bauer that as a Canadian, my obligations are to my country," said Eagleson in 1979. "If that means I have to pressure pro teams into playing against the Canadian Olympic team, I will."

Players had a $50-a-month training allowance, plus a $215-a-month living allowance. Married players got $50 a day for 75 days, as well as their training allowance. The stipends fit amateur rules enforced by the International Olympic Committee. In a CBC Radio interview just before the 1980 Games, general manager, Rick Noonan, said that the team would make close to $500,000 in gate receipts, exceeding initial projections five-fold. "It will certainly help the Canadian Olympic program continue on a comfortable note rather than having to worry every month whether [we're] going to be able to take on this project or do this project or that," said the GM. "The fact that our gate receipts have exceeded our expectations certainly encourages, I think, Hockey Canada and specifically the Olympic hockey program to seriously look at Calgary as being a definite home base in anything that might be undertaken in the future."

Looking back, Lang said the corporate aspect of international competition was not Father Bauer's strongpoint, so the decade of growth of Hockey Canada meant the team was on much better footing than any of the previous squads. "He was a funny guy because he didn't carry any power," said Lang, who was a part of Hockey Canada for 30 years, and knew Bauer from the days with the Nats in Winnipeg right up until the end of his life. Bauer was far better with players, said Lang, than corporate bigwigs.

During all the time he knew him, Lang believes, Bauer became more conservative—and more paranoid. "He was absolutely paranoid about people. He was absolutely paranoid his whole life about Al Eagleson. . . . I had, I don't know how many arguments with him about Eagleson or the people around, because he always thought they were loyal to Eagleson and not to him, which is bullshit," said Lang. "The big guys he really had trouble with, but he liked Tom Watt. . . . He always thought Watt was under the influence of Eagleson. . . . He was afraid he was under the influence of Eagleson and not him. I don't think Tom was under the influence of Bauer. I think you were under the influence or you weren't. You're either in or you're out. And when you're out, it doesn't mean you're totally out. I was, I think, the only guy who was on the fence. I wasn't in but I wasn't out. I was around because I controlled the budgets, and I controlled the agenda to a degree as the secretary of Hockey Canada. So he had to put up with me."

O'Malley said that Father Bauer often quipped, "If things are going too well, it is time to look over your shoulder." The O'Malleys, Debby and Terry, bought him a poster that read: "Just because you're paranoid, doesn't mean they're not after you . . ."

The media still felt an affinity to Father Bauer, with old pro scribblers such as Jim Coleman once again seeking him out, celebrating his "utopian plan" of a national team "composed of starry-eyed amateurs." Drake was appreciative that the media first went to Father Bauer, allowing the three coaches to stay "off the radar a little bit."

Heading into the Olympics, things were looking good for the Canadians. The fast, energetic, youthful team (aside from O'Malley) had defeated pro clubs from Houston, Edmonton, Winnipeg, and Toronto, and was competitive in the other games. There was little concern over the Americans, whom the Nats had beaten five times, and lost to twice in exhibition action.

Hockey Canada's Lou Lefaive tried to put things in perspective for *Sun* readers before the real games started: "The fact is that people have watched how well the pros have fared internationally over the last several years and they've come to realize, 'Heh, Father Bauer's teams of '64–'68 didn't do that much worse . . . maybe there's something to be said for a group of young players working together and aiming for a short series.' It's a different game, a different mentality. We're looking for guys who can peak instead of guys with the stamina to play 80 games. We want a different kind of hockey player."

The team's weakness, as the Olympics approached, was clearly goaltending. "We could not get a quality goaltender. We spent the whole year trying to get somebody," said Drake. "Father Bauer had made an initial judgment that a player that he was familiar with would be able to do the job, but it didn't turn out that way."

Three goalies were in the mix. One was Ronnie Patterson, who had played with the University of British Columbia Thunderbirds. Though young, he was a Father Bauer loyalist, seeing a surrogate dad in Bauer, as his own had died when he was a youth. He stayed true, even after being dropped just before the Olympics, travelling from BC to Ontario to see Bauer in his final days.

The hopes of the national team lay on the slim shoulders of Bob

Dupuis, a 27-year-old senior from North Bay, Ontario. He stuck with the team through thick and thin, and earned the right to be the number one goalie. In a syndicated column, Coleman said that Dupuis was not ready to be labelled "sensational," but he hung in there. "He played three games in three nights against Washington and Toronto. He gave up 15 goals but he stopped enough rubber to provide girdles for all the overweight ladies in Calgary," wrote Coleman.

Paul Pageau, however, was a surprise as a backup. "I flew in for games here at the pre-Olympic tournament in December and I flew out to Calgary for a couple of games there," Pageau said just prior to the Games. "I guess I wasn't really part of the team, but it didn't bother me. These guys are really great and I get along with people pretty easily." Pageau had been playing in Shawinigan, and had attended a New York Rangers camp as an overage junior. Did Father Bauer's known penchant for nationalism play a part in the addition of Pageau, the only French Canadian on the team?

"We should have named Ronnie Patterson. He was the type of goaltender that the team really wanted to play in front of," recalled Noonan. "I think it was the first time that I witnessed Father Dave become very concerned. His nationalism took over. We never really did have anybody from Quebec, and this Paul Pageau who was playing in Shawinigan was standing on his head in the Quebec league. We were kind of, not forced, but put in a corner where we had to give him a shot." Pageau just did not fit in with the team. "He never bought into the team. I felt sorry for him."

As for Dupuis, something went wrong, said Noonan. "Bob Dupuis was outstanding until we got to the Olympics, and then he just . . . I don't know . . ."

The tournament was divided into two groups: Red, made up of Canada, USSR, Japan, Poland, Holland, Finland; and Blue, with the Americans, Czechoslovakia, Sweden, Norway, Romania, and West Germany. With 12 teams, there was some difficulty scheduling practice time, meaning some early-morning and late-at-night workouts on ice that were occasionally shared with figure skaters.

In the round-robin format, the top two countries from each group advanced to the medal round. Bauer correctly predicted that the

February 16 game against Finland would mean everything. "Being realistic, we have to look at the bronze," Bauer told Wayne Parrish of the *Montreal Gazette*. "If we beat the Finns, we should come out of our group with the Russians. I think the Czechs and, the way they're playing, the Americans will come out of the other group, which would mean we'd have to beat the Americans for the bronze."

What no one guessed, though, is that the Soviets would seem so beatable, with both the Finns and Canadians poking the Russian Bear, and ultimately leaving it wounded for the famed Miracle in the medal round.

With wins over two of the weaker teams in the group, Netherlands (10–1) and Poland (5–1), Canada went into its bout with Finland confident. Then came Dupuis' faux pas.

At 17:07 of the second period, Finland's Jukka Koskilahti shot the puck from behind his own blue line. The puck slid 150 feet down the ice, and both Watters and Spring left it for Dupuis to handle. He whiffed. Deflated, Canada lost 4–3. Dupuis wouldn't even look into the stands to make eye contact with his father.

Like Gregg, Glenn Anderson lived the highs of the NHL after the lows of 1980. He knows the experience helped him as a hockey player, but that doesn't make it easier. "That was very painful because basically you trained for eight months, four hours a day, for that one moment in the game—and for the puck to go through our goalie's legs, it was just so devastating. I cried for like three days after that."

Drake spoke for the coaching group, defending its choice of Dupuis over Pageau. "It wasn't a sentimental choice, even if Bob has been with us ever since we went to training camp," said Drake after the game. "We had confidence in Dupuis."

"Looking back, and I've looked back a lot, we should have spent more time getting a goaltender," Davis told Steve Simmons of the *Toronto Sun* in 2005, just two years before his passing. "You couldn't really blame Bobby. He played really well for us. He was probably just the wrong guy for the job."

"It's a tough thing, because Bob Dupuis was an excellent goalie. He had an injury issue and he wasn't talking about it," said Pirie, referring to the keeper's suspected hand ailment.

Still, Canada wasn't eliminated. It beat Japan 6–0 and had a game against the Russians, whom the Finns had battled tooth and nail. The Finns were actually up 1–0 in the second period and 2–1 in the third, but unable to hold on, the Soviets winning 4–2, scoring three goals in 79 seconds.

Against the USSR on February 20, Pageau got the start for the Nats. The Canadians jumped ahead with goals by Jim Nill, Randy Gregg, and Brad Pirie, to just one, by Helmut Balderis. "We didn't seem to show any lack of confidence," said Captain Gregg. "I think the only time we saw that was maybe at the end of the second period against the Russians, the game we were up 3–1 with about three minutes to go in the second period, they scored their second goal. Really, it's the only time that I've been in a dressing room where I felt that kind of concern of questioning one's self. . . . It was arguably the best hockey team in the world at that point. They'd just scored a goal at the most dangerous time, at the end of the period. We still went out and played strongly, I thought. I don't think that it affected our game, but that 15 minutes in the dressing room struck me as odd in that we just seemed to, not looking behind our back, but just being a little bit more nervous than we had been in other games."

Alexei Kasatonov's goal, another dribbler with only 13 seconds left in the second, had the Canadians hanging their heads between periods.

Given the wisdom of time, and years in the Edmonton Oiler dressing room with such legends as Gretzky, Messier, and Fuhr, Gregg has a pretty good handle on the situation. "I think we all realized that we were a bunch of young Canadian amateur college players going against the best team in the world. Overwhelming. . . . I think it affected our players, as I said, but I think we realized the scope of the next 20 minutes when we got back on the ice."

In the opening minutes of the third, Boris Mikhailov and Alexander Golikov scored 12 seconds apart, giving the Soviets a 4–3 lead. There was a bit of controversy after the Soviets' third goal, as the Canadian bench protested the hook of Golikov's stick, and asked referee Jim Neagles for a measurement; Golikov left the ice before his stick could be measured, so Neagles let it go.

Dan D'Alvise tied it for Canada, but then Mikhailov scored the winner midway through the final period; a second goal by Golikov made for a 6–4 final. Hal Sigurdson of the *Winnipeg Free Press* reported from Lake Placid: "The Canadians played well enough to put at least a small dent in the Soviets' aura of invincibility. Frequently, they anticipated Soviet passes and intercepted them. They forechecked with an intensity which occasionally created confusion in the Soviet end."

Golikov's stick was a noted distraction. "His goal would have counted whether the stick was illegal or not," said Davis. "But it was definitely illegal. He should have got a two-minute penalty. After the game No. 6 [Valeri Vasiliev] traded sticks with one of our players. We measured it in the dressing room and it was illegal. Both Golikov brothers (Alexander and Vladimir) were playing with hooks much bigger than that."

In the postmortem, Drake said his team ran out of gas, outmuscled by the bigger, better-conditioned Soviets. "For a while there in the second period we had them running around pretty good."

In a Canadian Press story marking 35 years after the Olympics, the current GM of the Dallas Stars, Jim Nill, said the team was oh-so-close to beating the Soviets: "It's a game that could've gone either way. I think that game kind of showed that you know what, boy, these guys, they can be beat. We might've softened up the Russians a little bit, also. It was a high-intense, physical game. I think that put a little doubt maybe in the Russians, also."

After the loss, Father Bauer entered the Canadian dressing room. Centreman Dan D'Alvise called it "the most emotional moment of the year." Tears flowed instead of champagne. "Everyone was drained after the game. Nobody spoke in the dressing room for quite a while," said Drake after. "There's so little you can say when victory is within your grasp and then it slips away."

There was still a tiny chance of advancing, since Finland was playing Holland, and an upset by the Dutch, a team composed of many Dutch-Canadians, would put Canada through to the medal round. But Finland won with ease, 10–3. Though Canada and Finland had identical 3–2 records (the Finns were surprised by Poland, 5–4, in the opener), the Finns advanced based on the head-to-head victory.

A fifth-place game against Czechoslovakia loomed for the Canadians, but no one cared; they lost 6–1 and were wowed by the three Stastny brothers, Marian, 27; Peter, 23; and 20-year-old Anton, who combined for four goals in the first period and another in the third.

As for the actual medals in Lake Placid, the round-robin continued into the second round, with only the points the advancing teams earned against other finalists counting in the new, four-team standings. Convoluted? Sure. The issue was that the IIHF had decided that all participating nations compete for the medal awards in the games, rather than just a top pool.

Coaches encouraged their teams to run up the score against patsy foes to increase the likelihood of advancing. Since the U.S. and Sweden had tied, 2–2, each country took a point into the next round; the USSR had two; Finland none. The United States, by beating Russia (4–3) and Finland (4–2), finished with five points, one ahead of the USSR and three ahead of Sweden, the bronze medalist.

Post-Olympics, there was no federal commission exploring "the failure of Canadian hockey." The heart was there—but the game is also a cruel mistress. Just ask Bob Dupuis.

There was talk of a high-calibre, 16-team university league that would house the players for future national team efforts, but nothing came of it. At the time, O'Malley thought it would work: "If we can have a super hockey league in the colleges, we'll do better. We need something higher than junior hockey and a little less than professional hockey. This was a seat-of-the-pants operation."

In April, a disheartened Canadian team went to the Sweden Cup in Gothenburg, and didn't win a game. It even had a goalie with plenty of national team experience, Wayne Stephenson of the playoff-missing Washington Capitals. He'd been there at the end of the 1960s, and noted the differences in the European teams. "The Czechs are pretty much the same as the Russians, but the Swedes and Finns have changed," said Stephenson at the time. "The Swedes would never bodycheck—now they play more aggressively, and the Finns are a much stronger team than I expected."

Hockey Canada's Lefaive said the national team would take the place of playoff-less NHLers at the World Championships and at such events as the Izvestia Tournament. "It's pretty well agreed," he said. "To the extent that we can do it, the pros are not interested in doing it." Politics, and not hockey politics, helped end that talk; the Canada Cup scheduled for the fall of 1980 was put on hiatus on the heels of the boycott of the Moscow Olympics. It took place in 1981, but whatever funding the Canadian national team would have received from the gate in 1980 was gone.

The world had changed, noted Bob Hanley in his column in the *Hamilton Spectator*. It was time to give up on the Great Experiment, the Noble Dream. "Hopefully, the slaughter of Canadian hockey innocents abroad, in top-level international competition, is ended forever. Everybody hoped, everybody tried, but simple dedication was not enough," he wrote. "The man who dared most to dream . . . and to infect others with his beliefs and enthusiasm . . . was Father David Bauer, a very dear man, a very articulate one, who was able to convince the government and private supporters to give the old senior amateur idea just one more fling. . . . A few of the players from that squad may find professional employment, but by-and-large, the operation was a $900,000 exercise in running fragile heads against thick brick walls."

After the games in Lake Placid, Father Bauer sat down with Allen Abel of the *Globe and Mail*. He didn't offer excuses as much as an assessment: "The experiment has been fulfilled from the over-all point of view."

It was, after all, about more than hockey. "The whole rationale was to provide another option wherein some form of education could be involved, wherein some experiences other than hockey might be a part of human growth," he said.

There is little doubt the players grew from the experience.

Quoted in *How Hockey Explains Canada*, Paul MacLean credits the Olympic program for making his pro career possible. "That year probably made a difference between me playing in the NHL or not. Without it I may have remained a minor league pro at best. That year the ice time and the quality of workouts and practice time were key. I learned the intelligence part of the game. The IQ part of it was really enhanced in that year," he said, adding that Father Bauer cautioned the players to be proper young men, carrying themselves honourably, curbing foul language. "He had a certain way that he liked to play too. He thought the game was supposed to be played in a gentlemanly way. We were not to get carried away or dirty, like typical Canadian hockey can sometimes be. He frowned on fisticuffs."

After the Games, Watters was approached by Winnipeg Jets GM John Ferguson about signing a contract. He went home to Kamloops, BC, sat at the kitchen table with his mom and dad, and opted to return to Michigan Tech and catch up on his schooling. The NHL would be there in another year.

Graduating "was high on my priority list. I wanted to get a degree," Watters said. "It was my experience with Father Bauer and the national program that gave me that confidence that I could turn that contract down that year and go back to school for a year. That's the year that prepared me for my professional career, there's no question about it."

As for Glenn Anderson, he was easily the best player on the team, and Bauer knew it—Anderson didn't go to Russia for the pre-Olympic tournament lest the Russkies get a sense of his skills. The Hockey Hall of Famer speaks highly of Father Bauer, calling him a great mentor. "He basically comes into play every day of my life, his methods of thinking and psychology and how to approach life—always look at it from all angles," said Anderson. "Hockey's not the only thing that you can do in the world, there's so many other options that you have, so basically his philosophy was fantastic for driving me to become the person I am today."

In the end, Father Bauer's boys couldn't muster a miracle. Typically, he was able to set aside the disappointment, and later cracked: "Just think, if you guys could have scored a few goals against the Finns, I'd be a Cardinal by now."

Chapter 24

IN THE TWILIGHT

It's oddly fitting that Father David Bauer died in an Olympic year. Especially with the 1988 Winter Games in Calgary, and many of the hockey games played in an arena that now bore his name. The Father David Bauer Olympic Arena, originally named the Foothills Arena, and rechristened in 1986 after its ice surface was enlarged to international proportions, is the most obvious of his legacies.

There is also the Quest Program, which Father Bauer initially set up to serve students and teachers in Catholic education at Notre Dame College, in Wilcox, Saskatchewan. Part of the early funding came from an honorarium for his contributions to hockey in Japan. The program now runs in Ontario. "The Quest Program was really to fulfill a need that Father Bauer thought he had ignored so much because of his hockey involvement," said Terry O'Malley. "The Quest Program was about communicating faith in the modern electronic age. He was concerned with that aspect of what was going on in the world." Part of its funding came from the sale of the Bauer family cottage in Goderich.

Students can also seek a bursary in his name at St. Michael's College and scholarships at the University of British Columbia. The Father David Bauer Cup is an Alberta competition for teenage hockey teams. Father David Bauer Drive in downtown Waterloo, Ontario, used to be Civic

Drive; years ago, it was the site of a Seagram distillery warehouse where Rod Seiling, from the 1964 Nats, used to work as a teen and now calls home in a condominium. "It's the first place I worked and now I end up living in this building on a street named after Father Dave," Seiling said.

In 1979, the Father David Bauer High School Hockey Classic tournament in Toronto was the brainchild of Father Ted McLean, the principal at Father Henry Carr Separate School. Bauer and McLean's history dated to St. Michael's College; that they stayed friends through the years, even with Bauer based on the west coast, is perhaps a testament to something more than just a bond from the dressing room.

Coming to Toronto in his later years, Father Bauer dialled up Ross Morrison, one of the original Nats, and wondered about getting together, bringing Father McLean along. Morrison suggested the St. George's Golf Club, where he was a member. Tipping off the maître d' that he was expecting friends, two priests, Morrison was surprised to be asked to meet them at the door.

Without their clerical collars, they didn't look like men of the cloth. "I go to the front door and they've got the black suits on, plaid shirts. I said, 'Father, what's the deal with the . . . ?' He said, 'We didn't know if they would be acceptable here.' I said, 'Now I've got to get you a tie.' We kept a bunch of ties in the cloakroom. So I got them some crummy ties to go with those plaid shirts," Morrison said. A few drinks led to a few more, which eventually led to the cognac. "I said to the bartender, 'Bring over that bottle of cognac and just drop it here.' I think we put a pretty good dent in it."

Father Bauer made an effort to visit old friends and teammates wherever he was in the country, and it wasn't always to bum a ride somewhere.

Former Major Les Kozak was essentially Father's driver in the summer of 1961, just before the priest's reassignment to St. Mark's College. "We'd go somewhere and he would meet people. He always had fascinating, mysterious people that he would meet and spend 15 minutes, a half hour, an hour, talking to about some item that I didn't know what the subject matter was. Then we would head back. It was a wonderful, relaxing experience and great for me," said Kozak, who later worked as a scientist in Poland.

For the record, Bauer did have a driver's license. Besides the constant travel across the country and around the world, there are apparently other reasons he didn't always hop behind the wheel.

NHL vice-president Jim Gregory called Father Bauer, "the most spectacular person I ever met. . . . He married my wife and I. Our son is named after him. Everything I have to say about him, it would put you to sleep it's just so good. No negative stuff that I can think of. Except once, he was driving the car and he ticked another car . . ."

Morrison remembers going to the Bauer family cottage in Bayfield, Ontario, on the shores of Lake Huron. Father Bauer was admiring Morrison's car, and asked to take it for a spin. "He gets in and turns it on. In those days, when you turned it on, the aerial in the rear would come up. So he drives it under a tree and it just snaps the aerial. That night there's a huge storm and a branch goes right through the front windshield. . . . I'm driving back to Toronto and I've got this big hole in the windshield, the aerial is hanging off the side. 'I'll pay for it, I'll pay for it,' he says."

In 1984, the UBC Thunderbird Hockey Alumni Society established the Father Bauer hockey scholarships and awards at the school, with his blessing. Father Bauer never really gave up his coaching card with the T-Birds, and was often around the team, watching games and offering inspirational words in the dressing room. Bill Holowaty was one of Canada's best university hockey players, twice named Canada West MVP (1982 and 1985). "On a daily basis, [Bauer] wasn't on the ice, but he was in the rink all the time, he was around in meetings," said Holowaty. "He was able to influence our hockey acumen on a regular basis through one-on-one meetings, being in and around the team. He would not have necessarily been responsible and on the scoresheet in terms of having his name there, but he was a significant influence at that time."

Rick Noonan called Bauer "teacher, coach, friend" in the inaugural address for the scholarship. "As a coach, Father Bauer taught commitment, loyalty and integrity through his coaching philosophies. His theory of coaching was 'to play to win but not at any price,'" said Noonan. "Father Bauer believed that if team players could discipline themselves in one area, they ought to be able to master themselves in other areas.

Success in all levels of sport 'should not be an end but a means to an end' according to Father Bauer. Many players who experienced Father Bauer's coaching went on to be successful both in professional hockey and, more importantly, professional life and contributed to their respective communities."

Though Cam Kerr, who took Bauer's place on the trip to China to coach hockey, cannot truly confirm that the conversation happened, it is a fun story. Imagine Father Bauer chatting with Ernie "Punch" McLean, the colourful, profane coach for eons in New Westminster, BC. McLean was bragging about the hockey players he had sent to the pros, like Stan Smyl, Brad Maxwell, and Barry Beck. McLean asked how many professionals Bauer coached. "We have countless professionals—lawyers, doctors, teachers," was the reply.

Terry O'Malley didn't earn the nickname "Plato" for his partying lifestyle. He trusted his life to Father Bauer, from St. Michael's to the 1980 Olympic team, with Japan, Notre Dame College, and more in between. "Father Bauer, his prayer was that no one would be left wanting from the fact that they gave up their professional careers to be a part of this program," recalled O'Malley. "So if you go through your list there, I think you'll find that most people have done very well with their life."

A short list would include the lawyers: Gary Begg, Roger Bourbonnais, Paul Conlin, Fran Huck, Steve Monteith, Herb Pinder and Ken Dryden; educators: Terry O'Malley, Barry MacKenzie, Morris Mott, Hank Akervall; doctors: Randy Gregg, Jim Irving. Some of the miscellany is also fun, from the accountant Ray Cadieux; to Bob Forhan, who became Mayor of Newmarket, Ontario; to Jean Cusson, who runs one of the biggest sausage companies in North America.

Even those who went into professional hockey after their days with the Nats ended up in decent jobs outside the game. Or in it, like general managers Marshall Johnston and Jim Nill. Just about all have coaching experience, whether it's with their own kids, or in the NHL like Paul MacLean, or even in Asia, where Steve Carlyle coached the Chinese women's national team.

Brian Conacher was a player, coach, general manager, and arena manager, and worked in the media. He was fortunate to spend some final time with Father Bauer, including a 1987 Canada Cup game, the Soviets against Sweden, at Hamilton's Copps Coliseum. During the 1988 Winter Olympics, Conacher was the colour commentator on CBC Radio's broadcast of hockey games. He wrote about a last interview in his second book, *As the Puck Turns*:

> My most memorable interview of the hockey coverage was with Father Bauer, who still sat on the board of Hockey Canada and had attended some of the games. Alan Clark, head of CBC Radio Sports, became aware that Father Bauer was available, and knowing of my history with him was anxious for me to set up an interview. Because radio could be so informal, it was like a fireside chat. Father Bauer and I reminisced like old friends who hadn't seen each other for awhile. We talked about how far Canada's national hockey program had come since 1963, when he formed the first team. And the truth was, not very far. That year's Team Canada faced many of the issues and challenges the first team had struggled with. Hockey Canada, the CAHA and the NHL were still ambivalent, uncommitted and not united about how Canada should best be represented at the top level of international hockey.

Other than the direct impact he had on people, Father Bauer's belief that hockey and education could—and should—mix has left another legacy. Through his own decision to choose schooling over a path to pro hockey, and the fights with the National Hockey League to get players for the national team, Bauer was uniquely qualified to propel changes in the relationship between hockey and education.

Father Bauer wrote about his nephew's battles with the established system.

> Something of the character of the problem of junior hockey might be illustrated by the story of Bobby Bauer, the son of my brother Bob. When he was fifteen and playing midget hockey in Kitchener-Waterloo, he was drafted by the Niagara Falls

> Junior A team. His father wanted him to play his junior hockey in Kitchener or in Guelph so that he could remain at home, but neither father nor son had had anything to say about it. He had been drafted without knowing anything about it, Niagara Falls would not release him, and he could not play Junior A anywhere else. He wound up playing Junior B in Waterloo and when he finished his high school accepted a scholarship to Harvard University where he finally was awarded a travelling fellowship as Harvard's outstanding athlete and scholar and after a year in Europe returned to graduate school. Certainly not every case of a boy caught in this iniquitous system has turned out so happily. By what right do a group of junior operators, looking only to their own profit, determine that a fifteen-year-old boy must leave his home in order to play hockey at the level suited to his talents?

To Paul Conlin, sitting in his Ottawa office, it was a "noble cause" to "overcome the hockey system that required young kids at a very early age—and I'm not sure it's changed a whole lot even today—to choose between hockey and a continuing education."

In the Canadian Hockey League, the parent body overseeing the junior leagues of Ontario, Quebec, and Western Canada, education is now a part of the package. Two of the early proponents of changing the way education and junior hockey intertwined were—surprise, surprise—graduates of the Nats, brothers Herb and Gerry Pinder, who co-owned the WHL's Regina Pats from the summer of 1989 to January 1996. "When we took over the Pats, we instituted an education policy for two reasons—one, because we believed in it, and Herb and I had lived it; and two, because we were in competition to keep the best players with the U.S. colleges," said Gerry Pinder. "It was in our best interest to do it. We got severely criticized by the league commissioner and the other owners at the time when we did it. . . . That's largely the policy that they have today, is the one that we instituted in Regina. It's grown, and been refined, and it's better." In simple terms, the Pinders bribed the players to pay attention to school; it was $50 for each high school class passed, and $150 for each university-level course.

Today, many Canadian university hockey teams are stacked with graduates of the Canadian Hockey League. The three leagues, QMJHL, OHL and WHL, offer education, counselling, and career planning to players, who will have their education (tuition, textbooks, fees) funded at a post-secondary institution, which could be university or a trade school. There's an 18-month time limit on the cash-in—and a catch. Those who sign professional contracts with the NHL or AHL don't get the same ride. For the skaters still in high school, their progress is monitored on a regular basis. There is no doubt that many of the changes came as a response to top prospects being wooed by scholarships at American universities. As Herb Pinder said, "Father showed a different way."

Even Hockey Canada has an educational assistance program that was started in 1982 with funds from the 1981 Canada Cup open tournament. University coaches put forward names they think merit consideration, and a selection committee decides. The trio of arbiters the first year? Chairman Norman Wagner, Sam Pollock, formerly of the Canadiens, and Father Bauer.

Education, for Father Bauer, was a lifelong endeavour. After the Olympic program in 1980, he took some courses via correspondence from the Catholic Theological Union in Chicago, and Notre Dame University in South Bend, Indiana.

Father Bauer's influence on hockey waned in the 1980s. His attempts to keep the 1980 Olympic team together for a run at 1984 didn't work, and he was pushed aside from his role as steward of the program, despite having raised $400,000 from contacts for the road to the Games in Sarajevo. Stress from the fallout hospitalized him for the nerve-related disorder known as shingles.

The University of British Columbia paid tribute to Father Dave in a December 1983 oldtimers game, with Vancouver Canucks of the past playing against a bolstered UBC veterans team. How bolstered? Frank Mahovlich and Dave Keon came in to show their love and support for Bauer, and veteran NHLer Garry Monahan, fresh off time in Japan, played as a Thunderbird too. The 1,800 in attendance saw a goofy, fun game—goalie Dunc Wilson purposely scored on himself—but they also raised money for a Bauer scholarship. In a conversation with Dennis Feser of the *Vancouver Sun* at the game, Bauer was pleased by the scholarship, as "the costs of education are escalating." But more importantly, he seemed tickled pink at seeing old friends. "And the game shows the long-lasting value of friendship. That's one of the important things you get out of sport."

In 1985, former St. Mike's goaltender Gerry Cheevers asked Father to introduce him at his Hockey Hall of Fame induction. Cheevers wanted the priest because he met the criteria: "Who's important in your career."

Father Bauer's own induction into the Hockey Hall of Fame came posthumously. It was announced in March 1989, and he was enshrined on October 3, 1989, following a ceremony at the Toronto Convention Centre. R.W. Stevens read the citation and Father Bauer's brother, Ray, accepted the medal. Russian goaltending legend Vladislav Tretiak was also in that Class of 1989, and during the dinner, he approached the Bauer family and told them of his respect and appreciation for Father Bauer. The other name in the builder category that year was the executive director of the NHL Players' Association, Alan Eagleson.

The names of Eagleson and Father Bauer were tied throughout the years, especially as the Eagle gained power in international hockey circles. Chris Lang was a "lion tamer" in his role at Hockey Canada, and tried to keep the peace between the two distinctly different personalities. "He didn't trust Eagleson," Lang said of Bauer.

"We didn't have any grudges of any kind, but we had differences of opinion on everything," Eagleson said.

In 1997, the International Ice Hockey Federation Hall of Fame also honoured Father Bauer in Helsinki, Finland, as well as deceased Canadian hockey power brokers Gordon Juckes and Victor Lindquist in its inaugural induction class. The star of that induction day, though, was Canada's best-ever international goaltender, Seth Martin. Wearing a Team Canada jersey with "No. 1" sewn on the back, and his wife, Bev, with a Trail Smoke Eaters shirt, Martin gave thanks. "It's a really thrilling time to be back in Finland and meet some of the players you played against in the 1960s," said Martin, still celebrated by European fans.

Father Bauer was also part of the inaugural set of honourees for the Order of Canada. It was Canada's Centennial year, 1967, and The Advisory Council set out to honour those individuals "who had traditionally been excluded from such recognition," meaning sports and popular entertainment, as well as the traditional politicians, businesspersons, and artists. The Medal of Service went to hockey legend Maurice "Rocket" Richard, Father David Bauer, and golfing great Marlene Streit, who won the amateur titles of Australia, Britain, Canada, and the United States.

It would be fair to say that the new Order of Canada awards flew a little under the radar. Maurice Smith, grizzled veteran of the sports beat in Winnipeg, lamented after the 1968 Winter Olympics that there should be awards for the likes of Father Bauer and gold-medal-winning skier Nancy Greene. To his credit, he gave a mea culpa, and ran a letter from the Honourable Allan J. MacEachen, minister of National Health and Welfare, which gently chastised him, and mentioned that Greene, who sat on the bench during one of the 1968 Team Canada games in Grenoble, would be fêted in April 1969. "I am happy to be able to report these developments as I wholeheartedly endorse your views concerning the invaluable ambassadorial role which is played by Canadians such as Father Bauer and Miss Greene," wrote MacEachen. "I have had the pleasure of enjoying a close relationship with Father Bauer when he served as a member of the National Advisory Council and I was absolutely charmed by Miss Greene during her recent triumphant return to Ottawa. Both are most worthy recipients of awards under the Order."

Other organizations have also paid tribute to Father Bauer, including the Canadian Sports Hall of Fame (inducted in 1973), Waterloo County Sports Hall of Fame (1972), and the BC Hockey Hall of Fame (2009).

St. Michael's College in Toronto threw a fundraising dinner with Father Bauer as the guest of honour in April 1988. At the $75-a-plate event, Bauer mingled with his old teachers, students and friends. While on the podium, he donned a Majors hockey jersey. A memorial to Father Bauer was set up at the school in 1995.

Through the years, Father Bauer appeared a number of times on *Hockey Night in Canada* to talk about the national team program. During the Toronto Maple Leafs versus Edmonton Oilers game on November 12, 1988, play-by-play man Bob Cole talked over a graphic that appeared with 4:46 left in the first period. "The hockey world was saddened Wednesday with the death of Father David Bauer," said Cole. "The man was the founder and builder of Canada's national teams. Father Bauer gave much of his life to the sport and more especially to amateur hockey in Canada."

David Bauer's passing on Wednesday, November 9, 1988, at age 64, was not a surprise to those who knew him. He'd had surgery for a blockage of his pancreas in July 1987, and then it was revealed to be cancerous. As he fought pancreatic cancer, he went downhill throughout the year, and all his disciples did their best to be a part of those last months, whether through a letter, a phone call, or a visit. His final months were spent at the family cottage in Goderich; his last hours were spent at Alexandra Marine and General Hospital.

"In his last days Father Dave went through great suffering which he said he welcomed to prepare for death," Father Ted McLean told George Gross of the *Toronto Sun*. "He was quite willing to suffer as Jesus did for all of us. Never once did I hear him complain. He was always faithful to his family, his priesthood, his community, his students, his players, his friends and to the 'True Humanism' that he lived and taught."

Six of his former players made a road trip of it, and the photo of Ken Broderick, Marshall Johnston, Mike Smith, Mickey McDowell, Paul Conlin, and Roger Bourbonnais with Bauer, shrunken and grey-haired in a loose-fitting housecoat, leaning on a walker—"He was skin and bones," said Johnston—is at once sad and stirring. Terry O'Malley said his coach kept his sense of humour. "He reminded all of us that we are only TABs—temporarily able bodied," wrote O'Malley in his personal recollections on life with Father Bauer. "One time while visiting him at the hospital with Rick Noonan, the pain was especially severe, so he had us remove the crucifix from above the door to the foot of his bed where he could see it easily. Once in place, he gave it a particularly good Bauer scowl and we could see he was preparing for one of his 'encounters' with his Lord and Saviour. However, the nurse who came into the room as Rick was pounding the nail into the wall with his shoe gave us a 'you boys are a little odd' look."

On another occasion, O'Malley was there with some of the Bauer family, and Father Dave stopped breathing. "Everyone was really upset. They called in the priest to give the last rites. The priest begins to say the prayers for the dying at the foot of Father Bauer's bed, when, all of a sudden—'Uhhhh'—he gasps for breath. He sees the priest and he says, 'Get out of here. I'm not ready to go yet.' We all started to laugh."

How did he inspire such loyalty from so many people? "Father Bauer, he had something over us, whether it was the robe or what. I don't think so. He was just a man," said Terry Clancy, whose father, King Clancy, is in the Hockey Hall of Fame.

Dr. Randy Gregg, captain of that 1980 Canadian Olympic team, won five Stanley Cups as an Edmonton Oiler. Yet one of his most treasured photos isn't of Wayne Gretzky or Mark Messier. The children of Randy and Kathy Gregg were only two or three, and they didn't know who was at their house. "I did one thing at that point that I'd never done with anybody else. My young boys had been around Gretzky, Messier, and all the greatest, and I turned to Father Bauer and I said, 'Father, would you mind if I take a picture of my sons with you?' I never did that to anybody else, none of the great players. I just felt that someday . . . I want my sons to know who they were held by, because he was such a fantastic man."

The death of Father Bauer brought national attention and tributes from such iconic figures as *Globe and Mail* columnist Trent Frayne: "The personality of Father Bauer, who died yesterday, made a deep imprint on people. He was one of those of whom it is said, 'He can light up a room.' He had great energy, a calm presence, a quick smile and boundless enthusiasm. You couldn't walk away from him without having felt his impact."

Dave King, at the time the coach of Canada's Olympic hockey team, offered something different: "He was such an inspirational man. . . . For him, hockey was a means to an end to develop a better person."

The attention that came with his death, including an editorial in the *Kitchener-Waterloo Record*, would have made Father uncomfortable, wrote Archie McDonald in the *Vancouver Sun*. "Now that he is gone a man can tell the truth about Father David Bauer. The fact is he was as fine, as generous, and as caring a human being as ever walked into a hockey rink," he wrote. "If you would have put that in print while he was alive it would be with the knowledge that reading it would be excruciating agony for him. He treated personal publicity as if it were sin and to give him due praise caused genuine embarrassment."

What, then, would Father have made out of a family prayer service in Waterloo, two funerals, one at St. Basil's Roman Catholic Church in Toronto and one at St. Mary's Roman Catholic Church in Kitchener, and a separate memorial service in Vancouver at St. Mark's College?

Reverend T. James Hanrahan presented the homily in Toronto, and said that Bauer's association with hockey made him the most famous Basilian priest, ever. "There has never been a coach more concerned with team spirit, with developing a sense of mutual concern among his players," Father Hanrahan said. "Those who played with him became lifelong friends. During his illness, there was constant concern over the great number of people who wanted to see him, and people who he wanted to talk to one more time."

In Kitchener, Reverend Brian Higgins, who had known Dave Bauer at St. Michael's College, delivered the eulogy after the celebration of mass before 1,400 mourners. "His life was a challenge," Higgins said. "He dared to be a David who was inspired to meet the Goliaths of a materialistic society and put his life on the line again and again before God gave him rest." He was buried in the Bauer family plot at Mount Hope Cemetery in Kitchener.

Despite all he did for his faith, his country, and his game, Rick Noonan worries that Father Bauer's legacy is fading. "I've always maintained that Father Dave wouldn't want a book. There's been so many attempts. He was a very private person," said Noonan. "I remember one of the last things he told me, that he didn't want me making a hero out of him, because we had received his permission to hold a golf tournament to raise scholarship money at UBC for their hockey program—which he really put on the map. He said, 'On one condition, that we wouldn't grind people or make it a big focal point of anything.' I stuck to that promise and we lasted 25 years. Then we decided that the shelf life was getting old. People had forgotten who he was."

Chapter 25

THE BAUER COACHING MANUAL

Unlike his contemporary, Lloyd Percival of the University of Toronto, Father David Bauer never sat down and wrote a coaching manual. There are no known sketches of his plays, lineup sheets, or explanations of his desired style of play. But like Percival, who authored *The Hockey Handbook* in 1951, he had a great effect on a number of people. And Bauer's teachings lived on, through shift after shift of his protégés and students.

Dave Chambers, who coached the Quebec Nordiques after decades of coaching and teaching at the university level, has written a handful of books. He was asked what he carried through from his years under Father Bauer. "Speaking as a coach for so many years, he was able to handle the players," said Chambers. "His psychological aspect" was a strength. Religion was a non-issue. "His ability to relate to the player, even though he was a priest. At St. Mike's we had five or six Protestants—I was one of them—so it didn't matter; it was just him as a person."

The ability to motivate isn't necessarily teachable, but Father had it in spades. One time in the dressing room at St. Michael's, when Bob Goldham was the coach, Father Bauer, then the manager, went around to each player during one of the intermissions and shared what he thought they should do in the next period.

"As a motivator, his ability to handle players, and the great respect the players had for him, I think was the thing about him as a coach. He was a master at handling people and understanding people," said Chambers.

It's intriguing to see his philosophies and thoughts on the game, pieced together, if only because it offers more insight into his life in hockey.

For Howie Meeker, who knew Father when he was just Davey Bauer on the ponds of Kitchener, there was something instinctual about his style with the national team. "He had the cream of the crop of the amateur players in the country, and his teams always played respectively well. He had a feeling for hockey," said Meeker. "But he wanted speed, skill, and finesse. He didn't want any of this running guys into the fence, stickwork, things like that. He was really an amateur hockey player and wanted the game played according to the rules."

Billy MacMillan didn't travel a straight line from the man-made ice behind his Charlottetown, Prince Edward Island, home to St. Mike's to the NHL; rather he detoured to school, the national team, and into the pros. He won a Stanley Cup with the 1980 New York Islanders as an assistant coach, guided the Colorado Rockies for a season, and then moved with the team to New Jersey to become the Devils. Bauer was a defensive coach through and through, said MacMillan. "His theory was that a great defensive club would beat an offensive club," MacMillan said.

In Winnipeg, Gord Simpson had the unenviable task of merging the Nats left over from the 1964 Olympic program with his hometown Maroons team of mostly long-in-the-tooth veterans. Simpson had been around, but still took away knowledge from Bauer, who was essentially the general manager. "I learned a lot from him," he said. "He had ideas on how to condition his hockey players, and how to keep them going. That's what I'll have to say, is that all these boys that came from Father Bauer's team, they knew how to keep themselves in condition. There was no driving them or anything like that. They got out and did it."

Tom Watt took a little bit of Father Bauer with him on each step of his coaching journey, mostly gathered from their time together at the 1980 Olympics. From his ultra-successful days at the University of Toronto, to coaching, assisting, and scouting in the NHL in Toronto, Calgary, and Winnipeg, there are a number of ideas and concepts he took away. "Win or lose, you had to score the last goal of the game. If we lost 6–3, we've got to get that third goal. Because he always had this idea that whoever scored the last goal, that that was a big carry-over to the next game. And he was quite right. I've thought about that ever since that time, and it's a big deal," said Watt. "The other thing I learned from him too was that, when you're preparing for a big game, the last thing you do in practice is you scrimmage. Every player likes to play, there's not a player who doesn't like to play. So you let them scrimmage for 10 minutes or so, let them get into the scrimmage, let them get feeling good about themselves, you blow the whistle and you don't let them touch anything—send them right off, right away. Leave them a little hungry to play tomorrow."

Fast-forward to 1989, when Watt was an assistant coach with the Calgary Flames, under Terry Crisp. The Stanley Cup was on the line in Montreal—and the Canadiens had *never* lost a game at the Montreal Forum when the Cup was on the line. Though he wasn't alive, Father Bauer would have appreciated it, said Watt. "The pre-game skate in Montreal the day of the game, we went out and played shinny for about 15 minutes and we came off the ice. We won the game that night. I don't know if that was it, but that was the last skate before the game. We didn't do any shooting, we didn't do anything. We just went out and played shinny for about 15 minutes and then we won the game that night."

But Father was combative too, said Watt. There were times with the Olympians that Bauer wanted Watt and co-coach Clare Drake to do things differently. "Clare and I used to laugh, because he would watch us train and his criticism all the time after the practice was just about always the same: not enough one-on-one drills. Father's idea as a coach was that hockey boiled down to one-on-one battles in all areas of the ice. So we're not just talking about a defenceman facing a guy one-on-one on the rush, I'm talking about on the forecheck one-on-one, I'm talking about coming back with somebody one-on-one. His idea of hockey was that they were all one-on-one battles all over the ice. What he wanted in training was to see a lot of one-on-one drills. He wanted every player to be a sound one-on-one player. Actually his quote—you can probably find it somewhere—when we didn't win a medal in Lake Placid was that we weren't strong enough with our one-on-one play."

Terry O'Malley coached at Notre Dame College and at UBC. He always carried with him a mantra that Father Bauer shared: "You will be recognized as a great coach not with wins and losses but by how you treated the players whom you know you cannot play very much." Often O'Malley's mind drifts to the St. Mike's dressing room for bantam games, Coach Bauer going around the room, speaking to each player about his strengths, instilling the confidence to reach his potential in the game.

While Bauer was coaching at St. Mike's, Stan Obodiac, the long-time Toronto Maple Leafs publicist, wrote about Father Bauer in a Maple Leaf Gardens program. Obodiac called the priest the "Casey Stengel of Canadian hockey" for his penchant for moving players from position to position like the famed baseball manager of the New York Yankees, and specifically mentioned Gerry Cheevers, the goalie sent to the forward line for a number of games. "I am no Casey Stengel," said Father Bauer, "although I do like moving my players around. The evidences of this sound action were proven in the final St. Catharines game. Jack Cole was injured. I then had to shove another man in his position and he was ready to assume the new, strange position because he had been taught previously to do so. Every one of my boys can fill another position at a moment's notice."

The closest Father Bauer came to authoring a coaching manual was a column in four issues of the short-lived *Hockey Canada* magazine, published by the Canadian Amateur Hockey Association in 1962–63. Interestingly, in the first three columns, he is bylined as Rev. D.W. Bauer, and then in the last, as the hockey world became more aware of his plan for the national team, Rev. David Bauer.

Some highlights from those columns include:

> **Teams Must Play to Win, But Not at Any Price**
>
> **October 1962**
>
> We ought to remember that boys are human beings. Thus we should eliminate long schedules, boring practices and rough playing. We will make the game of hockey a game of skill and joy rather than brute force. Instead of trying to win at any price we will try to build up a boy's confidence and spirit by carefully

teaching him the technique and art of the game.

Boys are boys and they have their weaknesses. Therefore we ought to try to forge character out of their basic temperament, whatever that temperament might be.

Amateur sport plays a key role in the development of physical fitness, character and personality of boys. It develops their confidence and psychological security which is so necessary for their future in hockey and the world.

Defensive Skill First Essential To Be Winner
November 1962

My psychology is quite simple. Inside the framework of trying to win within the rules, I endeavour to build up a boy's confidence in himself by teaching things at practices which will most help him and the team.

Rather than making practices boring drudgery I try to make them interesting in order to increase the boy's confidence through acquisition of skill and technique.

I do not believe in aimless, useless scrimmages for the simple reason that I do not believe in practicing mistakes. Practice sessions, in their length and variety will vary according to the length of the schedule. The manner in which I build up a boy's confidence and positive thinking is by training him in the fundamentals; namely skating, shooting, passing and checking. As we generally do not need to teach a boy how to skate, shoot or pass because these are the things he naturally practises, I concentrate on teaching him how to check.

Peripheral Sight Development Is Useful Asset
December 1962

I give them drills which train them to maneuver easily in any direction. Secondly, I make sure that my boys develop split vision and entire perspective. This ability is basic to all other defensive maneuvers. By never taking his eyes off his opponent's eyes and yet being able to see everything else within 180 degree radius (sometimes called peripheral vision) the player will always be able to detect exactly what his opponent is doing with the puck as well as sense any change his opponent is planning to make in any direction.

Once the player has developed these skills he is trained in checking tactics. Maneuvering skillfully on his skates and using this split vision, he can impede the forward progress of his opponent without necessarily making severe body contact.

Puck Control Is the Key to Offensive Success
January 1963

Essential to offensive hockey, in my mind, is puck control. Here again split vision is very necessary. Short accurate passes are fed to men who constantly move towards any openings.

The puck should go to the lead man in order to avoid offsides, which serve only to hinder the forward progress of our offence. If a [player] has confidence in his checking abilities he will be not afraid to attempt more daring offensive maneuvers because he will know that if something goes wrong he will be able to recover himself effortlessly.

By switching players around and emphasizing checking and passing to the head man, a strong team spirit should develop. This prevalence of team spirit is far more important to winning the game and developing character and confidence than any technique.

But technique we must have, so I spend much time on skating, shooting, passing, winning face-offs and the power play. All of these things I try to combine into individual and team drills in order to utilize time and men effectively. Nor do I neglect the goal-keeper. But his practice is incorporated into our overall program.

Through his involvement in hometown coaching clinics, often tied to appearances by the national team, Father Bauer was able to share his thoughts with many coaches across the country.

He often advocated for more education for coaches. "Football and baseball have their coaching schools," Bauer said in the summer of 1961, at a dinner celebrating the championships for the two hockey teams at St. Michael's College. "We in hockey have been loathe to share our knowledge. The Canadian Amateur Hockey Association should seriously consider a recommendation from the Manitoba branch that a coaches' institute be formed."

In March 1966, the CAHA, along with the Canadian Interuniversity Athletic Union, finally heeded his words, and the first national coaching clinic was held at Macdonald College in Sainte-Anne-de-Bellevue, in suburban Montreal; a French-language clinic was also held at the University of Montreal. Roughly 150 coaches attended the nine-day course, financed by the National Fitness Council. Jack Kennedy of Hamilton's McMaster University was in charge, with the long-time pal of the Nats, Dr. Robert Hindmarch of the University of British Columbia, aiding him.

Father Bauer was there too, but he was also distracted by open tryouts for the national team being run by coach Jackie McLeod elsewhere in Montreal.

It wasn't an overnight process, and certainly didn't happen in isolation, but Father Bauer had a major hand in the National Coaching Certification Program, said Mickey McDowell, yet another former player turned educator and businessman. Judy LaMarsh, the federal Minister of Amateur Sport in the Liberal government, was the main proponent behind the NCCP, which launched in 1974, and she made numerous trips through the years in support of the Canadian national hockey team.

"The great Hockey Canada certification program that we all enjoy, which every kid can count on in hockey today, that came because Bauer was the guy asked to be the lynchpin to set it up. I was told that I was the first call he made when he got the nod," recalled McDowell.

Various divisions of hockey require different needs. A coach of four-year-old beginning players, falling like dominos as they pump their little legs chasing the elusive puck, will not have the skill-set of a driven, competitive—and paid—coach in the Metro Toronto Junior Hockey League. The NCCP set up a level system, where a trainee can progress from a basic, community-level concept to an Olympic-tier athlete, in a wide collection of sports.

McDowell, with a bachelor's and a master's degree in psychology at UBC, is quick to throw around such catchphrases as productivity, motivation, leadership. His task with the initial NCCP was group dynamics and exercises for the coaches. As well, Bauer called upon coaches he knew and respected, such as Fred Shero, Tom Watt, and Clare Drake, for input and consulting.

A motto in the UBC Thunderbirds hockey locker room reads, "Let technique be used but let the spirit prevail."

Those words, from former Leafs great Joe Primeau, were at the core of Father Bauer's beliefs.

In hockey, and in life.

ACKNOWLEDGEMENTS

It can be very humbling working on a project like this, knowing that others have gone down the road before. The greats of Canadian sports journalism—Jim Coleman, Scott Young, Dick Beddoes, Maurice Smith, Milt Dunnell, Trent Frayne, Jim Proudfoot, George Gross—have been there, done that. If it is possible to simultaneously leap for joy and weep at the beauty of a turn of phrase, then that's what I did when I found these words from Scott Young, the greatest of the greats in my mind (and not just for giving us Neil):

> I never saw a good idea die as silently, and with so few mourners, as our National Hockey team died.

That he wrote them in February 1970, a year before I was born, is a big part of the tale.

Growing up in Kitchener, Ontario (though I dispute Milt Dunnell's line from 1943, that the Bauer-Schmidt-Dumart Sauerkraut Line was named "in recognition of a delicacy that casts its enticing aroma over Kitchener"), I knew of the Bauer family, but not very much about it. As my writing took me further and further into the world of hockey, I yearned for even more. The idea for the book had percolated for a while, but it was Tom Watt, speaking at a Society for International Hockey Research gathering in the man cave of Mike Wilson, the Ultimate Leafs Fan, that pushed me over the edge. "Father Bauer is a great Canadian, but I could never get it straight—sometimes when you thought you were talking about hockey, the priest came out of him . . . and sometimes when you thought you were talking to a priest, the hockey came out of him." Like Young's words, Watt's were equally daunting and intriguing. And so I set out to write this book, only to learn that there had been other efforts in the past, often thwarted by both the complexity of the story and of the man.

There are many people to thank, but it always starts at home, where my mess of files drives my loving wife, Meredith, nuts, and where there's often a guitar practice off in the distance from my son, Quinn, while I transcribe interviews. We have taught our son well I think; he was seven years old when he came home from a trip with Grandpa Jim (to whom this book is dedicated) to the Waterloo County Hall of Fame at Doon Pioneer Village in Kitchener with scribbled notes about Father Bauer from a display there for me to use in the project. A happenstance bus ride with the mother of one of his classmates resulted in a day going through the CBC video archives for Canadian national team footage.

Michael Holmes at ECW Press believed in the project from the get-go, and helped me get through some rough patches. Jamie Melissa Hemmings aided with the transcribing when I felt overwhelmed. Though I don't know the statistic for sure, but I'm pretty sure that I am responsible for at least half of the interlibrary loans that come into the Jane/Dundas branch of Toronto Public Library; they have always supported me, and I am proud that my books are on TPL's shelves. Thanks, as always, to the Hockey Hall of Fame and its archivists, Katherine Pearce, Miragh Bitove, Craig Campbell, and others. Gregg Drinnan's website (gdrinnan.blogspot.ca) has a wealth of junior hockey information, and in particular, his research on past Memorial Cups was invaluable. Margarita Lopez, the archivist at St. Michael's College School provided file after file of information and some great photos, making me wish I had visited her earlier in the process. The files of Allan Stitt, hockey's preeminent collector of paperwork, revealed a couple of gems that I selfishly kept for this book on Father Bauer rather than use in either of the two books we have done together.

My friends in the Society for International Hockey Research mean a lot to me, from A—Jim Amodeo—to Z—Eric Zweig. Kent Morgan never failed to find me someone with a connection to Winnipeg, and Fred Hume at UBC was great too. Gary Mossman had been down the road with an authorized Father Bauer biography that was stalled by the Bauer family but, as a fellow SIHR member, provided the manuscript for my consideration. Then there's the hockey people. There is no book on Father Bauer unless you have Terry O'Malley and Rick Noonan on side. I was fortunate to have both playing on my team. Ken Broderick, who sadly died before seeing this book's completion, opened the door for a visit and let my son and I wear his 1968 Olympic bronze medal. It was Ken who invited me to a reunion of the Nats on Manitoulin Island, Ontario, held off and on since 1979. The remote Red Lodge Resort was booked for the crew, which came in from Newfoundland and Labrador and British Columbia and all points in between. There I got to witness the comfortableness that they share, even if they didn't play together, and that goes for the wives too, whether they are playing cards, drinking expensive cognac, or teasing each other about past transgressions: missed shots, costly errors, merry nights that extended into the wee hours of the next day. Andre Brin, a videographer from Hockey Canada, was there too, and brought in some vintage clips for the players to see. The jokes flew across the room, boys being boys in the safety of their living room:

"Let's show some offensive plays!"

"Is that O'Malley on his knees?"

"The Russians never let us have the puck."

A roar of laughter followed a photo of Roger Bourbonnais missing some of his teeth.

There needs to be a word said about the Word, too. The church I went to growing up in Kitchener, St. James'-Rosemount United, was about just about everything else besides religion for me. My nursery school was there, and I started my ongoing life in Scouts Canada there as a four-year-old Beaver Scout. There were church-organized camping trips, the youth group provided lots of fun for an awkward teen, and many of my parents' friends came from there.

But for many in Canada, the main religion remains hockey. It unites us as Canadians, and no one ever preached that better than Father Bauer.

BIBLIOGRAPHY

Many of the sources are cited in the text. The following list is some of the other sources that helped flesh out the book.

Berton, Pierre. *The Comfortable Pew: A Critical Look at the Church in the New Age*. Toronto: McClelland & Stewart, 1965.

Best, Dave. *Canada: Our Century in Sport*. Markham, ON: Fitzhenry & Whiteside, 2002.

Boyd, Bill. *Hockey Towns: Stories of Small Town Hockey in Canada*. Toronto: Doubleday Canada, 1998.

Brignall, Richard J. *Forgotten Heroes: Winnipeg's Hockey Heritage*. Winnipeg: J. Gordon Shillingford, 2011.

Cole, Stephen. *The Canadian Hockey Atlas*. Toronto: Doubleday Canada, 2006.

Conacher, Brian. *As the Puck Turns: A Personal Journey Through the World of Hockey*. Mississauga: John Wiley & Sons Canada, 2007.

Conacher, Brian. *Hockey in Canada: The Way It Is!* Richmond Hill, ON: Simon & Schuster Canada, 1970.

Daniels, Calvin. *Guts and Go: Great Saskatchewan Hockey Stories*. Surrey, BC: Heritage House, 2004.

Dixon, Joan. *Trailblazing Sports Heroes: Exceptional Personalities and Outstanding Achievements in Canadian Sport*. Canmore, AB: Altitude Publishing, 2003.

Dowbiggin, Bruce. *The Defense Never Rests*. Toronto: HarperCollins, 1993.

Eagleson, R. Alan, and Scott Young. *Power Play: The Memoirs of Hockey Czar Alan Eagleson*. Toronto: McClelland & Stewart, 1991.

Foster, Susan, and Carl Brewer. *The Power of Two: Carl Brewer's Battle With Hockey's Power Brokers*. Bolton, ON: Fenn Publishing, 2006.

Gallagher, Beth. *Profiles from the Past, Faces of the Future: Waterloo 150*. Waterloo, ON: Waterloo Public Library, 2007.

Gruneau, Richard, and David Whitson. *Hockey Night in Canada: Sport, Identities and Cultural Politics*. Toronto: Garamond Press, 1993.

Henderson, Paul, and Jim Prime. *How Hockey Explains Canada*. Chicago: Triumph Books, 2011.

Kidd, Bruce. *The Struggle for Canadian Sport*. Toronto: University of Toronto Press, 1996.

McCreery, Christopher. *The Order of Canada: Its Origins, History, and Development*. Toronto: University of Toronto Press, 2005.

Quarrington, Paul. *Hometown Heroes: On the Road with Canada's National Hockey Team*. Don Mills, ON: Collins, 1988.

Shea, Kevin, Larry Colle, and Paul Patskou. *St. Michael's College: 100 Years of Pucks and Prayers*. Bolton, ON: Fenn Publishing, 2008.

Szemberg, Szymon, and Andrew Podnieks. *IIHF Top 100 Hockey Stories of All-Time*. Bolton, ON: Fenn Publishing, 2008.

Waterloo Centennial Programme: The History of Our City's Growth (1857–1957). City of Waterloo, 1957.

Watson, Alan. *Catch On and Run with It: The Sporting Life and Times of Dr. Bob Hindmarch*. AJW Books, 2012.

Wells, Don. *Flight of the Thunderbirds: A Century of Varsity Sport at the University of British Columbia*. Vancouver: Department of Athletics and Recreation, the University of British Columbia, 2007.

Wilkins, Charles. *Breakaway: Hockey and the Years Beyond*. Toronto: McClelland & Stewart, 1995.

Young, Scott. *100 Years of Dropping the Puck: A History of the OHA*. Toronto: McClelland & Stewart, 1989.

Young, Scott. *War on Ice: Canada in International Hockey*. Toronto: McClelland & Stewart, 1976.

INTERVIEWS

It's funny how projects can overlap, where a book on Toronto Maple Leafs documents—*Written in Blue & White*—leads to interviews for three different books. Thank you to all who took the time to share their memories on the record, and to a number who did so off the record.

Reg Abbott
Lou Angotti
Glenn Anderson
Roger Bourbonnais
Ken Broderick
Arnie Brown
Doug Buchanan
Ray Cadieux
Terry Caffery
Dave Chambers
Gerry Cheevers
Terry Clancy
Don Collins
Brian Conacher
Paul Conlin
Cam Connor
Jack Costello
Jiri Crha
Jean Cusson
Ab DeMarco
Clare Drake
Ken Dryden
Alan Eagleson
Ken Esdale
George Faulkner
Susan Foster
Emile Francis
Stu Gibbs
Brian Glennie
John Gouette
Randy Gregg
Jim Gregory
Chuck Hamilton
Bill Hay
Derek Holmes
Bill Holowaty
Jim Irving
Bruce Jessup
Marshall Johnston
Red Kelly
Dave Keon
Cam Kerr
Les Kozak
Chris Lang
Chuck Lefley
Ted Lindsay
Jim Logan
Barry MacKenzie
Billy MacMillan
Guy Maddin
Ted Maki
Cesare Maniago

INTERVIEWS

Jack Martin
Bob McAneeley
Johnny McCormack
Mickey McDowell
Brian McFarlane
Bob McKnight
Jack McLeod
Howie Meeker
Grant Moore
Ross Morrison
Morris Mott
Rick Noonan
Terry O'Malley
Bob Pallante
Ross Parke
Gerry Pinder
Herb Pinder
Brad Pirie
Tom Polanic
Noel Price
Gord Renwick
Larry Riggin
John Russell
Phil Samis
Rod Seiling
Gord Simpson
Harry Sinden
Mike Smith
George Swarbrick
Ted Toppazzini
Gene Ubriaco
Tim Watters
Barry Wilcox

STATISTICS

David Bauer

SKATER STATISTICS			
SEASON	TEAM	LEAGUE	TOURNAMENT
1942–43	Toronto St. Michael's Majors	OHA-Jr. A	--
1943–44	Toronto St. Michael's Majors	OHA-Jr. A	--
	Oshawa Generals	OHA-Jr. A	Mem-Cup
1944–45	Toronto St. Michael's Majors	OHA-Jr. A	--
	Windsor Jr. Spitfires	WnCHL	--
	Ottawa Canadian Postal Corps	ONDHL	--
1945–46	University of Toronto Varsity Blues	CIHU	--
	TOTALS		

		REGULAR SEASON					PLAYOFFS				
	No.	GP	G	A	P	PIM	GP	G	A	P	PIM
	10	20	10	11	21	10	6	2	8	10	2
		25	12	25	37	20	12	7	5	12	12
		--	--	--	--	--	7	4	5	9	4
		1	1	1	2	0	--	--	--	--	--
		6	2	5	7	2	--	--	--	--	--
		10	2	5	7	4	--	--	--	--	--
		5	1	5	6	2	1	0	1	1	0
		67	28	52	80	38	26	13	19	32	18

Courtesy the Society for International Hockey Research

INDEX

INDEX

INDEX

INDEX

ALSO BY GREG OLIVER

Blue Lines, Goal Lines & Bottom Lines: Hockey Contracts and Historical Documents from the Collection of Allan Stitt

Written in Blue & White: The Toronto Maple Leafs Contracts and Historical Documents from the Collection of Allan Stitt

The Goaltenders' Union: Hockey's Greatest Puckstoppers, Acrobats, and Flakes (with Richard Kamchen)

Don't Call Me Goon: Hockey's Greatest Enforcers, Gunslingers, and Bad Boys (with Richard Kamchen)

Duck with the Puck (with Quinn Oliver)

SLAM! Wrestling: Shocking Stories from the Squared Circle (Editor, with Jon Waldman)

The Pro Wrestling Hall of Fame: Heroes & Icons (with Steven Johnson)

The Pro Wrestling Hall of Fame: The Heels (with Steven Johnson)

The Pro Wrestling Hall of Fame: The Tag Teams (with Steven Johnson)

The Pro Wrestling Hall of Fame: The Canadians

Benoit: Wrestling with the Horror That Destroyed a Family and Crippled a Sport (with Steven Johnson, Irv Muchnick and Heath McCoy)

Get the eBook FREE!